Steel Wheels
and
Rubber Tyres

Volume Two

A General Manager's Journey:
Manchester
Plymouth
Great Yarmouth
Halifax

by
Geoffrey Hilditch
OBE, Ch Engr, FI Mech E, FILT, FCIT, MIRTE

THE OAKWOOD PRESS

© Oakwood Press & Geoffrey Hilditch 2004

British Library Cataloguing in Publication Data
A Record for this book is available from the British Library
ISBN 0 85361 616 7

Typeset by Oakwood Graphics.
Repro by Ford Graphics, Ringwood, Hants.
Printed by Cambrian Printers, Aberystwyth, Ceredigion.

Front cover, top: A once famous advert drew attention 'To what one could do', but the AEC double-decker that took a header down the Shibden Valley embankment required *two* to regain the vertical. Two AEC 'Matadors' that is, so despite the author's pose it was far from being all his own work. Recovery provided a very interesting morning for those so engaged. Note the damaged lower saloon nearside, through the gap a lady passenger and her little girl left the vehicle - or so I am told!

Front cover, bottom: During the time the M62 motorway was being constructed around the west and south of Halifax certain highways had to be cut. Near Dean Head a cutting was excavated to be spanned by a high bridge and here a temporary and very steeply-graded 'track' was constructed taking vehicles down from the original road level to the motorway surface level and back up again. Here Leyland 'Leopard' No. 237 is just about to regain the original road. This was a bottom gear climb not even to to be attempted in bad weather.

Rear cover, top: Five Roe-bodied Daimler CVG6 machines arrived in Great Yarmouth in 1961, there being two 30 ft 72-seaters and three 27 ft 65-seaters. Thanks to the very different operating terrain these vehicles with their semi-automatic gear boxes were basically trouble free. Here fleet No. 12 one of the latter (Nos. 11-13) is ready to leave the Leeds works for the homeward run.

Rear Cover, bottom: The standard Halifax double-decker became the reduced height Northern Counties-bodied Gardner '6LX' engine powered Daimler 'Fleetline'. Here two typical examples stand in the Skircoat depot yard on what was tipped ground. Halifax Town's Shay football ground is behind the concrete fencing, formed when spontaneous underground combustion began to effect the whole areas in the early 1900s. With the tram depot in danger, desperate measures had to be taken to put the fires out.

Published by The Oakwood Press (Usk), P.O. Box 13, Usk, Mon., NP15 1YS.
E-mail: oakwood-press@dial.pipex.com
Website: www.oakwood-press.dial.pipex.com

Contents

The old order changes. One of the last three ex-Todmorden lowbridge 'PD2s' now No. 357 passes brand new 'Fleetline' No. 296 at Todmorden Market Place. Another 'Fleetline' and a Plaxton-bodied dual purpose AEC 'Reliance' stand on the left.

Introduction to Volume Two

Volume One ended at the point where I had, with some reluctance, tendered my resignation and so left Leeds City Transport for what at the time seemed to be a very uncertain future. On the face of things my chances of ever finding myself holding the job of General Manager of a municipal transport undertaking were just about nil, but one never knows just what this life is going to bring, and if one is lucky enough to possess ambition, background and appropriate technical qualifications then who knows just what might be possible?

Achieving such a post in those days (alas, so few municipals remain in this year of 2004) depended also on a whole series of other factors, when good luck and a wife who never objected to frequent household removals and coming to live in strange areas of the country were of paramount importance.

In the event as you will read I managed to make it, but once the chair was yours you speedily found that life was very different to what it had been as a lowly member of staff, or a departmental head, or even a deputy General Manager. The buck really did stop with you!

Any new General Manager can expect to have something of a 'honeymoon' period during his first months in office, which is just as well, for to hold that office in a strange undertaking one has to learn as quickly as possible where the buses actually run, what local tribal customs are in respect of union agreements, duty schedules, etc., and just what are the relationships between your outfit and other bus concerns that impinge on your territory, and even more important those that exist or otherwise with other departments in the municipal structure, and their chief officers.

Last but by no means least, what do the members of the council come to think about your efforts and how does any resulting atmosphere impact during Committee or full council meetings?

Two things become very obvious in no time at all. A considerable sense of humour is a decided asset as is a very thick skin, for here the pages of your local newspapers will soon reflect what their readers, who are not always bus passengers, think of you and your managerial efforts. Do you really base your timetables on *Old Moore's Almanac* or the *Liverpool Tide Tables* as some correspondents are sure is the case?

But this is for future pages. Let us start here in the afternoon of Sunday 1st November, 1953, as I caught a No. 9 bus from Oldham Star Inn to Ashton, and changed there onto a trolleybus that took me to Guide Bridge station wondering all the while just what the next day would bring.

Chapter One

Daimler Days

I travelled to Coventry the Sunday afternoon before I was due to start work at the Daimler Radford Works via an unusual route, catching the afternoon Manchester London Road to London Marylebone express from Guide Bridge for 'old time's sake', eventually alighting from it at the Rugby Great Central station and then taking a Midland Red single-decker on to Coventry. This caused me some surprise due to the very large quantity of notices transferred onto the bulkhead and sundry other places. In fact there seemed to be the best part of a quarter of an hour's reading material on display.

I duly presented myself at my new office around 8.45 am to find, as I had seen on the day of my interview, that it was quite large. Most of the men were employed on private car production, for at this time the very successful 'Conquest' saloon was being made - well it was priced at £1,066. This left a residue of 10 draughtsmen or so, and of these several were working out the design of a Daimler tractor which was certainly a departure from the normal sort of production. This machine was to take two forms, having either tank-like tracks, or more conventional but still sizeable tyred wheels. A good deal of effort did come to be expended on some prototypes, but as apparently was often the case at Daimler another innovation never reached bulk production.

The only type of buses being built were the Gardner-engined home market 'CVG5' or 'CVG6' with the preselector gear box, and a straight-framed export single-decker fitted with a Daimler 'CD650' engine that since first introduction had been the subject of a series of modifications, but was an engine that I was destined to come to know more about within the next two years. The number of chassis actually passing down the line at this time was not large, although a Manchester order for 90 'CVG6s' that became bus Nos. 4400-4489 was just about complete, as was a large Birmingham order. There was a degree of uncertainty abroad as some little time previously the Senior Bus Engineer and a fair number of the staff had been made redundant, and this caused me to wonder just what sort of a concern I had joined, but it was rather too late to worry overmuch about that aspect of the matter.

My first jobs were to scheme out an arrangement to allow an external radiator water filler to be fitted into the front fibreglass cowl of the new look bonnet assembly, redesigning brake drums and producing an assembly drawing in cross section of a front axle and king pin assembly. Daimler buses were built in sanctions, and a new one was now being agreed, which provided the opportunity to introduce various modifications, the basic aim here being to reduce both weight and cost. Once again the change in atmosphere from my previous employment was very marked but even though I was miles from home and amidst strangers, the fellows around me proved to be both friendly and helpful. This sense was heightened when after three or four days at Radford I came to meet the then head of our side of the business, Len Hartsilver, whom I came to like. Another personality that I came to know was Peter Windsor Smith, later to become Daimler Chief Engineer and later still involved

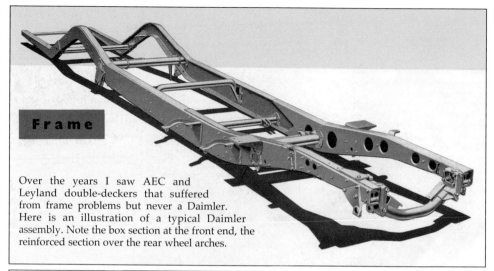

Frame

Over the years I saw AEC and Leyland double-deckers that suffered from frame problems but never a Daimler. Here is an illustration of a typical Daimler assembly. Note the box section at the front end, the reinforced section over the rear wheel arches.

Above: The Daimler standard preselector spring loaded gear box was a very reliable unit which at first sight was very complicated. Understanding just how the various gear trains did their stuff was a bit difficult initially, but the operating mechanism was quite straightforward. This type of component was not readily open to driver abuse, unlike the later two-pedal control Daimatic versions. I well recall riding on a foreign 'Fleetline' one night when I could not help myself and so gave a surprised Lancashire driver a badly-needed gear change lesson.

Right: Daimler began to design an oil engine before the last war, which was just as well because Gardner could not produce sufficient power units in early post-war days. The Daimler 8.4 litre 100 hp product was very smooth running, if not as economical as a Gardner, and a considerable number were fitted into the resulting 'CVD6' chassis. Unusually the timing gear was located at the rear of the crank case (Dennis oil engines were similar) it being maintained that the arrangement reduced torsional vibrations. After about 1952/53, however, few came to be produced.

Above: A detailed view of the front end of an almost complete Daimler 'CVG5' chassis. The front engine mounting sandwich blocks, the chassis double pressings and the front spring front brackets are closely seen. Between the frame pressings were aluminium bridge pieces, two of which are visible. Note how bolts holding the front cross-member pass through them.

1. Cylinder head cover breathers.
2. Timing case breather.
3. Cylinder water drain cock.
4. Exhauster oil drain pipe.
5. Sump drain pump.
6. Exhauster oil suction pipe.
7. Dipstick.
8. Fuel drip tray and pipe.
9. Engine oil filter.
10. Bottom cover.
11. Oil filler cap.
12. Fuel oil filter.

The resulting Daimler 'CVD6' chassis was also to become the basis of not only double- and single-deck buses but also luxury coaches which provided the company with what was virtually an additional market. Here the inherent smoothness of the engine with its flexible mountings offered a high degree of refinement. Unfortunately Daimler lost out later by not producing a medium power horizontal engine and fitting it into a lighter weight single-deck chassis.

Bullock & Sons was one of the few private companies to buy Daimler chassis before 1939, then between 1943 and 1945 fourteen Daimler utilities entered service. Two were 'CWG5s' the rest 'CWA6s', fleet numbers 259 and 260 and 261 to 272. The Daimler engine first appeared in two further 'CWD6' utilities, Nos. 273 and 274, in 1946, the post-war 'CVD6' chassis coming next later in 1946 in the shapes of two Barnaby-bodied 35-seaters, Nos. 281 and 282. Bob Mack took this photograph of No. 282 in Wakefield bus station. Bullock's bought Barnaby bodies on a regular basis both pre- and post-war. Another 14 'CVD6s' (12 double-deckers and two single-deckers) came up to 1950 when the 150-strong fleet was sold to West Riding company, at that time also in private ownership.

with me in some interesting development work, and I met Bob Crouch who was then and for years later the Daimler Bus Sales Manager.

I had been at Coventry about four weeks when I had a stroke of luck. A batch of buses had been built for either West Bromwich, or Walsall, I forget which, and these had the unfortunate habit of coming out of gear when in motion, which was surprising as the Daimler-built preselector gearbox was usually a well developed, and very reliable, component.

I was given the job of trying to locate the cause of the trouble, a task which by a pure fluke took all of 10 minutes. Originally the gear selector device consisted of a lever mounted at the side of the steering column which worked in a quadrant. This had a series of serrations on the underside, each of which corresponded to a gear position and acted as a fairly positive location for the lever, whilst at one end a spring-loaded stop prevented a driver from accidentally picking up reverse.

Now instead of a quadrant the selector lever was housed in a box, also mounted on the side of the steering column, the lever working in a vertical gate, which gave much better control, as when driving there was no need to look where the lever was, feel alone being completely adequate. To engage a gear you moved the lever to the required position, and then pressed the change speed pedal which replaced the usual clutch pedal mounted in the cab floor. Movement of the lever worked in turn a series of rods, the motion thus imparted travelling via the rods and various relay levers to the camshaft mounted inside the gearbox. This in turn positioned the gear strut so that when the pedal was pushed down the spring-loaded bus bar positioned the strut, and so when the pedal was released the spring and strut ensured the gear band or brake was tightened up to prevent the gear drum from turning and so bringing its internal epicyclic gear into action. This sounds very complicated, but was simple to follow through on an actual chassis.

In this case the layout drawing done to a reduced scale for obvious reasons was totally accurate, but when the detailed drawings of the components involved were produced someone had taken the distance between two centres of a relay lever as being correct when measured on the drawing whereas that distance needed to be twice as great to allow for the half-size scale of the drawing. As a result the gearbox camshaft was not being turned through as many degrees as it should have been and this allowed struts to be incompletely engaged. This was one of those instances when luck comes to be on your side.

Luck was about to be on my side again, for I now saw an advertisement for a technical assistant with Manchester City Transport (MCT). Although I had only been with my Coventry employer for some seven weeks, I asked Mr Hartsilver if he would mind my applying, and also give me a reference which in retrospect was rather pushing things. He kindly consented, and also allowed me to have a day off with pay to attend for interview. This took place one Monday afternoon, so I was able to have an extra night at home. I kept my fingers crossed and as I left home said to my wife that if I was lucky enough to be given the job I would be a Municipal General Manager within 10 years, a forecast which was just 50 per cent wrong - on the right side.

The interview, which took place at 55 Piccadilly, Manchester, was very different to the one at Leeds and was conducted by the General Manager Mr A.F. Neal, and his Chief Engineer, then Cyril Oakham, who had previously

MODEL "650"

SIX CYLINDER - 5" x 5½"

Lockheed fluid pump unit
included in illustration as
an example of additional
driven auxiliary.

Daimler 650 engine, complete with that six plunger hydraulic fluid pump. This power unit was well regarded by the Halifax engine fitters and gave a good life once a couple of early problems had been solved (*see text*). This was another Daimler design that needed more development but like so much else from Radford was allowed to fade away. As it was, a prototype 'CVG6-30' (or 'CVD6-30'?) chassis with one of these engines gave quite a performance when tried in Halifax.

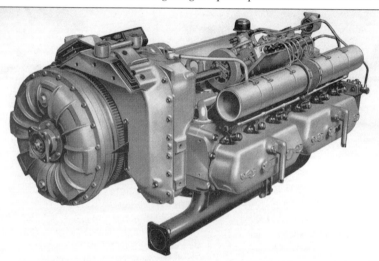

Daimler next went on to produce its larger engine - the 650 cubic inch model in both vertical and horizontal form producing up to 150 bhp at 2,000 rpm. The former was used in the CD650 double-deck chassis and various export models; the latter in the underfloor-engined 'Freeline'. These chassis normally had a certain hydraulic brake system. Sales were moderate. Again Daimler missed the market. A design to compete with the AEC 'Reliance' or Leyland 'Leopard' should have been produced but none was. Here is the horizontal version of the larger engine.

The 'CD650' horizontal engine plus a five-speed (overdrive) preselector gear box when put into the Daimler 'Freeline' chassis gave a spanking performance, even if the braking system did have its 'tender' moments. The net result was an expensive assembly with a fairly high consumption but quite a few came onto UK roads under luxury coach bodies. Red House Motors of Coventry purchased this example with the classically-styled Burlingham 'Seagull' coachwork.

Fluid flywheels consisted of two mechanically unconnected parts. The near portion was connected directly to the crank shaft. The inner runner to the output shaft. Oil, the working medium, took the power from the input vanes to the output ones, but that oil had to be kept up to the right level. At idling speed, take off the hand brake and the bus would creep on level ground. Because 100 per cent slip was never possible a fluid flywheel and conventional gear box were not compatible. Prolonged idling in gear was not desirable - the oil heated, internal pressure rose and seals could suffer. Driving vanes at the rear coupled direct to the crank shaft. Driven rotor towards the front - no direct connection to former.

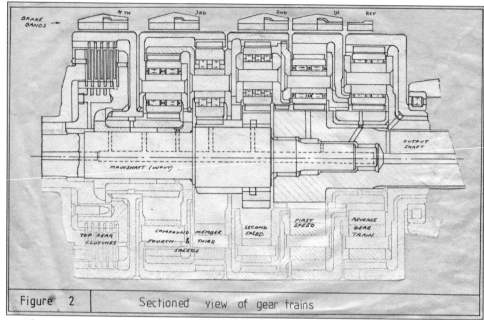

Figure 2 | Sectioned view of gear trains

The answer, if a fluid flywheel was required, was to fit an epicyclic preselector gear box. It looks from this illustration to be fiendishly complicated but a spring-loaded Daimler box was very reliable and those in Halifax often covered 400,000 miles before needing overhaul. Later air-operated semi-automatic boxes were never as good.

Three-axle buses were, as we have seen, popular in the 1920s and a few were built in the 1930s. It was therefore quite surprising after World War II when Daimler built a batch of such chassis with Gardner 6LW engines for a South African export order, but no home operator was inclined to invest in any.

been with London Transport. They asked me a considerable number of questions about where I had been and what I had done and then surprisingly asked me if I was in a hurry to return to Coventry. I replied in the negative, and so I spent the later portion of the afternoon in a waiting room. The staff clerk, who was marshalling the other candidates, told me that this had not happened before and he was sure in consequence that the post was going to be mine; I fervently hoped that his forecast turned out to be true. Eventually at around 5 o'clock I was taken back to Mr Neal's office and told that I had been selected, so when could I start? A date was agreed and I left for Coventry much later than intended and gave Mr Hartsilver my notice the following day, when he indicated he had felt all along that I would be successful.

In my view anyone who became a technical assistant at Manchester was very fortunate indeed, and a whole series of men who held one of these positions became General Managers in due course, for example, Jack Thompson at Manchester itself, Frank Thorpe at Bury and Newport, Derek Hyde at Barrow, Coventry and Blackpool, Colin Clubb at London Country and other NBC concerns, Peter Bland at Ashton under Lyne, and Allan Wright at Sunderland to name a few. As a training ground it was virtually unbeatable but some last comments about Radford.

My stay at the Daimler factory, which had been greatly damaged in the Coventry blitz but had now been rebuilt, was only of exactly 13 weeks duration, so I was never able to visit every part of the premises, but three areas that I did see were of some interest. The first of these was the experimental department located behind the building which contained our offices, where George Fabel and the other members of the staff worked on various development projects. The second was the area of ground at the far end of the works, used for testing completed chassis. I was fortunate in that I quickly made friends with one of the senior men so engaged, with the result that most of my Saturday mornings were spent with him. He showed me what he did and how he did it, and this gave me the chance to try my hand behind the wheel. The third area of interest lay on the other side of the road to our office, a road that ran from the main gates right through the factory.

Here was the bus assembly line located at one side of a shop that, from a floor area point of view, would have swallowed the whole of Seddon's Woodstock factory production space, with lots of room to spare. Beyond the single line devoted to PSV assembly were the ranks of new cars in the process of assembly. To reach the bus line you had to pass through the car finishing bay, where numerous Daimler 'Conquest' saloons were being cleaned and polished by a number of female employees, the place having that atmosphere redolent of new leather, new paint, and new polish.

I used to look at those cars with envious eyes, and wonder if I would ever be able to afford a Daimler 'Conquest' at £1,066 or £1,512 with purchase tax. It would have been possible if on my weekly wage of £12 5s., less tax and insurance, I had neither eaten, drank nor lived under a roof for around two full years. These, though, were but the cheap end of current Daimler production. The maroon and grey sports cars with the initials NHD in old English script on the doors, used by Lady Docker, was in another class altogether, as were various expensive limousines that could frequently be seen. It was all rather off-putting to a member of the proletariat, but one had to have hope!

Between late 1937 and early 1938 Manchester put into service 40 Leyland 'Tiger' TS8 single-deckers with MCW/Crossley 32-seat bodies. Some of these were allocated to Queens Road garage and then began to appear on the Oldham area Nos. 2, 10 and 13 express services. Although fitted with comfortable seating they had no door fitted to the Scottish style cut away rear entrances which made them rather draughty in winter. Mr Pilcher's streamline swoops were prominent in pre-war days but when Roy Marshall took this post-war photograph they had been deleted. This view of No. 76, new in January 1938, was taken in Piccadilly - until the 1940 blitz the terminus of the above services. Then with frequencies halved double-deckers took over and the routes were cut back to Stevensons Square.

As mentioned in the text I passed my PSV driving test on a 'bomber', a pre-war Crossley streamliner fitted during the war with a Gardner '5LW' engine which replaced the original Crossley unit. With a central accelerator, a crash gear box and noise and vibrations in profusion it provided ample food for thought. DVR 600, fleet No. 628, had an English Electric body. It went into service in October 1937 and had a life of just 13 years, being withdrawn in October 1950. It was intended for exhibition at the 1937 Commercial Show but for some reason failed to make it.

Chapter Two

Technical Times

At the time of my arrival at 55 Piccadilly, Manchester, the Department's rambling head office, the engineering headquarters were at the front of the building on the third floor. Our office space was on two levels, the higher housing the drawing office. The lower and larger portion had at the rear, looking into the light well, Mr Oakham's room, and there were also rather small partitioned-off offices housing Mr Atkinson, the chief technical assistant, who had been with MCT for a considerable number of years and had had a rather chequered career, and Mr Thompson the Garages Engineer. He had prime responsibility for the depots at Hyde Road, Rochdale Road, Queens Road, Birchfields Road, Princess Road, Parrs Wood and Northenden, plus the service fitters, who with their small vans attended to any breakdown calls from vehicles out on the road. There were also three other Seniors reporting direct to Mr Oakham, namely Mr Eversfield the Electrical Engineer, Mr Lees the Car Works Superintendent, and the Constructional Engineer, whose empire since the end of tramway operation and the abandonment of the track had been greatly reduced. Each of these three gentlemen were located in the Hyde Road complex.

The technical assistants were four in number, one being attached to the electrical department, whilst the three involved in bus engineering shared a table in the main office where several clerks were also located, but on the table by our places were little stands bearing the legend 'Mr . . . . out at' and below that were simple holders into which could be slipped cards with such words as Parrs Wood, etc., which you duly set up each time you went out on safari.

I was told to become fully mobile by being passed for both motor and trolley bus driving so I was duly taken out by the chief driving instructor in one of the department's Morris staff cars. After I had driven him around the centre of Manchester for half an hour he expressed himself satisfied, and so I moved onto the next rung of the ladder. At Hyde Road in the area where tram scrapping had taken place, an area once the home of the Manchester City Football Club, was a circular track where trainee drivers first tried their hand on a double-decker, for which purpose numerous elderly Crossleys well past their service days were retained. I had about half an hour on one of these, which still retained its Crossley engine, and then I was told to begin stage three.

For this I met another instructor in Piccadilly bus station one lunch time, and he indicated that I should climb into the cab of yet another Crossley, start the engine, and have a gentle drive via Market Street and Deansgate to Trafford Park, when he would assess my performance. As I have said before, in *Looking at Buses*, this vehicle made my hair stand on end. It was of the 'bomber' variety.

In other words a solidly mounted Gardner engine had replaced the original Crossley unit, the gearbox was of the crash variety, and variety was enhanced by the accelerator pedal being positioned between the clutch and brake pedals. Throw into these factors some busy city streets, and make this the first time ever

The standard Crossley type 'DD42' chassis was basically well engineered but really needed some more development time. The power unit certainly let the whole assembly down as Crossley bodies were excellent. I viewed the collapse of the company with some sadness after the AEC takeover but the earlier move out of Manchester to Errwood Park, Stockport did not help- as Manchester's orders came to a pretty abrupt end.

The first batch of 91 post-war 7 ft 6 in.-wide Crossley double-deckers were new in the spring/summer of 1946 and provided the garages with their first experiences in maintaining their 8.6 litre Crossley 'HOE7' engines. With an unladen weight of 7 t. 6 cwt 1 q., a Crossley constant mesh gear box and reasonable steering thanks to king pins having roller races they were not bad to drive and most of the batch, like No. 2917, shown here, lasted for 15 to 16 years. Some, however, were given Leyland engines from withdrawn pre-war 'TD5' engines between 1950 and 1954. Surprisingly they sported only a single headlight.   *Roy Marshall*

you have tried to drive a big vehicle on the open road, and you will realise that I came to experience a whole series of palpitations.

We did manage to reach the site of Trafford Hall without hitting anything, and I began to relax when Mr Worthington said that my performance could have been a lot worse and with some more practice I should be able to pass the test. For the next week or two I drove more modern Crossleys in and around Manchester taking turns with various would-be service drivers, allocated to the same instructor and training vehicle, and then followed the driving test. I was required to take yet another 'bomber' from Piccadilly to Trafford Park via a different route to my first trip where my reversing skills were put to the test by the Department of Transport Examiner. He, after asking various highway code questions, pronounced himself satisfied and wrote out my pink success slip.

The more modern Crossleys had either crash gearboxes in the early post-war models, or synchromesh boxes in the later ones, which as one of my colleagues said was the best crash box ever made. They were easy vehicles to handle in the main, the low bonnet line giving an excellent view of the nearside kerb, whilst the driver's seat and the riding characteristics were comfortable. Remember, though, that on these occasions the buses were empty, and so the steering on those with thrust buttons as opposed to roller races in the front axles, whilst feeling heavy, did not border on the almost impossible as could be the case when a full load of passengers was being carried.

I next took out various Daimler and Leyland buses to gain further experience, and should add here that by now the 4400-4489 series of Daimlers were coming into service. These and the 4100s, having Gardner '6LW' engines with flexible engine mountings, were quite pleasant to handle but the 4000 series were definitely not. They had heavy Brush or Crossley bodies and only five-cylinder Gardner power units, so noise and vibration were high whilst performance was very, very, low. They were about as unpleasant as the 'bombers' and I for one would not have wished to have driven one for a full eight hour shift. The other hazard with a Daimler was the so called 'Daimler knee' syndrome, in other words having to press the quite heavy gear pedal every time a ratio change was required meant that your left leg really could begin to ache, but here do not be lazy. If you failed to push the pedal right to the end of its stroke, before letting it come back quickly but still under control, that pedal could and would fly back under the influence of the very strong spring inside the gearbox, and if it should hit your ankle or shin you suffered. Pain or not, it had to be forced back into position, so put the selector lever into neutral, stand up, grab hold of the steering wheel, put *both* feet on the pedal and exert as much pressure on it as possible. It would then go back so as to be just a few inches above the cab floor, to adopt different heights as different gears were brought into use. There was little doubt that once you were proficient with a preselector gearbox, you could save some valuable seconds as you moved away from stops on busy city routes. Never use a change speed pedal as if it were controlling a clutch.

The Leylands were different again, coming into four different categories. The first consisted of the pre-war machines having the Leyland 8.6 litre engine, with a cylinder head covering all six bores, and housing an overhead camshaft. These

Daimlers 4400 to 4489 went into service between November 1953 and February 1955. They found the technical assistants some work in solving their initial 'engine shutting down' problems as the vehicles came to a stand and then investigating brake and lining life problems.They were very successful buses. Roy Marshall took this photograph of No. 4421 on what must have been a cold day judging from the appearance of the unauthorised radiator blind. Cab heaters were not a Manchester luxury when these buses took the road, so drivers sought to keep their feet warmer by using newspapers or cardboard as a blanking plate.

vehicles had crash gearboxes, orthodox pedal layout, and push-on handbrakes, this being a standard Leyland arrangement in the 1930s. Now used almost entirely on part-day services, they provided the technical assistants with little work, but they handled from a driving point of view very well.

Series two came into a very different category, comprising the 'PD1' models of early post-war delivery. The first batch were only 7 ft 6 in. wide and weighed around 7 tons 10 cwt, but the later ones came out to the 8 ft dimension and so were very much heavier at 8 tons 3 cwt. With their Leyland 7.4 litre E1817 engines they were poor performers, for if the fuel pump stops were set to give a clean exhaust there was insufficient power, raise the fuel delivery and one had more urge but also more smoke. The gearbox although also of the crash variety did not help, as going (say) from second to third, one took the foot off the accelerator, moved the gear lever to neutral as the clutch was depressed and then counted one, two, three, four and on five moved both clutch pedal and the gear lever simultaneously. By this time the engine revolutions had died down, so on any but the slightest adverse gradient, a change back down to second could well be necessary. I was not a lover of the 'PD1' and it was some time before I came to be master of those unfortunate gearboxes.

Variety three was very different. The 'PD2' had the 0.600 9.8 litre engine, a spanking performance (until the fuel input was cut down in the interests of economy), and, wonder of wonders, a synchromesh gearbox. Well not quite, as bottom gear was of the crash form, and had in addition a very low ratio, so low in fact that many drivers would, before trying to engage it, come to a stand. This meant having to hold a laden bus on a hill on the handbrake which now was of the pull-on form (the 'PD1' was similarly fitted), but this was not a problem in the Manchester area where there were few steep gradients, and where second gear starts were the norm in consequence. Once on the edge of the Pennines, however, for example on the number 10 route to Greenfield, there were places where first gear had of necessity to be engaged, but once it had thanks to the ensuing low ratio of 6 to 1 a 'PD2' would climb a mountain.

A 'PD2' was also in standard trim rather speedier than either a Crossley (with its lower power output), or a Daimler (as their 112 hp Gardner engines were governed to 1,700 rpm), thanks to the 125 hp available, but of course top speed really depended on the governor setting and the 'PD2' as it came from Leyland had a combined pneumatic/mechanical unit. The pneumatic part controlled idling speed, the mechanical part maximum revolutions of 1,800 rpm. One such bus came in my time to be fitted experimentally with an all pneumatic governor, and before this was set to give standard performance the question was asked just what would happen if it was left in its unadjusted form?

I found myself driving the vehicle and performance was initially exhilarating, and then very worrying. The speed was in the mile a minute category before sense prevailed as the steering began to feel like jelly, and so a speedy conclusion was reached before anything came adrift.

The last series of Leylands, 30 in number, were the Department's first underfloor-engined buses. They took the road when industry opinion had not come to any very firm conclusions as to just what form such vehicles should take, so management had elected to experiment. As a result Nos. 1-18 followed the traditional Manchester single-deck body pattern and were fitted with a rear passenger entrance. Nos. 20-23 followed what was soon to become the accepted configuration and had front entrances so that they were potentially suitable for one-man-operation. Nos. 24 and 25 were different again having 33 seats within their Northern Counties bodywork, centre entrances, and maximum standing capacity. Needless to say they proved to be most unpopular, and a trial spell on the famous No. 53 route came to be of short duration. Finally Nos. 30 to 35 struck a very different note as they had bodies of the half-deck pattern. In other words the rear portion was higher than the front part to provide considerable space for luggage, as these six machines were intended for use on the city centre-Ringway airport service. It follows from the foregoing that there were no buses with the fleet Nos. 19, 26, 27, 28 and 29, but between them the 30 did provide the technical assistants with a fair amount of work; I will leave further comment until later.

Manchester did, of course, have another type of bus in service in this era, namely the electric-powered trolleybus and so an early task was to learn how to drive these interesting vehicles so as to become 'fully mobile'. Thanks to the full-width cab, the instructor could seat himself comfortably, on the nearside, and so give advice to his trainee, for if the controls were simple the overhead

Manchester's pre-war and early wartime trolleybuses were well built and had long lives but towards the end of their days did become decidedly run down. Here No. 1012 an original Crossley new in March 1938 stands in Stevensons Square on a Moston service in 1952. This was the type of trolleybus on which I passed my driving test. No. 1012 was withdrawn in July 1955.   *Roy Marshall*

system certainly was not. There were only two pedals coming up from the cab floor, the left one for power the right one for brake, whilst a conventional handbrake lever was located to the right side of the driver, and in these respects the two basic breeds of trolleybus were quite similar. The two varieties consisted of the pre-war or early wartime intake, the earliest examples of which dated from 1938, these being of Leyland or Crossley manufacture and having either two or three axles. The post-war buses were of all Crossley manufacture and again had either two or three axles, a subject to be considered in due course, but let us at this stage return to driving.

The standard method, when about to move off, was to pull on the handbrake, put on a modicum of power to firm up the drive as it were, and then slowly release that handbrake as the power pedal was depressed in a like manner. In this way a smooth take off could be achieved, but now came what to me was always a trolleybus surprise, because once you reached what can be best described as 'cruising speed' let the power pedal come back and, thanks to the motor armature acting as a flywheel, one's trolleybus would roll for quite a considerable distance on a flat piece of highway. Now, though, could come a snag for when restoring power one needed to put the pedal down to the point where power became appropriate to speed otherwise a nasty snatch could result, this state of affairs only applying to the earlier buses. The post-war Crossleys had automatic acceleration and so did not suffer similarly.

Trolleybus driving was an art of its own, every such Manchester vehicle had a white painted '0' on the rear panel to remind you as a trolley driver *not* overtake the one in front, otherwise there could be a mix up of two sets of booms, and prepare yourself for trouble. The overhead too had to be learned. In some places, for example on Oldham Road, the overhead was so far away from the kerb that if you tried to run by it dewirement would follow. At such places (here before Miles Platting) a string of fairy lights was run aloft to let you know just where it was. In those pre-smokeless fuel times, Manchester, like most other urban areas, suffered from days of 'pea soup fog'. On such occasions one normally used the kerb as a marker but at these places you needed swivelling eyes. One looking down to make sure you did not hit anything, the other looking up to allow your vehicle to follow the lights in the wires.

Then there were the points. If I remember correctly at most places in Manchester you coasted under the overhead skate to go right, and to go left, slowed before the skate, then with the trolleys under it put on the handbrake, and took more power when the points would move over and the signal marker lights fitted to an adjacent traction pole would indicate that the line was set for the required route. Needless to say, however, there was at least one place in the

There was a time in the 1950s when the idea of using buses with centre doors, low seating capacity and a lot of standing space occupied various managerial minds. Lancashire United and the SHMD Joint Board introduced such vehicles as did Manchester with its two Northern Counties-bodied Leylands, Nos. 24 and 25. Not surprisingly passengers preferred seats to standing space and the design fell out of favour. Manchester's were given 41 seats in 1958 and ended their conventional PSV careers in 1963. No. 25 subsequently escaped the scrap man and now resides in the Manchester Queens Road museum, where David Wayman took this photograph on a very wet day.

system where overhead point setting had to be done in reverse, i.e. power to the right. Then you could have a memory lapse with dire results. One day I had a vehicle out on test and arrived at Audenshaw Snipe. Reversal here meant going backwards into a narrow side street, and then coming out again to return towards Manchester. Being on my own I felt that going backwards was not a good idea, so I continued under Ashton wires to Chester Square. At that place an Ashton trolley coming from Guide Bridge was approaching the junction; as it was in service I gave the driver priority, and so began to follow him into Ashton town centre. We ran together along Old Street and as we reached the left-hand curve to take us into Warrington Street the Ashton driver braked, I had to do likewise but for an instant forgot what I was driving and pressed the left-hand pedal down, only it was not the clutch, it was the power pedal. My trolley took off, we went straight ahead, and the poles left the overhead wire which began to vibrate somewhat alarmingly. The Ashton conductor too looked alarmed for he was on his rear platform as my bus shaved past his.

Fortunately every Manchester trolleybus was able to move under battery power, so I hauled the poles down with bamboo provided, put the control box handle to battery forward, pressed the floor stud and ran along Old Street until we were back under the wires again. By a miracle nothing in the overhead came adrift, so with electric power available once more I left Ashton with grateful thanks to the trolleybus Gods, and never heard a thing about what could have been a very nasty affair. I never forgot again.

I had by this time passed my test in a way which was very unusual. My instructor was sitting in the back of my training vehicle as we came up to the *Daily Express* building in Great Ancoats Street when he came forward, opened the sliding window in the bulkhead, and pointed to a man walking on the pavement ahead who was carrying a sizeable brief case. 'Stop by him', said my teacher, 'I know where he is going, we will give him a lift'. I duly stopped, the stranger came on board, when my instructor asked me if I could find my way to the Manchester City's Ground at Greenhays which meant running over what with its numerous corners was Manchester's most difficult trolleybus route. We crossed Ashton Old Road, and Hyde Road, and then travelled via Brunswick Street and Lloyd Street to Greenhays (Platt Lane), where I put the bus into the loop. At this point the passenger came round to the front, opened the cab door, and asked me did I have my driving licence with me. Wondering somewhat I passed it to him, when he opened the briefcase, took out a pad of pink slips, and proceeded to write one out for me, adding as he did so that he was the MoT trolleybus driving examiner and he now had no doubts as to my competence. What a lovely way to be tested!

There was another driving hazard to be negotiated situated at the entrance to Hyde Road depot. This was a steel-framed washing bay that was over long, and not over wide. For the sake of safety the overhead was left normally dead so a driver had to approach the structure carefully, make sure his trolleybus was 'dead-centred' and then apply sufficient power to ensure it ran right through the structure and so back onto live wires. Initially at least negotiating could be a heart-stopping experience but after several encounters a more relaxed attitude could be adopted and one simply sailed through it.

When I was given the job of trying to improve the steering in 1954 of the sixteen 1951 three-axled all-Crossley trolleybuses they looked almost brand new having done very little mileage. The modifications were very successful but conductor opposition to working a 66-seater (58 seats on the two-axled version) continued to keep them on peak hour work. No. 1247 is here so engaged on a short working to Denton in April 1959, two years before withdrawal. *Roy Marshall*

Fortunately here the steering had to be set straight ahead, for post-war Crossley trolleybus steering characteristics were not all they should have been.There were 38 two-axled vehicles that could be classed as having heavy steering, and 16 three-axled vehicles with very much heavier (impossible) steering. I was told to see what could be done to ease matters, for these machines were only used on part-day tracks because of this fault, and, although around three years old looked almost new.

With their air brakes, there was quite a lot of space in the vicinity of the front hubs, due to the small size of the brake cylinders, and so one bus had different wheel discs fitted that brought the centre line of the tyre meeting at ground level the centre line of the king pin if projected downwards to that level. A series of wedges having different angles were then tried between the axle forging and the bottom of the springs to provide different castor angles, and after three or four trys we struck lucky, and some very acceptable steering came into being, the testing taking place on my Greenhays driving test route (*see diagram overleaf*).

The next step was to have several union representatives go out with me to try the modified bus for themselves. They found it to be much easier easier to handle than any of the previously more acceptable two-axled buses and so agreed after a little more negotiation that if all the remaining members of the batch, Nos. 1240-1255, were modified similarly they would become acceptable for all-day operation. So flushed with success I had orders placed for the necessary material, and Hyde Road Depot put the modifications in hand.

The Monday morning came a week or two later when all were to be used all day on the Piccadilly-Hyde-Gee Cross service, and so I travelled direct to Hyde Road to see how things were progressing, but I need not have bothered. The ones which

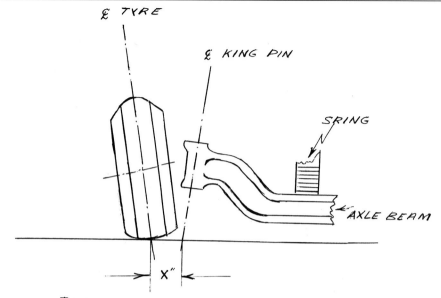

IT IS USUAL TO HAVE SOME DISTANCE HERE
TO REDUCE TYRE "SCRUB". REDUCED TO
"NIL" ON CROSSLEY

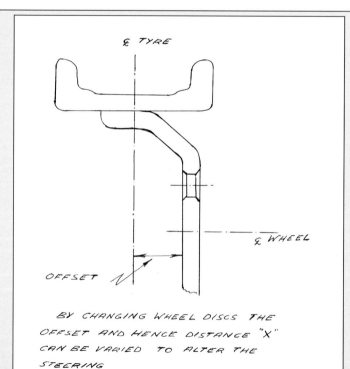

BY CHANGING WHEEL DISCS THE
OFFSET AND HENCE DISTANCE "X"
CAN BE VARIED TO ALTER THE
STEERING

at about 9.30 am were still on the road were coming in because now the conductors objected to having to deal with 66-seaters, whereas the other contingent in the series, 1200-1237, had only 58 seats. The request was then made 'Could the latter 38 be treated similarly to the now improved 16?', but we gracefully slid out of answering that question in the affirmative, and I transferred my attentions to Crossleys with internal combustion power units that were pretty much the same.

In their cases the size of the vacuum brake cylinders came in the way of fitting new wheel discs with different offsets, so a mounting plate was designed that moved these 'servos' inboard. Then we could change the discs and start more wedge experiments, when once again what had been very dead and heavy steering was suddenly much improved. There was, though, more Crossley work to do.

The superintendent of Birchfields Garage was Mr George Yates who suffered in two ways. Firstly his allocation of around 160 buses was all Crossley, and secondly, when the depot fuel consumption returns came out for the various periods, Birchfields was always bottom of the table. Could type '7' engines be made to drink rather less in the course of their daily excursions? By this time the Crossley Company was no more, having been taken over by Associated Commercial Vehicles, but Alf Jones who had been on the Crossley technical staff and was now similarly employed by AEC was consulted and offered several thoughts. Various experiments followed. We provided cold air induction to give a more 'dense' charge, amended the valve timing setting, adjusted fuel pump timing, and made other modifications which did effect some improvement, but we could have done more. I had a chat with Alex Dixon, then Oldham's rolling stock superintendent, who had four varieties of Crossley in his fleet, namely 10 single-deckers and 10 double-deckers of 1948 vintage with standard type '7' engines and four single-deckers and four double-deckers that were new in 1950 that had the later down draught engine. Mr Dixon showed me some figures which indicated that a down draught Crossley was better in service than a Leyland 'PD1' but was not, needless to say, up to the performance or fuel economy of a 'PD2'.

At this time Manchester had in use 290 Crossley oil-engined vehicles of post-war construction that had been delivered in batches of 71, 109, 50 and 60, the oldest of which dated from 1946 (excluding No. 2960 the original prototype), the newest from late 1949, so being less than five years old they still had a lot of life left in them. Negotiations with Errwood Park, where many ex-Crossley staff were still working, followed and a scheme to convert our later engines was costed, but in the end management refrained from taking any further action. Perhaps if my stay at Manchester had been longer we might at least have had some experimental engines running to prove the point to MCT satisfaction one way or the other. The price for a kit of parts was about £110.

I must, though, pass comment on what appeared at this time to be the standard Crossley response to our various failure claims. It basically went, 'We are surprised! We do not appear to have experienced anything of the sort previously, but rest assured it will now receive our urgent attention'. Perhaps if Crossley's had remained independent it might have done, as it was it did not.

Some of the newer rolling stock presented us with problems, and the single-deck Leylands began to claim our attention. Clutch life was to say the least low, and invariably a new flywheel insert had to be fitted as well as a new clutch plate.

The vehicles that in the main kept me interested and occupied during my time in Manchester were the 8 ft-wide all-Crossley double-deckers of the 109, 50 and 60 vehicle extracts. Being heavier at around 8 tons 3 cwt than their 7 ft 6 in.-wide predecessors they gave the maker's type 'HOE7' power units more to do and thanks to different front axles with king pin thrust buttons steering was decidedly heavy until modifications based on three-axled trolleybus work were made. The 109 contract Nos. 2000 to 2108, new in 1947/48, had constant mesh gear boxes as had the 50 contract Nos. 2110 to 2159 of 1948/49. The last 60, series Nos. 2160 to 2219 had synchromesh boxes, No. 2160 shown here was new in July 1949 and survived until October 1964.   *Roy Marshall*

The vehicles allocated to the Airport service not being subjected to numerous stops and starts per mile did not offend similarly, but they were fitted for obvious reasons with internal body combustion heaters instead of relying on the radiator cooling circuit. The clutch problem was eased for the depot staffs, but not for the drivers, by fitting stronger clutch springs, but we had not by the time I came to leave really found out why the heaters seemed to fail so often. Apart from looking into these various problems we also drew up specifications for new vehicles, and also for various components that were bought through the medium of the tendering process. These activities gave one the chance to visit our suppliers' works, and especially so if the associated products were not behaving as well as the engineering department thought that they should.

Other new rolling stock problems that we encountered concerned the 30 Northern Counties-bodied Leyland 'PD2s' Nos. 3300-3329, and the 90 Daimler 'CVG6s' Nos. 4400-4489. From the former came a front end 'bumping' noise when in motion, and this took some finding, which meant taking several rides whilst perched on the nearside front wing, with the bonnet open, or preferably removed. Eventually we found that there were in effect two dashplates one behind the other with no packing between them, which meant that the requisite degree of silence could only be obtained after some dismantling had been effected.

The Daimler problem was quite interesting. All too often when one of the buses was in service the engine would shut down as the vehicle came to a stand, and as buses stop on average four times a mile, or more often when in city traffic, this became more than a nuisance. The driver then had to engage neutral and press the starter button, which to say the least did not do much for his morale. Now the usual method of driving a Daimler with a preselector box was to come to a stand whilst still in top, engage bottom or second if few passenger movements were involved, and so be ready for a quick move off, but shutting down prevented all that. We carried out various experiments, with stronger fuel pump rack springs, or putting up the idling speed, but in the end found that all this was due to Daimler incorporating a more efficient fluid flywheel, so a solution came with the fitting internally of a baffleplate when wear and tear on the driver's thumb was considerably reduced.

These same Daimlers also had a revised brake linkage, and this seemed to put much more braking effort onto the rear brakes. An experiment was then carried out using twin piston servos. These were mounted in tandem on a single piston rod, so that, theoretically at least, twice the braking pull came to be exerted on the operating levers. I found myself one wet Saturday morning testing the first example to be so amended, and there was no doubt that when the brakes were applied things were different. The front wheels locked and an uncontrollable skid developed that could well have had sad consequences if it had continued for a few more feet, so we began to seek other alternatives.

Manchester being a very large undertaking had of necessity to buy vast amounts of engineering material, when low price and high quality were sought from our suppliers. In those now far-off days there were a large number of brake lining firms in existence, e.g. Mintex, Capasco, Ferodo, Duron, Top Dog, Chekko, Tenoid, Don, to name but a few, and all of these were desirous of receiving Manchester orders. As a result a great deal of time was spent seeing how various test sets performed and taking the vehicles involved for brake tests on the very quiet and wide Hardy Lane. The object of the exercise was to discover which linings suited each type of bus best, by giving adequate stopping power and low wear without achieving that low wear rate as a result of the material rapidly increasing the internal diameter of the attendant brake drums. At the time few brake testing machines existed, so a Tapley meter had to be used, and obtaining the standard of 30 per cent handbrake efficiency as required by the Ministry of Transport examiners was often rather difficult to reach. A strong arm at such times was very desirable.

This search for improved efficiency came to include exhaust brake experiments. The idea behind such devices was to fit a unit as near to the exhaust manifold as possible. This consisted of an operating mechanism controlling a horizontal flap valve that could be so moved into a vertical position that the exit of the exhaust gases from the cylinders was largely prevented. This 'muffled' the unit, so that the back pressure so created provided a braking effect. There were two ways of bringing exhaust brakes into operation. One was by having a footbrake pedal pad that incorporated a switch, so that each time the brake was applied the exhaust brake came into effect, thus taking it outside the control of the driver, whilst the second was to mount an independent lever under the steering wheel so that 100 per cent selection was available. Well they did work to a degree, and perhaps if we had been running buses up and down alps we would have persevered, but in the end it was decided that they were bound to have an adverse effect on engine life and another endeavour was left for posterity to record.

The 30 Leyland 'PD2s' with Northern Counties bodies, Nos. 3300 to 3329, were smart vehicles and found little work for the technical assistants once the bumping noise coming from the front end had been traced and eliminated. Note the wide upper saloon front centre window pillar. This housed the trunking which connected the perforated upper saloon ceiling panels to the engine air intake thus providing upper saloon ventilation. Drawing copious quantities of cigarette fumes into the power unit did not appear to induce lung cancer or other bronchial ailments in the attendant 0.600s. *Roy Marshall*

By 1954 economy was the order of the day, hence the purchase of 20 Daimler 'CVG5' chassis with MCW lightweight bodies having 64 seats, Nos. 4490-4509, of which No. 4490 was based on an almost unique Daimler chassis with as much weight as possible having been eliminated. Note No. 4492 shown here has an external radiator filler, one of the design tasks in which I was involved in my Daimler drawing office days. This photograph was taken in Piccadilly bus station in August 1955. *Roy Marshall*

Saving staff time was another factor that exercised our minds, and topping up engines was an expensive nightly chore. The usual drill was for an engine oiler to go down the lines once the buses were parked up, lift the bonnet unless there was a suitable access hole provided, and then take out and wipe the dipstick before checking the sump level. If it was on the mark move on to the next bus, if not leave the bonnets up. Once this preliminary survey had been completed go round with the engine oil bowser and add the amount of lubricant necessary, making a careful note of vehicle number and quantity required. Sump-topping figures when turned into mpg gave a very good indication as to engine condition. For example a brand new Gardner could use next to nothing for weeks, but eventually as ring and bore wear took place a figure of say 1,250 mpg could drop to 250 mpg, and by then some attention, if not before, was indicated. I used to think that if my monthly mpg figure for the fleet averaged over 800 miles per gallon then there was not much to worry about, but all this is an aside.

Someone had a bright idea. Mount a reservoir container with a sight glass on the front panel in the space behind the front wing. Run a pipe from the reservoir to a unit mounted on the sump and fit this with a float valve. As the oil is burned due to bore and ring wear, the valve will open, lubricant will flow into the sump, and then when the right level is restored it will close up again. No need to lift bonnets, and wipe dipsticks, one look at the sight glass will tell you all you need to know. We fitted a few and monitored them carefully but once again it was felt that engine repair costs being what they were a competent engine oiler was much more reliable than an automatic device.

We thought then that fuel costs were far too high so improving fuel consumption figures was in everyone's minds, and so we came to the 'lightweight' era when a batch of 20 Daimler 'CVG5s' was ordered to be fleet Nos. 4490-4509, but I will save my comments on this particular phase for later. I must, though, say something about Crossley's former Errwood Park factory's final effort. There were some 165 trolleybuses in the fleet, and some of these dating as they did from 1938 were, by 1954, not exactly in the first flush of youth. It was in consequence decided to order 62 new vehicles from the BUT organisation which was jointly owned by AEC and Leyland, when any home market trolleybus order came to be based on Southall designs whilst Leyland took care of export market requirements.

As a result Errwood Park came to build the 62 chassis, but for a variety of reasons production was badly delayed which had a very adverse effect on Burlingham's of Blackpool who took the body order. This firm had expected that they would be erecting double-deck trolleybus bodies for Manchester in that part of the year when luxury coach production was minimal, but thanks to the aforementioned delays famine and then feast followed in that order and there was 'woe' in the land, and not least within our Piccadilly Headquarters.

I was by now quite convinced that being a Manchester technical assistant was the best job that I had ever had, even if the pay was identical to that which I had been receiving at Leeds. Working at Piccadilly was pure joy, and I found myself often impatient on Sunday for Monday morning to dawn, when thanks to my treasured 'Official's Pass' I could travel at will on our buses, and those of the joint operators in our area. But I still had ambitions, and so an advert put out by Halifax Passenger Transport for an Assistant Engineer at all of £695 to £760 took my eye.

I made a few inquiries, to find that the title was rather unfortunate, due to the head of the undertaking being styled General Manager and Engineer, so that the holder of the post being advertised would in fact be head of the engineering department and so would report directly to the chief. The fact that the Halifax fleet strength of 164 buses was a little less than our Manchester trolleybus numbers was not important, this would provide more in the way of all round experience, so I asked Mr Oakham if he would mind if I submitted my application and he kindly replied in the negative.

A week or two later I received a letter telling me that I had been selected for interview, an event scheduled to commence at 2.30 pm. On the morning in question I knocked on our Chief Engineer's door, to ask if I might leave in time to catch the 11.35 am bus to Halifax. As he replied 'of course' he gave me a curious smile, and then said that he would tell me something the following morning irrespective of whether I had been successful at Halifax or not. I tried to discover just what this implied without success, which certainly left me wondering.

I arrived in Halifax around 1.00 pm, had a quick snack and walk round, and then made my way to the Town Hall to find myself involved in a standard Municipal full Transport Committee affair. What happens is as follows, the candidates are received and ushered into a waiting room where you sit with your opposition until called into the room where your inquisition is to take place, usually appearance takes place in alphabetical order. After one's formal interview you are shown into a second room where you may or may not discuss what transpired before the Committee with your filleted fellows, until the last victim is brought in, and then you wait while the Committee members debate what their choice is going to be. Once that choice is made the Committee Clerk, usually a member of the staff of the Town Clerk, comes in and asks Mr Successful to step forward, then the Committee Chairman offers congratulations on one's appointment and asks if you have any questions. That moment represents your only chance to suggest that more salary might be offered, or can the figure of removal expenses quoted be varied upwards, only at this time the latter consideration did not apply as none were then being paid.

My turn came when the then Chairman, a very senior Alderman, introduced me to the Committee and also to the General Manager (Mr Roderick MacKenzie) stating that the latter had a few questions to put to me, when the word 'awkward' should have been included. They were snorters! Fortunately I had done some homework, as we had copies of past Halifax annual reports back at Piccadilly. When asked what I thought tyre costs might be in Halifax I was able to say that ours in Manchester were then 0.39 dpm, whereas thanks to the local roads and gradients in Halifax and district something under 1.0 dpm could be regarded as satisfactory. The costs reported the previous year were 0.93 dpm. Then we moved onto fuel and repair costs, so I utilised my local knowledge to say that no Manchester bus had to face routes with the geographical characteristics of those to, say, Heptonstall or Brighouse via Brookfoot, and so was able to provide answers that seem to satisfy. The Chairman then inquired why it was that I appeared to know the area so well, so I replied that my wife was a local girl, and whilst I had been working for Leeds City Transport we had for a time had a house in one of the nearby hamlets. The interview took around 25 minutes, and then I was dispatched to waiting room No. 2, to await that momentous decision.

By good fortune it was in my favour, so I was called back to be offered the post when my intended General Manager left to have a word with my former competition. Once he was no longer in view another Alderman came up to me, shook me by the hand, and said, 'Tha did weel, reet weel, but don't let yon B..... upset you, he's just the bloody same with us', that gave me something more still to ponder over. As it was I found him a most capable General Manager, who knew his own mind, who was good to work for, and invariably very supportive, but he could be off-putting until you came to know him well. After we left the Town Hall he took me to Skircoat Road to look over the premises, and then for a meal to tell me what would be expected from me. He indicated that my competition had not been as good as he had expected, and if full justice had been done then I might not have been sitting where I was. But as these words were uttered with the ghost of a smile, were they really meant?

I went home on the Oldham bus thinking that life was going to be decidedly hectic in the days to come, and here I was not wrong, but pleasure at my success was then completely dissipated by my finding Uncle George in hospital where he passed away that night (*see Volume One*). The following morning I was at Piccadilly early but not as early as Mr Oakham who called me into his office as soon as I reached my desk. He then congratulated me on my Halifax appointment (just how did he know that I had been successful by that time?) and then said he had promised to tell me something so now was the time. Did I really want to go to Halifax, or would I rather stay in Manchester with the title of senior technical assistant on the same salary as that offered over the Pennines?

I asked for a day to think the situation over, but had in the end to say that whilst I was very grateful for the offer I felt that it would be in my long term interests to leave. As I saw it at Manchester I would be ever more immersed in the technical aspects of the job, whilst at Halifax as a departmental head I would be seeing every facet of engineering activity including control of the engineering labour force. So a few weeks later, feeling rather sad, I left Manchester and all the good things City Transport had provided, plus, whisper it softly, another factor in the overall balance.

As technical assistants we had a roving commission so we were to be found not only in head office, but also at Hyde Road works or in the garages at Rochdale Road, Hyde Road, Princess Road, Queens Road, Birchfields, Parrs Wood, and Northenden where we always received a friendly welcome from their respective superintendents. If anyone had bothered to check on our whereabouts around lunchtime, fortunately no one did, they would have found that we gravitated towards two of these that will still remain unidentified. Why? Well the lunchtime food served at these places was simply delicious, and the company too was excellent.

Not every fleet engineer of that time had the ambition to progress to managership, being very content to deal with the 'nuts and bolts', whilst of those who had ambition, by no means all achieved the desired result. Was I in the end going to make it? The answer I felt would depend on what opportunities presented themselves in the future and then just how lucky I was, but even if I never did, being head of an engineering department of a bus undertaking was far better than working in Gorton works or shed. I had a lot to be thankful for.

North Western purchased 10 all-Leyland coaches, fleet Nos. 600 to 609, in 1952. With 41 seats they lasted until 1963. Roy Marshall took this photograph of No. 600 heading out of London. The location of the front nearside seat I was occupying when we came 'adrift' on Windy Hill in January 1955 is clearly visible. Unfortunately I cannot remember the fleet number of the 'Royal Tiger' involved, but they were very comfortable vehicles.

Bus No. 229 in the JOC fleet is a typical 7 ft 6 in.-wide AEC/Park Royal product, with the thinness of the main pillars all too plainly displayed. This bus has the original JOC insignia on the orange panelling which contained within the garter the Halifax, LNER and LMS insignia. Not really appropriate after 1st January, 1948 it lasted into the regime of Mr MacKenzie when only the above-200 fleet number readily identified a JOC vehicle.

Chapter Three

Assistant Engineer, Halifax

On Monday 3rd January, 1955 I left our Oldham home at around 7.40 am and made my way to the Halifax bus stop. This was then located in the lower part of Greaves Street against a low wall that had formed a part of a now demolished cotton mill and behind the wall was a now derelict site later occupied by a small café-cum-snack bar, only that facility was not yet open. Of shelter there was none, so one stood on a rising gradient in a very windswept location.

At this time six services used Greaves Street as a terminal or picking up point, these being:

The joint Yorkshire Woollen/North Western X12 express service to Halifax and Bradford scheduled to depart at two minutes to the hour.

The remarkable Mersey-Tyne-Tees long distance operation with its six partners running to Leeds, Newcastle and Middlesbrough that left at quarter past the hour, something I had used frequently in my Leeds days.

The Hanson two hourly service to Huddersfield via Uppermill timed to leave at five minutes to the even hour. Once the haunt of Albion single-deckers it now found work for a Roe-bodied 'Regent III' double-decker.

The Oldham-worked 'P' route to Uppermill via Scouthead and Delph station that left at quarter past each hour. Pre-war single-deck-worked, it now utilised one of Oldham's Leyland deckers.

The reverse of the above from Oldham to Uppermill via Lees. This was worked by North Western as service No. 153 and left at a quarter to each hour. Both of the above workings were in fact circular, going out one way, and coming back another. On Saturday evenings however Oldham buses put in the odd appearance on the 153 but then ran into Peter Street on their return to the town, a thoroughfare now covered by the Spindles shopping centre.

Finally there was another North Western service to Huddersfield via Delph introduced pre-war, ostensibly to keep Hanson out. Not now on a regular interval basis, it was finally withdrawn on 31st December, 1970 when no local authority subsidy was forthcoming. To that date it was timed to leave at five minutes to the odd hour sometimes. At first it passed our third Delph house in Huddersfield Road then it was altered to run through the village but loadings were never brilliant so that in pre-war days a Dennis 'flying pig' one-man single-decker was the usual allocation. In other words one of the six 1934 vintage Dennis 'Ace' chassis with a four-cylinder petrol engine, a short wheel base and 20-seat Eastern Coach Works body, fitted for one-man-operation.

It was more than chilly as I stood waiting at this far from delectable spot and sad to say the 7.58 would on this of all mornings fail to appear. All I could do was to wait for the 8.58 which finally came into view only about 20 minutes behind time. This of course meant that instead of reporting to my new General Manager just after nine of the clock I was not able to knock on his door until around half past ten, when he bleakly, or so it seemed, accepted the profound excuses that I came to make on behalf of North Western Road Car Ltd.

On Tuesday morning I stood in Greaves Street once more hoping that the 7.58 would arrive on time, but needless to say it did not, but still 8.25 was a lot better than 9.20, and as a bonus we had not an ordinary bus, but a *coach*, one of the Leyland-bodied 'Tigers', with a centre door, and a seat right at the front besides the driver. This was unoccupied on arrival, and I began to think myself truly blessed as the heaters were working, and a pair of rather icy feet began to gently thaw out. Greaves Street over the years must have made a considerable impact on the health of several generations of would-be bus passengers, until in May 1965 the short-lived North Western combined bus station and garage was opened in adjacent Clegg Street.

As it was we swept through the Mumps Junction, up the gradients to Grains Bar, through Denshaw and so over the top of the Pennine range to Windy Hill towards the place where the M62 motorway intersection now stands. Here we were travelling quite fast when the driver decided to apply the brakes which was a pity as we were at the time on a nice sheet of best Yorkshire-style black ice. There was a 'swoosh' as we spun through 180 degrees taking out a perfectly innocent telegraph pole in the process to finish up with the driver on the floor, and the coach beginning to run backwards down the gradient. I reached over, pulled up the handbrake and we came to a halt, but the pole had not done the rear end a lot of good so now we had another service car that was not going to see either Halifax or Bradford that day. It was facing whence it came, and so it stayed.

We stayed where we were until the 8.58, late of course yet again, came to the rescue so even more profound apologies to be made after I had knocked very late yet again on a certain door. This did not seem to be the ideal way to start a new job, but worse was to follow. On the Wednesday the 7.58 was actually on time, and made it safely to Ripponden but at that point thanks to my freezing wait on Monday I had to surrender to a dose of influenza, and as a result my Halifax career really began not on 3rd January but on the 10th, when I began to make some interesting discoveries.

There were then 164 buses in stock but seven of these stood delicensed in Skircoat garage consisting of five Roe-bodied and two Weymann-bodied AEC Mark I double-deckers, these being the last survivors of the pre-war fleet. Mr MacKenzie was adamant that only 7 per cent spare buses should be kept over maximum service requirement, so what had we that were allegedly available for use?

Almost brand new were 22 Daimlers with Gardner '6LW' engines, 10 for the Joint Committee having MCW lightweight bodies, the other 12 Corporation members having Roe coachwork. I felt that these would be no trouble for some time to come which was sadly very incorrect. Then there were the six Daimler 'CD650' machines with East Lancs bodies, Daimler 10.6 litre engines and a hydraulic system that was a Chinese puzzle in itself. These were members of the Corporation fleet, as were nine Leyland 'PD2s' with synchromesh gearboxes (our only buses with conventional transmission) and three AEC Mark III single-deckers with Roe rear entrance single-deck bodies. Another 19 single-deckers were contained within the Joint fleet, some still having their original rear entrances others painted cream having been fitted with forward doors so as to make them fit for one-man-operation on the more rural routes.

The balance of 98 buses consisted of vehicles based on the AEC 9.6 litre-engined 'Regent III' chassis. The first eight of these were historic as they were built to

LPTB standards, and were the first such to enter provincial service. They had Roe bodies, but no saloon heaters which made them very unpopular with their conductors in winter. They dated from December 1946, whilst the last of the 'Regent III' breed came new in 1951 and also had a London look about them as they had Park Royal metal-framed bodies of four bay construction. These were not at all bad, and the same could be said of another 10 'Regent IIIs' that had Roe bodies. Two of these should have been Corporation fleet single-deckers, but when the decision was taken not to restore the pre-war Bairstow Lane route Nos. 73 and 74 emerged as double-deckers entering service on the 1st January, 1950.

The remaining 74 'Regents' had Park Royal timber-framed bodies that were to say the least unfortunate. Purchased between 1947 and 1949 through the medium of loan sanction, they were delivered during a period of rapidly increasing prices via a rise and fall type contract. Consequently to keep the price down to something approaching the original quotations the idea of including proper window pans in their build was dropped, and some none too wide main pillars were rebated to accept windows with rubber seals kept *in situ* by wooden fillets. Fifty-eight of these were 7 ft 6 in. wide and originally had 56 seats, they were not good, worse however were the sixteen 8 foot-wide specimens, all Joint Committee vehicles, that came into use in December 1948 or January 1949. These will be mentioned in greater detail later.

When I arrived Halifax buses were covering some 6½ million miles a year. Just under three million miles were worked by the Corporation or 'A' fleet as it will be described hereafter, whilst the Joint Committee or 'B' fleet made up the balance. There were then three single-deck and 75 double-deck buses in the 'A' fleet, plus seven delicensed = 85, and 19 single-deck (5 with rear entrances and 14 with front entrances) plus 60 double-deckers in the 'B' fleet. Remember here that these were high mileages for the time, mileages over roads that all too often contained some very indifferent surfaces and were infested with steep gradients and sharp bends. In many places the roads our buses used were little more than country lanes, and remote ones at that. Intense operation was the order of the day, and vehicles could easily run up over 6,000 miles in any four week period. Add to all this the extreme weather that winters could produce in the 1950s, and the scene was set for some interesting times.

Now one cannot maintain a fleet of buses without equipment and men. Halifax had two garages, Elmwood, which had three pits, the greasing equipment and an Essex washing machine, was opened on 4th November, 1932 at a cost of £23,500 having been built to house the 'B' fleet, and Skircoat the old tram shed that over the years had been adapted and extended. The parking bays thanks to 3 ft 6 in. gauge tramway dimensions were too narrow for comfort, but Mr MacKenzie had made some useful alterations to the workshops contained therein, and one could not say that there was a shortage of plant. I should also mention here that being of a tidy mind he had a fleet renumbering exercise put in train so that by the time of my arrival all 'B' fleet buses were numbered over 200, 'A' fleet buses coming below that figure.

From a staffing point of view I was fortunate. Men who have served their time to a trade were in that period of high employment very secure, and so were not prone to be continually moving from one job to another. The same could be

Sixteen AEC 'Regent III' 8 ft-wide buses with thin-framed Park Royal bodies originally Nos. 235 to 250 went into service from 1st December, 1948, and these provided even more structural problems than their 7 ft 6 in.-wide compatriots. Later as fleet Nos. 335 to 350 they were taken out of service between November 1960 (No. 240) and September 1965 (Nos. 347 and 348). All were JOC owned. When new they were regular performers on the Halifax to Huddersfield and Hebden Bridge to Brighouse services.

The 12 Daimler/Roe 'CVG6' Nos. 87 to 98 went in service from February to March 1954 so were just about 12 months old when I came to know them and their engine problems. So why were they subject to premature wear/failure? We never did discover a single cause so perhaps it was a combination of factors - 8 tons unladen weight - Coalene fuel mixture - and low power equals much low gear use.

said of those who were designated as being 'semi-skilled', although in many instances the description 'semi' was a misnomer, they really knew what they were about. The net result was that we had a high proportion of staff members who knew their jobs, and without them successful maintenance would have been impossible. The full list of staff in the Department on 31st March, 1955 was as follows:

Electricians	5
Electricians' apprentice	1
Mechanics	33
Mechanics' apprentices	3
Coachbuilders	17
Coachbuilders' apprentices	2
Coach painters	5
House painters	2
Running repair men	14
Mason	1
Greasers and oilers	6
Works labourers	14
Shunter cleaners	8
Cleaners	22
Storekeeper	1
Stores issuers	2
Works foremen	5
Garage foremen and superintendent	8
Engineering assistants	2
Rolling stock superintendent	1
	152
Plus this author	1
Total	153

The full departmental staff then numbered 772, there being 262 drivers and 197 conductors plus 86 conductresses and 17 traffic inspectors, with administrative/ clerical personnel in addition.

Although not then officially recognised as such there were really two parts to the engineering department, namely major repairs and servicing. The former was undertaken in the Skircoat-based dock, fitting, body, paint and electricians shops where skilled tradesmen went about their various tasks, each shop having a foreman and a chargehand. Servicing was a garage function, where washing, cleaning, oiling and greasing and road calls were attended to. These functions were supervised by the garage superintendent Jack Kitchen and his seven garage foremen who had come up through the ranks usually via a cleaner, shunter/cleaner, shift man progression. They worked on shifts covering every hour of every day, and also had one other important job, for Halifax had a very economical system.

Every day the traffic office produced output sheets for each of the two garages. These listed each signing on time for the staff destined to work the same, and also their various names. At the material time they would report to the garage foreman who would tick them off and hand out their route plate which showed their scheduled journeys. At the same time he would indicate which bus had been allocated, and just where in the garage it could be found. You will understand from this that the life of a garage foreman could be particularly hectic when early morning fleet output was in progress, and especially so if one of the front buses parked in line in a Skircoat narrow bay failed to start, and so was blocking in those in the queue behind it, or someone failed to show up when spare men had to be found and allocated.

Supporting each foreman during his period on duty were two shift men. They did minor maintenance tasks such as fitting new light bulbs or helping non-starters to do just that. They also covered the road calls and so found themselves often faced with some awkward situations, especially during periods of bad weather.

As I began to digest all the foregoing plus a variety of other associated topics two things struck me. Firstly, up to that time I had responded to the instructions given to me by my superiors, now unless Mr MacKenzie was going to be very much in control of the engineering department what might happen in the future would be down to me. Secondly, my title was, as mentioned earlier, rather more unfortunate than I had at first thought. Mr MacKenzie held the post of General Manager and Engineer, so I was labelled Assistant Engineer but I had an assistant, who at the time was exactly twice as old as I was, had years of practical experience behind him, and was known as the rolling stock superintendent. For quite some time if we met anyone new, he was received as if he was head of our Department whilst I was treated as his assistant. This certainly did little to make life easy for I was told that he had been promised the top job earlier, but a sudden change in circumstances took place to his ultimate disadvantage. That was not anything I could help so the big question facing me was where did I begin? That question was solved for me within two hours of my first arrival, that Monday morning.

Deciding to go into town for lunch I left Skircoat garage, and walked to the bus stop opposite the yard. A vehicle obviously taking up service came from the Elmwood establishment and stopped for me. I then went upstairs and sat on the nearside front seat. We reached Wards End and began to negotiate the roundabout there when the front frames opened and a gap appeared between the edge of the window glass, and the pillar. I put a pencil in the gap, and as the bus straightened up to descend Horton Street I could not remove it. Then we turned another corner and I could. In King Edward Street at the loading barrier I introduced myself to the driver and asked if he would take it back whence it came, and tell the foreman on duty from me that it must not to go out again until I had cleared it.

After lunch I found it parked outside my office, and questioned our highly competent body shop foreman Leslie Boulton as to what he knew about it. Leslie knew a lot, and also about the 30 or so others that were in a similar condition. Those missing window pans were having a much greater effect than anyone could ever have imagined. This was not something that could be put right in a day. We opened this example up to find frame movement everywhere so a whole series of pillar brackets, tie bars and fabricated stiffeners were produced and fitted and also to every one that subsequently passed through overhaul. But the whole structure as designed and modified simply was not up to Halifax conditions and the attendant loading, accelerating and decelerating forces. With a 9.6 litre engine, air brakes and an unladen weight of 7 tons 11 cwt these were a good driver's bus even if they were a body maintenance nightmare. There were then 74 bodies of this general design in the fleet. All in due course had to be similarly strengthened.

Trouble was coming my way from a much more substantial quarter, but before looking into this matter a spot of arithmetic is necessary. You have 157 licensed buses and your GM says 7 per cent spares only, that gives you a float of 11 against a peak output of 147. Subtract never less than three in the body shop on overhaul plus a fourth accident damage, three in the paint shop, and several on dock including two waiting for a new Certificate of Fitness and there is little left to cover emergencies. Add to that the fact that the fleet has a surplus of single-deckers and around 3.00 pm each afternoon you could well find yourself in crises. Here one hopes one's newest buses are doing their stuff, but are they? Answer in the negative, as you begin to appreciate that Manchester and Halifax operating conditions are poles apart.

The 12 Corporation fleet Daimlers (Nos. 87 to 98) were about nine months old and had begun life as one would expect with Gardner '6LW' engines using little or no lubricating oil, returns of anything over 2,000 miles per gallon being the norm, but this happy state of affairs was no longer apparent. Consumption was down into the few hundreds or even worse, so in an attempt to discover just what was happening locks were placed on the filler caps and very intensive topping up checks were made. Results showed that oil was being burned. Then came a spate of failures. Pistons seized, cylinder liners were pulled down, and then bearings began to fail, something that was almost unheard of. Then the 10 JOC buses began to suffer similarly but not, thank goodness, to quite the same extent, so what could be the cause? Gardner staff came and went whilst I made various visits to their Patricroft headquarters, and they pointed the finger at the lubricating oil we were using and also our special 'blend' of fuel.

Now at this time every Halifax bus had a very distinctive smell, thanks to the use of Coalene. This was a by-product of a coal distillation process, and arrived by the tanker load. It was pumped into an above ground storage vessel that bore all the signs of having begun life as a Lancashire-type boiler. Next a derv tanker came on the scene and its load was dropped into an underground tank; and once this process was completed one of our two engineering assistants unlocked the coalene tank valve and ran the requisite amount down to join the derv, to give a two parts derv to one part coalene mixture, if indeed it did mix properly as coalene had a heavier specific gravity. So 4,000 gallons of derv equals 2,000 gallons of coalene. Now these Gardner engines were of the then quite recent 'K' type design having an output of 112 bhp at 1,700 rpm and they had a low compression ratio. Slipper type pistons were fitted and these had a reduced number of compression and scraper rings, when, alas, they found the coalene mix to be very indigestible indeed. Starting even on a warm morning was not a quick process and volumes of white smoke would be emitted, together with sundry coughs and bangs, until in due course sufficient heat had been generated but heat also came from other sources.

The nadir came one morning around 10.00 am when there was a knock on my office door. My invitation to 'Come in' found a driver and conductor standing before me when the latter said in words etched on my mind: 'Mr Hilditch can

1947/48 saw much of the pre-war Halifax fleet replaced and the arrival of seven all-Leyland 'PD2' double-deckers as Nos. 335 to 341, all entering service on 1st November, 1947. Two more but with enclosed under canopy heaters followed as Nos. 342 and 343 on 1st March, 1948. All were later renumbered as 100 to 108. Of these Nos. 101, 104 106 and 108 were sold to Oldham Corporation Transport in 1965/66 overhauled and repainted by Halifax before dispatch. For a short time from September 1965 No. 108 became a JOC fleet member as No. 308 as shown here prior to preparation for its move to Oldham.

Mr Cook, appointed General Manager in September 1947, went to the 1950 Earls Court Commercial Vehicle Show and there saw the Daimler 'CD650' exhibit. Obviously impressed he ordered six for the 'A' fleet which with H30/26R East Lancashire bodies went into service in November 1951 as fleet Nos. 349 to 354 to become 81 to 86 under the MacKenzie scheme. Alas, he had no way then of knowing just what problems their braking systems would provide. All were taken out of service between July and September 1962. Mr Cook too was to have a short life sadly suffering a fatal heart attack whilst in office in October 1951.

tha do owt abaat these bloody Daimlers. The one we 'ad wouldn't bloody go in fact it were so bad, that ah got off as we left depot walked into town, and ah were theer afore my mate.' It was true too! Gardner's did not supply reconditioned engines but in the end in order to help the firm provided us with reconditioned crank cases. We had to build them up into complete replacement power units which did begin to strain our resources, but as the Leyland, Daimler and AEC engines did not suffer anything like as badly I began to wonder.

The Daimlers weighed around a ton more than the 'Regents', had 61 seats and were 8 ft wide. They had vacuum brakes, and spring-loaded preselector gearboxes so pushing down the change speed pedal was much harder than it was on a 'Regent III' with its air assistance. Consequently the Daimlers were not exactly a 'good drivers' bus' and spent more of their time in the lower gears than did the other buses in the fleet. I perhaps foolishly advanced this argument during a visit to Patricroft when I gently suggested that at least 125 bhp would be of advantage. The net result was that on return to base I found an angry GM waiting for me asking who did I think I was to tell Mr Hugh Gardner himself that his engines were not big enough? Perhaps my boss was cross with me for also suggesting that, 'With the work load now facing us a seven per cent spare quota was much too low, so please could we return those seven pre-war 'Regent Is' to duty.' They had preselector transmission, the gear selector lever coming up from the floor and looking for all the world like a normal gear stick. In the event he did agree but not for long for our two Weymann-bodied examples left for pastures new, the five with Roe bodies surviving rather longer, until the last three departed forever.

Gearsticks were yet another problem, and here I must turn to our nine Leyland 'PD2s' (Nos. 100 to 108). They were our only orthodox transmission (i.e. in 1955 terms) buses and there was no doubt that they were much more demanding in terms of physical effort than a 'Regent III'. They exhibited a whole series of defects. The gear levers snapped quite often, the synchromesh system did not always work, propeller shaft welding gave way, their rubber bushed spring shackles caused them to lean badly, and take off from rest could give rise to a series of kangaroo-like leaps that was quite disconcerting. There was only one thing to do and that was to bring in each one in turn and give it a thorough overhaul, when as many of these faults as possible could be eradicated but here we were back with an engineering truth. If we had had 98 Leylands and only nine 'Regents IIIs' it was almost certain that the latter would have been the unpopular buses, but a few years later when back in Halifax I began to think that this maxim might not be wholly accurate. As it was we made a start with No. 105.

Looking back after so many years I am sure that there was a recipe that would have provided Halifax with a fleet of well nigh indestructible buses, and we actually had the basis of such a salvation already in our hands in the forms of the six Daimler 'CD650' vehicles, Nos. 81-86. But on the other hand if you really wanted to experience 1955 problems here were one's subjects all ready and waiting. As it was a 'CD650' with an improved engine, proper power-assisted steering and air brakes would have been a winner. If only!

PW. 1313

The 10 Daimler 'CVG6'/MCW vehicles JOC fleet Nos. 284 to 293 (later 290 to 299) weighed 7 t. 2 cwt 3 q. and provided less in the way of engine problems - but bodies were another matter until some local modifications were made. No. 293 received that turbo-charged Gardner '6LW', whilst No. 299 was given a second-hand Daimler 'CVD6' power unit. Nos. 296 to 299 were sold to Derby in 1967/8. The most striking member of the batch was No. 285 which went into service on the Washer Lane route on 8th August, 1956 in that very short-lived reversed livery - green below the lower saloon windows, orange above. By an odd coincidence a certain Assistant Engineer lived in that area!

Amazingly after what had gone before, the last five Roe-bodied 'CVG6' vehicles of October/November 1956 were excellent performers. Unladen weight was 7 t. 12 cwt 3 q. seating capacity 37/28. These had teak lower deck frames, and light alloy upper ones. Originally 'A' fleet Nos. 15 to 19 they became Nos. 115 to 119 in 1960, more alterations followed in 1971 and 1972. This photograph was taken in George Square, Halifax.

These Daimlers, like all buses of that make, had a very strong chassis that possessed double members from the front to the rear of the front spring rear brackets, so nothing was going to sag in old age. All the mechanical components such as the rear axles were substantial and gave no trouble unlike those in the 'CVG6' versions where their 5.4 to 1 worm wheels were showing signs of over-rapid wear, but more of that later. The engines were tough when two initial problems had been solved, namely the way in which piston rods could split down the centrally drilled oilway and the habit of air intake filters being drawn down into the induction manifolds. True fuel consumption was on the high side but they did weigh over 8 tons, and were employed on heavy 'A' routes. Some more development work could have been undertaken if only Radford had put its mind to the task so just what was their real trouble?

The answer lay in their hydraulic systems. The heart of this was a seven radial plunger engine-mounted pump. This took high-priced special fluid from a large bulkhead-mounted supply tank, and pushed it into two frame-mounted hydraulic accumulators. These had an internal rubber bag, and this was inflated by compressed air to a pressure of 450/500 psi. The fluid was pumped in, compressing this bag as it did so, up to a pressure of 1,200 psi when it was ready and waiting to do its thing, or rather things. Applying the brakes sent pressure down to the cylinders, so making retardation possible; turn the steering wheel, there is a hiss, and one has power assistance, only there is no self-centring action which can be alarming to the unwary. Press down the change speed pedal and once again power assistance is available whilst putting on the handbrake finds a similar benefit. As the fluid both went out from, and then returned to, the supply tank there was no shortage of chassis piping so all this Engineer can add is - 'If only it had all worked'. 'Well we have to try new things haven't we?' Actually it was all too complicated and one could not rely on the brakes working properly, as I found out for myself on one momentous occasion. I was driving one of the six down the steeply-graded Gibbet Street when braking assistance virtually disappeared. As a result I had to proceed with extreme caution, but then for no apparent reason full braking effort suddenly became manifest once more rather to the surprise not only of the driver but also of a full standing load of passengers.

It was very seldom that one of these vehicles was not to be seen on the brake repair pits and so, when fluid consumption was virtually above that recorded for lubricating oil, and it was several times the price, drastic action had to be taken. All the various seals in the system were replaced, mineral oil was substituted for hydraulic fluid, piston type accumulators replaced the air bag variety, the power steering assemblies were removed and straight manual units went on instead, and the handbrakes and gear change pedals lost their power servos. Reliability was thus very much improved, but they were still suspect, and so came to have quite short lives. It had to be said that the East Lancashire bodies gave not a scrap of trouble, and so Leslie Boulton was often heard to sigh for many more but here his luck was out. Still we had the 10 MCW group lightweights and they also gave us food for thought; we also had one 'CD650' that experienced two crank case explosions - the only times I ever encountered such phenomena.

Conventional wisdom decreed that if you saved a ton in unladen weight you saved around one mile per gallon in fuel cost. Here was the basic thought behind this design, and so the unladen weight of the complete 'CVG6' came out at just over seven tons complete with 8 ft-wide 59-seat body, but alas too much had been sacrificed in the interests of economy. There were for example no exterior panel straps. One panel overlapped another, and all were pop riveted *in situ*. Vibration caused the rivet holes to open out and then panels came adrift whilst the upper saloon floors were improperly sealed so that in rainy weather water collected in the upper deck cove panels, and then found its way into the lower saloon which could result in wet seats. Compared to what we had to do to the Park Royal bodies these were in the minor 'pin prick' category.

Without doubt the Roe teak-framed composite bodies did well. Framing body rot even in the most likely places was virtually non-existent, but as time wore on the single-deckers modified for one-man-operation began to deteriorate. When new with rear entrances, their emergency doors had been placed at the front on the offside right behind the driver's bulkhead. Now, though, another big hole had been cut in the framing to take the amended position of the main passenger entrance, so it was not over surprising that movement occurred at cant rail and roof level, or that doors began to rattle badly unless frequent checks and remedial attention took place.

These all represented some of the basic engineering problems that confronted one each day, so what about some of the others? Here one only had to turn to the changeover sheets kept by the garages. Generally speaking requests for a changeover coming from a driver highlighted problems that occurred with unfailing regularity, and after so many years I can still clearly recall them.

With the 'Regents' fuming, fuel leaks, rattles from underneath, slipping in all gears, vibrations when pulling hard, and brake problems were most frequently recorded. Fuming, assisted no doubt by our Coalene fuel, usually resulted from an injector or injector leak-off pipe union letting fuel drip onto a hot exhaust manifold, so tightening the offender up would solve the problem, but a fuel filter bracketed onto the manifold was another cause. A solid pipe led from the cast aluminium filter cap, which had coils in it to take up vibrations, but it was still far too stiff so replacing this by a flexible pipe went a long way towards stopping that nuisance.

Rattles from underneath usually came from the stabilisers. There were two of these by the front and rear axles. They consisted of a torque tube positioned across the frames and connected to the axles via links and shock absorber-like devices that allowed a certain amount of 'roll' to take place before coming into action, when the tubes did their stuff. I should add at this point that the eight LPTB models did not have these stabilisers and had a reputation for rolling and swaying badly. If this was true then there was a resulting benefit as they seldom if ever suffered from damaged panels. I did drive them from time to time but never had any heart-stopping moments with them. Stopping the rattles was, however, quite easy. We had some gauges made up, and set the links up to them but let's talk about road springs later.

Slipping in all gears meant that there was insufficient fluid in the fluid flywheel, which originally had packing glands. Leaks therefrom was a fact of life, but in due course two lip seals were substituted on the basis that if one failed the second would still be available; only it did not work out like that. The inner one would fail first when you would find that the outer one had been running dry for most of its life, so the seal was non-operative. In due course bellows glands virtually cured flywheel leaks once and for all but before that time we had tried to resort to other alternatives. These were centrifugal clutches designed to exactly replace a fluid flywheel. When new they worked quite well, but as the friction linings wore, so engagement required a higher rpm; in due course a snatch resulted so fluid flywheels returned. Years later a combined fluid flywheel/lock-up clutch solved some, but not all, of the problem. Vibrations denoted a worn centre main bearing, and these were very pronounced at times, so one did not want to see many of these problems as rectification really meant removing the power unit and examining the condition of the crank and bearings. Brake problems meant that either the linings were worn, or the slack adjusters were not adjusting so here were tasks for our two resident brake fitters who, despite having to deal almost daily with the 'CD650s', were never short of other work.

The same went for our road spring men, two in number, who did little else than replace broken ones. Operating conditions were mainly to blame here and in one particular period of 12 months those 162 then - working vehicles used no less than 443 road springs. Later, making sure we fitted brand new as against repaired springs either on overhaul, or when required as a result of premature failure, did reduce consumption.

As a result of all this I determined on some drastic changes. As I have said Elmwood Garage had three pits, one of which contained the greasing equipment. The other two were now used for a series of 10 working day inspections. A fitter was allocated to each pit, and they were joined by an electrician and a body maker. We started on the first day with every bus whose last fleet number was a figure 1, in other words 31, 41, 251, 291, etc., were either left in in the morning or booked back later. Each was then checked over when minor faults could be rectified, major ones being reported to the respective shop foreman for immediate or later attention. Next day all the 'twos' followed, and then all the 'threes', until 10 working days later it was the turn of the 'ones' once more. By this means everyone knew what were the subjects for the day, a check was kept on any missed and they were given the treatment on the Saturday. If a Bank Holiday intervened then every vehicle dropped back by two days, but it took some time before the benefits of this closer attention became apparent. Chassis greasing was done on the same basis, better too much than too little and at the same time fluid flywheels were checked. Then to add a belt to braces they were also checked on nights the following week, but here one had to be careful. One night a shunter/cleaner was checking his list of wheels when he ran out of oil, so walked to the stores to replenish his can, leaving the flywheel cover up and the top plug out. Another shunter came along to move the vehicle, did not realise its condition, and started the engine. Result one lower saloon front half saturated with a very smelly ex-flywheel working medium, which took some cleaning up.

Now Mr MacKenzie never did interfere with my doings, although of course I outlined my various intentions to him before putting them into practice, but he did on a very early day have something to say about vehicle cleanliness. We

Nineteen AEC 'Regal III' Roe-bodied single-deckers with 32 seats began to enter the JOC fleet from 1st July, 1949 as bus Nos. 251 to 269. Three for the 'A' fleet, Nos. 344 to 346, followed on 1st December, 1949 later to become Nos. 70 to 72 in 1952. All then had rear entrances. These with 9.6 litre engines and air-operated preselector gear boxes were sprightly buses but had one bad feature in that the top of the windscreen was too low for comfort for any driver over average height. Most were taken out of stock in 1962/63.

recruited a gang of lady day cleaners and tied their activities into the day inspection system, so four-weekly full interior cleans and exterior soap washing went a long way to meet my Chief's requirements, as no more criticisms followed, but there was one more memorable morning when he vented his ire on me.

The previous midnight I met Jack Kitchen our garages superintendent close to his home at King Cross and we walked down Free School Lane to see just what the night staff were doing, such excursions being a part of our regular routine. We stayed longer than intended and so at a little before 4.00 am were standing on the Skircoat forecourt talking to the foreman before getting into the car and going home for a little more 'shut eye'. I can picture the scene now, it was a calm cold pre-Christmas night with no moon, but the stars were out in full force and conditions were still thus when I stepped through my front door. I awoke just after eight to a very different world of odd light and quiet because, whilst I had been sleeping, heavy snow had fallen, and one look outside made it obvious that Washer Lane had seen no buses that morning, nor had many other routes. I was up and dressed in no time, but had to walk all the way to Skircoat to find an angry General Manager in the garage asking why we had failed to anticipate the turn in the weather and prepare for it. It was, to say the least, really and truly memorable and I had never seen my henchmen move so quickly as he issued a string of instructions.

This, though, was a very isolated occasion. He was a very good General Manager whom I greatly respected, and I would gladly have worked for him anywhere else at any time. He could be off-putting and especially so when he gave you a cold look as you put some proposition forward and inquired, 'So tell me would you spend the money involved if it was your own?' A single hesitation at that point, and that scheme was certain to founder. He had many other qualities. The Halifax Bank Holiday agreements at the time were very complex so I asked him one day for some advice as to how to administer them. He then proceeded to dictate two memoranda that set out the situation very clearly, and which I used then and for several years thereafter when I came to return in another capacity.

I was therefore very sorry when in early 1956 he left for his native Scotland and the position of General Manager of Scottish Omnibuses before later moving on to higher things, but here let me touch on vehicle painting. The Halifax livery was unusual in having three main colours namely orange, green and cream. Originally Halifax trams had been painted blue, but when Ben Hall from Wigan became General Manager in 1922, he adopted a maroon Wigan-like paint style. This was then applied to both buses and trams until the arrival of the pioneer AEC 'Regent I', namely MT 2115. Intended for demonstration in Glasgow it was finished accordingly in green, orange and cream but *en route* to that city was shown to the municipal managers who were in conclave at their annual gathering in Great Yarmouth. There it was seen by Walter T. Young who had in succeeded Ben Hall in 1926 and he asked that in due course it could be tried in Halifax. It arrived and made a big impression so that both the AEC 'Regent' chassis and the colour scheme were adopted as Halifax standards. The timing was fortuitous as the Joint Committee was in the process of formation, and so a new livery seemed very appropriate in the circumstances.

Mr MacKenzie had mounted a blitz on painting times. The external paint style with its black lining-out was expensive to apply, whilst interiors in these preplastic days had ceilings that needed frequent attention and particularly so on the upper deck where tobacco fumes caused the white paint to turn caramel even when a nicotine stain resistant paint was being applied. Then all the interior woodwork was polished and varnished and this had to be removed for refinishing. Consequently he decreed that a full repaint had not to take more than 165 man hours and to achieve this figure had the exterior layout simplified. Now I did not like the end result, although it was an improvement on what might have been after one vehicle was turned out by way of a trial with embossed and unpainted lower panels, but luckily it did not prove to be successful.

After he left us for Edinburgh there was a period of some weeks before our new GM could take up office, so I sought out our paint shop foreman, Fred Ingham by name, and suggested that if he got a move on, and I took the chance, we could restore those buses that had had the treatment to what had gone before if the work was completed before we saw our new boss. Fred was not at this time noted for alacrity but he did not like the new scheme either, and so it came to pass. I held my breath expecting strong repercussions to descend upon me any day but surprisingly not a thing was said in higher circles and so we came to have a single and original double-deck livery. Echoes, however, of this period were apparent in 1999 when a certain firm began to put out models of Halifax buses. One of a 1954 Daimler 'CVG6' with MCW body came out in the old and much-liked livery but another, a Leyland 'PD2' with Leyland body, displayed the MacKenzie arrangement. I wonder just how many purchasers ever knew why one was different to the other?

The body shop made a neat job of turning those rear entrance Roe single-deck bodies into front entrance one man units, but they were not really ideal and cutting a hole in the near side framing right opposite the emergency door did not promote structural strength. Painted cream when first converted, the survivors were restored to orange, green and cream as shown here.

Chapter Four

Change at the Top

Before Mr MacKenzie departed for his new Scottish pastures he had finally accepted that our original spare vehicle allowance was indeed too small, and so he arranged that the last five pre-war AEC Mark Is should be replaced. Another five Daimler 'CVG6' chassis and a like number of Roe bodies were ordered, rather to my regret as I had been hoping for something more substantial in the engine room, but as it transpired these vehicles, which were delivered after our new GM took over, never gave anything like the trouble that their 12 'A' fleet predecessors did, even though the new intake was also a part of the Corporation fleet. New in October and November 1956 they were initially fleet Nos. 15 to 19. Perhaps this was due to two factors.

Firstly, they had a new Roe 65-seat body which still had the old and well tried teak lower framing but now the upper saloons were framed in light alloy thus giving an unladen weight of 7-11-3. Secondly, our rolling stock superintendent had inadvertently solved the rear axle worm wear problem. That came about because we had sold the earlier Mark Is to a well known Potteries operator, namely Berresfords Motor Services, who had also taken a quantity of spares for them. These were paid for, thanks to his negotiations, partly in cash, and partly by giving us a a brand new Daimler differential assembly which had a 6.2 to 1 ratio. When the next unit failed on a bus of the 87-98 batch this unit was fitted, and as a result, hill climbing performance was very much improved even if top speed was not, so we carefully monitored its performance.

Our new boss did not seem over-interested in the contents of this last order, so I managed to slip in a few thoughts of my own. As a result the destination layout was amended so that the main blind could be turned and sighted easily by the driver, the saloon bulkhead panels were covered in green ribbed rubber (I never did like checker plate aluminium) and motors were fitted into the under canopy heaters. I should add here that the earlier 22 Daimlers also had this type of heater unit, but someone had ruled out the provision of motors on economy grounds so that little heat ever penetrated the lower saloon in cold weather unless the bus was running at high speed downhill into a strong facing wind. Such a combination seemed seldom to occur! As it was 22 more heater motors began to appear and were quietly fitted.

Our new General Manager took up his position in June 1956 and was a very different personality to Mr MacKenzie. He was of course Mr R. LeFevre who came to us from a similar position at Bury where he had been since 1944 and where he had changed the livery from maroon and cream to green and cream. I well recall seeing the first such repaint one day in Manchester, and went out of my way to walk over to Cannon Street bus station to discover just where this phenomenon had come from. He was to later make a much more startling change to the Halifax colour scheme when he had one of the MCW-bodied Daimlers, No. 285, given green lower panels and an orange upper deck. I drove this out of the paint shop and into the yard after completion when the sight of

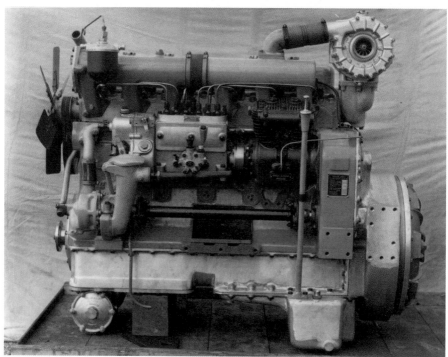

The Daimler 'Mark VII' engine was a reliable unit that had no problem coping with the extra power fitting a turbo-charger could produce. Here is the resultant assembly after the BSA boys had done the necessary. Fitted in my days as Assistant Engineer it was still running happily when I returned as GM nearly five years later. By then Daimler engine production was a thing of the past.

Leyland also went in for turbo-charging fitting this power unit to an experimental rear-engined double-decker. This bus STF 90 was run on trial by Hebble and my friend, chief engineer Douglas Cane, kindly invited me to drive it when it was being used on the steeply-graded Halifax-Queensbury-Bradford service.

it almost stopped the traffic on Skircoat Road. It also prompted a member of the Authority to ask one night in Council how was it that he had seen the lower deck of a double-decker floating over the walls and hedges adjacent to his home. Needless to say it did not last long, but for some reason I completely failed to take a colour photograph of it.

It did not take long to discover that Mr LeFevre had a very different bus-buying policy in mind and Leyland chassis and MCW group bodies were going to be the order of the day. But before they were little more than an expression of future intent he firmly grasped the nettle of the short life of those '6LW' engines. The end result was also startling in its way. One of the 12 'A' fleet buses disappeared to the Leyland factory at Chorley, and emerged a wee while later sporting an 0.600 engine that gave it a weird sound and a good deal more urge. Leyland then produced another 11 sets of parts and so the whole batch came to be similarly converted. He also had some sharp words with our Daimler friends who promised to supply sets of replacement differential units at very advantageous prices, so thanks to that earlier piece of bartering we obtained new 6.2 to 1 ratio worms and wheels, and so laid another problem to rest. Here too the higher governed speed of an 0.600 power unit went some way to bring back maximum road speed to its former level. Needless to say by this time the words Gardner and Daimler were not highly acclaimed in official circles.

I, though, had been involved in some interesting development that was also to produce a couple of engine changes in due course. The BSA company that then owned the Daimler business was working on the production of a series of turbo-chargers that could be fitted to diesel engines, and had a Birmingham bus which possessed a Daimler 8.6 litre oil engine modified to accept an early experimental unit. They wished to find out just how its performance measured up to that obtainable from the naturally aspirated and larger 10.6 litre 'CD650' engine. What better place to find out than Halifax?

As a result the Birmingham bus laden with tests weights and one of our 'CD650s' similarly fitted began to run tests between Halifax and selected points on some of our more steeply-graded routes. These trials took place in September 1957, and soon showed that turbo-charging could be a practical proposition; remember that whilst many power units today incorporate such devices, this was certainly not the case all those years ago.

In fact Halifax had experimented before 1939 in endeavours to obtain more power than was available from a standard AEC 8.8 litre engine. The desire was prompted by the conversion in May 1939 of the Huddersfield Corporation tramway route from West Vale to that town, a route which also served Elland. From Elland the trams were paralleled by the buses working the through Halifax to Huddersfield No. 43 service when Halifax provided three of the four vehicles involved, but no form of receipts sharing existed, each kept what it took. Now the new trolleybuses that replaced the trams simply swept up the steep Ainleys gradient as they came out of Elland and Halifax takings were, on the face of it, heading for a very steep decline.

As a first essay to prevent this occurring, Mr Craven, the then General Manager, had an almost new Roe-bodied 'Regent Mark I', No. 64, fitted with a supercharger. This was mounted below the lower saloon floor at the front end, and driven by belts, but both the supercharger and the belts came to be badly affected by road dirt, water, etc., thanks to being in a very exposed position, so No. 64 was soon restored to as-new condition. Mr Craven persisted and in April 1939 four new Roe-bodied 'Regents', Nos. 201-204, took the road and were unique as they were equipped with 9.6 litre twin carburettor *petrol* engines. These proved to be more than capable of holding their own against the trolleybuses, but had the nasty fault at times of catching fire when there was a misfire back through the carbs. Their life too was not of long duration as petrol consumption was coming out at 3.5 mpg, so within 12 months of the war starting all received the standard 8.8 power unit.

In direct contrast to all this was another, and much more recent, Halifax experiment to produce an 8.4 litre power unit out of a standard 9.6 litre 'Regent III' engine. I believe the reasoning behind this was that if a Gardner '6LW' engine of similar capacity can give such a good level of fuel consumption is it possible to make the undoubtedly thirstier 9.6 engine learn to consume less? Now Skircoat Workshops were equipped with a very useful dynometer, so we did some bench testing with the unit that had originated in the time of my predecessor. Whilst it was not very difficult to line up the bores and provide new piston assemblies that reduced the compression ratio, redesign and production of new cylinder heads was rather beyond the normal operating capability and so a quite interesting endeavour was brought to a gentle end. As it was, bench testing of a series of other engines seemed to produce evidence that using a coalene standard mix as against straight fuel did produce a slighter greater maximum brake horse power, thanks possibly to its higher specific gravity, but on this possibility those conducting the tests decided to remain silent. Coalene on a one third basis gave a more advantageous price per complete gallon. Still used in 1963, it was gradually phased out thereafter, and with it went the unique aroma.

Now one booking frequently made by the drivers was 'bus pulling poor' but if nothing amiss was visible or audible how did you prove the point one way or the other? We came up with a solution. Not far from the garages was a road about ¾ mile long on a continually rising gradient. We marked a kerb stone at the foot of the hill with white paint, and then took out several vehicles that had never been the subject of any such complaint, and with a stopwatch, timed how long it took to reach another marked kerb at the top. We also marked the places where it was desirable to go from first to second, then to third, and finally if possible to top. These timings were then averaged out, so that thereafter if a vehicle which was alleged to be non-standard made it within a few seconds of the norm we just returned it to service without any further investigation.

There were two statistics that did merit prompt attention. Our General Office was headed by a lady, Miss Turner, who was assisted by several other members of the same sex, and the one thing they could do in those pre-computer days was to produce fuel and engine oil usage statistics quickly after the end of each four-weekly period. These came in tabulations with each batch of buses grouped together, and also showed not only individual figures but also the group average. Any bus that showed a low lubricating oil consumption was brought in, checked for leaks, and if nothing was apparent was booked for investigation. Similarly with fuel consumption, if it was obviously over 1 mpg below average the question was asked why? Well, its mileage might be low because it had been stopped for some reason, say accident repairs or awaiting parts, but if a reasonable mileage had been performed then its fuel pump siting, and injector condition, etc., were booked for early attention.

By now more routines were in place, having been prompted by the need to overhaul the Leylands, and so we reached the stage when on a Saturday morning a bus that had been given 'the works' the previous five days went off for a test run, and was given any necessary attention thereafter. Whilst it was out, the labourers cleaned up the pit on which it had been standing, and then out from the fitting shop came an overhauled engine, front and rear axles, a gear box, a steering column, and in the case of a 'Regent III' the combined air tank and valve assembly. Later in the morning next week's bus was put onto the pit, and so on Monday morning the process could start all over again.

We also had a system of 'A' docks undertaken at 12,500 mile intervals when all the injectors were changed automatically, and at twice that figure the cylinder heads were dealt with similarly. I am sure that present day bus engineers will hold up their hands in horror if or when they read these lines but we are talking about a time almost half a century ago when bus construction, metallurgy, and above all oil technology was nowhere near present day levels of excellence. If you wanted to keep the Halifax wheels turning with as little fuss as possible then regular routines were essential.

Alas, however, despite one's best efforts one never could achieve the ultimate. By late summer the fleet would be looking reasonable, and once we had found a manufacturer that could produce an orange paint that did not fade, it was not too easy to spot which panels had been replaced since a last full sojourn in the paint shops. But when the weather turned nasty buses began to slide on ice, or in more rural parts dry stone walls would collapse just as a vehicle was passing them. Have black ice form just before the fleet was turning out, and you could bet that from 10 to 20 panels would be needing removal in the body shop by lunchtime. On one calamitous morning the total came to around 40, but that was exceptional.

At this time neither the County Borough nor the County Council had any really efficient gritters or snow ploughs. If snow fell, and it did often, then efforts were made, when oft-times an open lorry would be laden with a mixture of salt and sand, and two men with shovels would take their place on the pile, and distribute this as the lorry moved slowly along. The only trouble then was that what was on the highway would melt in patches so our buses were having to negotiate a form of tank testing ground that did nothing to promote long spring and body life. After such a spell our troubles magnified alarmingly. Bus routes became snowbound, with vehicles marooned perhaps not all that far as the crow flies from the town centre, and there they had to stay until the road was open once more. Again many of the rural roads were narrow, and flanked by dry stone walls; drifting snow would fill them and no bus is going to plough its way through three or more feet of the wretched stuff. Now the Transport Department did have two remedies in the shape of two AEC 7.7 litre-engined 'Matador' ex-Army gun tractors. These had four-wheel-drive and power winches and were fitted with quite cosy home-built cabs. A 'Matador' was a very useful tool and they could be fitted not only with snow chains but also a large snow plough, one being of the 'Vee' type, the other having a side-cutting blade.

One snowy night I set out for Mount Tabor to try to rescue the crew of a single-deck staff bus that was stuck there, but realised as I gained the top of the hill above Woodlesford that I was never going to make it even with the 'Vee' plough before me. Even if I had we could well have found that the pressure it could generate would push down the roadside walls, which our resident mason would have to go out to repair.

I elected to return to base via Pellon and King Cross, and had no problems until I reached the top of Free School Lane to find that snow had drifted right across the road by the Crossley and Porter Schools and was by now at around 2.30 am decidedly deep. There were no stone walls here, so engage bottom gear plus four-wheel-drive and 'Charge'. For some reason I know not why I stopped, got out of the cab, and waded through the snow to the drift and there almost invisible in it was a car containing four people, who were truly frozen. I shudder to think what might have happened if I had gone ahead. As it was we pulled them out of the car, loaded them into our warm crew cab, and gave them lodgings and breakfast at the depot. Mention of the 'Matadors' leads me on to their other essential uses, namely vehicle recovery after some spectacular occurrence or a conventional vehicle failure on the road.

Some recovery was possible without recourse to the 'Matadors', and a case in point took place one winter morning at Shibden. The terminus here had been dug out from the hillside (as had several others on the system) and here drifting had done its worst; so when the first bus of the day reached the end of its outward run, just below the top of the valley, reversal was impossible. Just to make matters worse the road to Shibden was narrow and twisty and lined with snow deeper in some places than others. There was only one thing to do, and that was to put the 'Regent III' into reverse gear and back it down the 1¼ miles or so down to Stump Cross where there was room in the main road to change direction. Such an exercise certainly gives the muscles in one's neck something to think about.

Winter was not alone in making reversal impossible. I went into Elmwood garage late one evening to be told by the foreman on duty that he had just received a message from a driver to the effect that he was too scared to turn his bus (another 7 ft 6 in. wide 'Regent III') round at Blackley, a hamlet quite high on the hills above Elland. I left in the car to find out what the problem was, the answer - wind. It was quite calm and balmy at Skircoat, but at Blackley there was a howling gale. On arrival there it was usual to back one's vehicle into a space at one end of a large stone barn, and this is what our driver had done, but when he had brought his bus part way out again it began to feel the full force of that wind. At first I did not believe him, so tried it for myself and then had to agree, being mindful that two Halifax tramcars had once been blown over on the Queensbury route so that thereafter a wind gauge was installed at Skircoat. When it registered a dangerous level either open top or single-deck cars replaced the closed top double-deckers normally working the route. As a result I bade the crew to join me in the car, and that 'Regent' slept out for the night.

Now for the spectacular. My first experience of what might be described as transport-style 'field sports' occurred on the evening of Sunday 15th July, 1955. I received a call to the effect that single-deck AEC No. 258 had run into a ditch high on the moors above the Calder Valley whilst working a circular tour service. At the time we had two such licensed runs that were low-priced, gave a ride of about three hours duration and were very popular. Operating afternoons and evenings at holiday periods they found work for all the otherwise spare 'Regals' that had been altered to front door configuration, and as mentioned previously painted cream.

It was a warm and fine summer evening which was just as well as this little incident had occurred over the 1,000 foot contour line when 258 was traversing a very narrow part of what was in effect a tarred-over moorland track. This was not much wider than the bus itself and had ditches on either side that were around two feet deep. The offside front wheel had managed to leave the road surface, so after unloading the passengers it did not take long for one of the 'Matadors' to have it back where it should have been with no damage done and the passengers back in their seats, and with something rather out of the ordinary to chat about.

You will appreciate that when in the morning of the 5th September the Elmwood foreman rang me to say that we had a bus in a ditch at Outlane, I was not unduly perturbed. Particularly as I had only returned that morning from a week's holiday, but the pile of accumulated paper on my desk prompted me to jump into the car, to see what it was all about, when I found that this was some ditch. Now Outlane could also be described as being in the clouds. The village was then served by a Huddersfield - formerly tram - trolleybus service that used a decent main road. We ran an hourly JOC service from Halifax via a series of minor roads that suffered all the usual winter problems, but there was no snow and ice this morning. A 'Regent III' had left the terminus and was working back towards Halifax, fortunately with no passengers on board. As you came out of Outlane the vehicle had to negotiate a series of bends, the road being narrow of course, and bordered by the inevitable stone walls. On the right-hand side was a field whose surface was three or four feet above the road, but on the left-hand side was a virtual ravine. Here the bed of the stream it contained was probably 15 ft to 20 ft below the road level and into this our double-decker had plunged going straight through the wall. The front of the vehicle was embedded in the other face of the ravine, the rear platform being jammed up against the wall which on the stream side was quite high. The radiator was damaged, as was the sump, but thanks to the angle at which the bus rested, fuel from the tank was flowing by gravity into the fuel pump, the rear wheels were still turning due to it still being in gear, and few 9.6 litre engines could have sounded better on tick-over. Goodness only knows how the driver had managed to put it in that position, but that was a matter for other authorities, the job of the engineering department was to restore it to its rightful place on the highway.

The first task was to stop the engine which proved to be a mite difficult, and then resort to sheer brute force. We had an old 'Regent I' which had been converted into a utility crew cab/flat wagon so this was run into the field some way from and parallel to the road at the point of the accident and then anchored

Some ditch! After being told we had a bus in a ditch at Outlane, this was the sight that greeted me on arrival at the scene! How did the photographer from the *Halifax Courier* get there before I did? There are places to put double-deckers, but this wasn't one of them! Thank goodness recovery could take place in a period of mild dry weather on 5th September, 1955.

The road to the Outlane terminus is to the left, there was a lane to the right, so why did bus No. 272 take the centre path that led to a solid stone gable end? The coping stone over the nearest upper window is the one that came down during evening operations. No. 272 is in the modified MacKenzie livery.

Halifax Courier

in situ. The two 'Matadors' were then placed at right-angles, but facing it and secured to the utility. Then after some of the field wall had been removed (more farmer involvement) both winch ropes were run out and after a modicum of non-Parliamentary language had been uttered, those ropes were looped round the rear axle of the bus. Power was then applied to the winches, and those present stood well clear. The 'Matadors' and the utility moved but not the bus, so still more anchoring had to be employed with stakes driven down into the ground to aid overall security. Then another attempt was made, and to our profound relief out came the 'Regent' like a cork from a bottle. Again we had fine and warm weather conditions, but if it that field had been wet and muddy we would never have got that 'Regent' out. I should also add that when I arrived it was to find the driver sitting on the wall looking at the results of his endeavours and smoking a cigarette, well I suppose that he just had to calm his nerves.

The next 'outing' also took place on the Outlane route this time with a bus travelling *uphill* to that terminus. At Sowood was a fork in the road, route to Outlane to the left, minor lane to the right. In the fork stood a shop, so how come our 'Regent' had done its best to demolish the same? We pulled it out, I recall that one of the front wheels was in the cellar, and did what we could to sheet up the building prior to it receiving builder's attention but that was another morning event. I was called out in the evening as a high wind had sprung up, and the police said that wind was getting under the ceiling of the room behind the former gable end, and making the roof rattle. It was another dark but starlit night as I helped to secure more sheets and ropes with our shift fitters. A fortuitous glance upwards made me move very quickly as the upper window coping stone you can clearly see in the photograph of the incident was on its way down to land just where I had been kneeling.

Not too long after that and in bed my approaching slumbers were disturbed by a loud crash coming from the nearby main road. Here a single-deck AEC 'Regal' working a staff bus heading from King Cross towards Sowerby Bridge had managed to get into a skid on a wet stone cobbled road surface and entered the bar area of a public house, only this entry had been made by the front wall and window. One public house was 'open' that night rather longer than usual.

All this, though, was small beer compared to what was to follow on 5th June, 1956. The roads from Bradford and Leeds to Halifax join at Stump Cross where they also meet the valley road from Shibden. From that point the main road follows a straight and rising course to the brow of the hill which is situated in Godley cutting, but before it reaches that spot it has to cross the Shibden valley virtually at right-angles, and to do this the road builders constructed a very sizeable embankment. There was no wall on the right-hand side as you approached the town centre only a rather stunted hedge, but if you looked carefully you could, and perhaps still can, find a few feet of metal piping acting as a form of stiffener. Here piping, not an 'X' marks the spot.

That morning yet another 'Regent' was returning to base, and all its driver had to do was to pursue a straight course, apart from avoiding a Corporation gulley emptier that very inconsiderately was dealing with a nearside drainage matter. Sad to say our bus hit it, and then as nothing was coming in the other direction did a sharp right-hand turn, crossed the carriageway, went through the hedge, and

This *Courier* photograph clearly depicts the scale of the Shibden Valley embankment down which our straying 'Regent III' took a dive. Recovery was not possible until it had been slid to the middle of the field. It was taken back to base via the lane at the rear - a lane complete with overhead line poles. Goodness only knows how neither crew or passengers were seriously injured or killed in the accident.

disappeared down the 70 ft or so 1 in 2 slope of the embankment. This is retained at the bottom by a wall so our straying member of the flock careered over this and did a somersault when it finally arrived in the adjacent field. At this point the gentleman who had been smoking in the upper saloon emerged from the upper deck emergency door unhurt, but saying a few interesting words about the sort of service being offered, the lady and her little girl who had been thrown onto the road through the initial collision and front nearside damage were picking themselves up, also unharmed, and the conductor, who with great presence of mind had left the rear platform as his bus took its dive, was surveying the scene. Even the driver who had no option but to stick to the wheel was intact and active so now it was up to us.

Needless to say the field was wet and muddy in parts, and it was also occupied by several animals which quite unreasonably took exception to this orange, green and cream monstrosity that came out of the sky and also to the inevitable wrecking crew and 'Matadors' that were soon on the scene. 'Nay lad it were all a reet to do! By gum nathen then!' That's local parlance. I had other words for it.

You will see from the photograph that the bus was not in the best place for recovery, so the always helpful winches came into play, pulling it almost into the centre of the field where fortunately it was rather drier, and there one 'Regent III' was returned to the vertical. Well almost so, for as a result of its over-exciting morning that 'Regent' no longer had a front axle, as the springs had virtually disintegrated, and a suspended tow was necessary. One of our two 'Matadors' carried a crane, whilst the other had a flat platform behind its crew cab. Eventually the 'Regent's' front end was secured via chains to the crane hook, and a solid tow bar was arranged so that the bus could not swing forwards when under tow and so come into contact with the rear of the 'Matador'. All that then remained to do was to move the equipage under 7.7 litre engine power out of the field, onto the main road, and so back to Skircoat, but here came a snag. There was a lane at the edge of the field away from the foot of the embankment, but it was as usual narrow and sunk into its borders were several overhead line poles. Can a 'Matador' bend an overhead line pole you might ask? I can tell you from practical experience that it can, but let's pass over that aspect of the matter.

The usual inquiry followed but we won't dwell on that either, apart from saying that our General Manager later had a very diplomatic conversation with the then Traffic Commissioner, or was it the other way round? Anyway by the time this took place it had been firmly established that there was no contributory fault on the 'Regent', and that member of the flock was about to be restored to service once more.

Up to now I have dwelt on nuts and bolt matters, but these only took up a part of one's day. I was having to cope with quite an amount of correspondence, most of which had to be passed to the GM for signature in the time honoured manner, and seeing the large number of representatives from various firms who were trying to sell us their wares. Anything from buses complete, via bus parts to cleaning rags came into these categories and then there was the staff. We did not have too many labour problems, and doubtlessly some of those that we had were of my direct making, but our works shop stewards did hunt in a pack of three, and so life was never dull. It was seldom the case that Mr Le Fevre our new GM exerted any undue pressure on the engineering department, with one possible exception. He had been to some conference or other where a speaker had given a talk on the way in which thin oils could promote better fuel consumption, and he was very anxious to see a large scale trial begun. I dragged my feet. Over three years the average fleet lubricating oil consumption figure had risen from 320 mpg to 924 mpg, this being with a straight SAE 30 material, and as engine condition had also improved in other ways the fuel oil figures had also shown an improvement. We had one dubious fuel figure improvement attempt before us in the shapes of 10 lightweight bodies, and using a thin SAE 5 oil under Halifax conditions did seem to be asking for trouble. There were of course no multigrade oils then available, materials which thanks to long chain polymers thicken up as their temperatures increase. In the end the six big 'CD650' Daimlers were chosen as guinea pigs, but when after my departure some AEC 9.6 litre engines were given the treatment my predictions tended to come true.

Our Chief's relationships with Leyland provided me with a great deal of interest when in February 1957 we received the prototype 'Atlantean', registration number ATC 201, for testing under Halifax conditions. This machine had torsion bar suspension, and various other ideas that never made it into production, and we were not able to run it in service carrying passengers. I was able to drive it over most of our routes and was quite impressed with it, as it was certainly a big improvement on its two predecessors with their small rear platform mounted power units.

He also had no objection to my carrying out a little experimentation of my own. It seemed to me that as we had spent time and fuel on co-operating with our BSA friends in their turbo-charger experiments we ought to have something back, and in due course my requests brought results. We were given a turbo-

The prototype Leyland rear-engined bus that arrived in Halifax for our perusal was very different to STF 90 with its rear platform. Here was a 30 ft-long front entrance double-decker based on this rolling platform. The 0.600 engine at the rear was standard but at the other end was independent torsion bar front suspension, plus a very luxurious driver's seat. I drove it around Halifax and was impressed as it went very well but the body had an odd feature with two mini bulkheads at the front of the rear wheel arches to provide additional rigidity.

Towards the end of my time as head of the engineering department a prototype Daimler chassis arrived at Skircoat. This was 30 ft long had a semi-automatic gear box plus - wait for it - a Daimler 650 engine. I took it out on test and was impressed by the clean layout, substantial build and handling characteristics. When the 30 ft design came on the market a Gardner '6LX' engine was the standard fitting. If Mr Le Fevre's 30 bus order had not been placed then the 27 ft alternative would have been my recommendation as several routes had places that would not allow 'Fleetline' operation at that time.

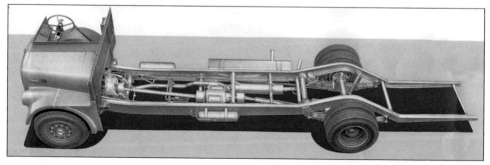

charged 'Mark 7' Daimler engine that was fitted into bus No. 291. Daimler was still rather spasmodically developing its 8.6 litre 'CVD' power unit, few of which were being sold at this time, and the 'Mark 7' was about the last manifestation of these endeavours. It proved to be a very reliable unit, and was still in use when I returned to Skircoat some five years later - which sadly was more than could be said for offering number two.

I persuaded my friends to take one of our now surplus Gardner '6LW' engines and fit this with a turbo-charger. They did so, the resultant assembly was fitted into bus No. 293 and the results were startling. We ran it in, and then took it onto our test hill. The stop watch was set at zero, and I pushed the accelerator down to have the seat squab hit me in the small of the back. It was a flyer, but the crank and bearings just weren't up to the working pressures involved so that '6LW' came to have a short life but a very merry one.

Life too was by now beginning to cause me to think. Did I try to obtain a bigger engineering job, or did I endeavour to break into general management as I had always wished? This is a dilemma facing most engineers at some time in their careers but oft-times what happens is dependent on which vacancy occurs and when.

I saw an advert for the Chief Engineer's post in a much larger undertaking, so I applied, and received a letter telling me to meet the General Manager of that undertaking in a well known railway hotel for afternoon tea. Odd! I showed it to my GM who said, 'That's typical', so wondering I boarded a through train that then ran from Bradford and Halifax to London. Arriving at my destination just prior to lunchtime, I decided on a spot of reconnaissance, and as I was hungry what better place to have lunch. I entered the dining room, was shown to a table by the head waiter and was about to start the main course when who should come into the room but that same General Manager and one of my colleagues who was very obviously a competitor. To make matters worse the GM, who had no idea who I was, was led to the next table, so that every word that was spoken was more than just audible. There was only one thing to do. Leave the meal, head to the station refreshment room for a sandwich, and see if any of the locomotives I had known in earlier days were still running in the area. Consequently I spent the afternoon either bus riding or trainspotting, but sad to say I did not get the job, and to add insult to injury the afternoon tea that I was given was nowhere near as substantial, nor appetising, as the lunch provided for my competitor. The only good thing here was that he was not successful either.

Perhaps it was fortunate that I was not offered that particular post as not very long afterwards something much more suitable came on the market. Before I was in a position to do anything about that the new regime made its vehicle preferences very plain with the ordering of nine Weymann-bodied Leyland 'Worldmasters' to be Nos. 1 to 9 inclusive for the 'A' fleet, and eight Leyland 'PD3s', again with MCW group bodies, for the 'B' side. These were to be numbered 201 to 208 inclusive, and moquette upholstery was also out. In future all double-deck buses would receive brown hide on all seats, whilst single-deckers would display a green leather. All interior side panels would be painted to suit and another indicator layout would be adopted as standard. It made me wonder just what I would want if ever I reached the dizzy heights of General Manager, but we might well find out before the end of these pages is reached.

On the day of the interview for the Deputy General Manager's job Bretonside bus station still had to be opened. By the time I took up the post it was in full operation. Purpose-built it was situated below the main road viaduct, and in my day was well used, but the pace was never as frenetic as my later bus/coach station experiences in a certain Norfolk seaside resort.

Chapter Five

Deputy General Manager, Plymouth

The advert that I had seen read as follows:

CITY OF PLYMOUTH
Deputy General Manager & Engineer

Applications are invited for the above post, in the Passenger Transport Department. The salary is accordance with scale 'C' (£1,295-£1,515). The appointment is terminable by three months notice. Candidates must have had experience in traffic administration, and must possess a recognised engineering qualification. Associate membership of the Institution of Mechanical Engineers, and of the Institute of Transport will be an advantage. Candidates should not be over 40 years of age.

Applications should be submitted not later than the 14th March, 1958 to the Town Clerk, and should give the names of two persons to whom reference can be made.

I could not say that I was well versed in traffic administration, but I was under 40, with eight years to spare, and I did possess both of the stipulated qualifications, so as the salary was at a minimum £550 per annum more than I was receiving at Halifax, and the job obviously would represent another step up the ladder if successful, I posted off my application.

A short period elapsed, and then a letter came to say that I, and one other, had been selected for interview, an event that was to take place in Plymouth some six days ahead. I did an immediate assessment of likely opposition, and then rang one of my former Manchester technical assistant colleagues who now had a job like mine in another place, but I did not have time to pose the question before he said, 'So, it's you is it?' We had a chat and agreed to meet on Stockport station so we could travel to the City together. There were of course no motorways in 1958, and travel to Plymouth by train took most of the day, so we did not reach our hotel until late in the afternoon The next morning, having time to spare, I looked up an old acquaintance in the form of Sidney Mayall the former Oldham traffic superintendent, who had left that job largely for health reasons and who was now in charge of the Torpoint Ferry. We had a chat and he told me to be sure that I told him the outcome of my application, our interviews being timed to commence at around 2.30 pm.

The Chairman of the Transport Committee at that time was Alderman Medland, who was rightly regarded as a power in the land. He had for a time been one of the local MPs and he had a rather abrasive interviewing technique. This became manifest when he told me that Plymouth's bus route gradients were worse than those to be found anywhere else, a statement I gently but politely contradicted, saying that those in Halifax were decidedly worse. An explosion followed but to my surprise the reigning General Manager J.G. Timpson agreed with me. But then he should have known, as in earlier pre- and post-war years he had been Assistant Engineer at Halifax and had been involved in those turbocharger experiments of 1939, his time there being interrupted by wartime service as an officer in the RAF.

The first Plymouth Crossley I ever saw was No. 336, numerically the last of the batch of six that in my period as DGM were normally to be seen on the Mount Gold service. Of lowbridge design with a Crossley body here No. 336 stands in a blitzed city centre in front of two lowbridge wartime utility Guy 'Arabs' on 23rd June, 1951. I had always hoped to have a drive with No. 336 but managerial edict spelt the end of that ambition.   *Roy Marshall*

By 1958 it was obvious that bus development was underway in several chassis building establishments but on arrival at Plymouth I was back to basics on my home Western National operated route as rugged Bristol chassis and economical Gardner five-cylindered-engines were the norm. So it was a return as a passenger to the noise and vibrations experienced in days in Manchester or as a North Western Road Car passenger. Here is a typical example of a long-lived production family. Sadly in January 2003 the last part of the Gardner business went into receivership.

Eventually I was called back to be told that I had been selected subject to passing the medical examination that promptly followed. A starting date was agreed upon and I was left with two tasks, firstly to tell my wife, Muriel, about the events of the day (her response was to say that she was starting to pack forthwith), and then to visit Sid Mayall and give him the news. The outcome was not what I had ever expected. He took me to his home which was quite close to the ferry's Cornwall side, and then he and Mrs Mayall said that until we had a house in the area I was to stay with them, and so I was introduced to my future bedroom. It really is a small world.

A few weeks later I started my journey to my new office at Milehouse, not by tram, bus, trolleybus or train as in the days of old, but by the ferry. Once the novelty had worn off I found this part of my commuting trip rather tedious, and to some extent the same could be said of my new employment, because at first I had very little to do. It was quickly impressed upon me that despite the word 'engineer' in my title I was *not* to become involved with what went on in the workshops and garage. My first task was to look into passenger complaints which then averaged three or four per week, and then take an interest in the doings of the traffic department. A department which must have had the most complicated form of duty schedules known to man. There were main route duties, chain break duties, rest day duties, rest day relief duties, rest day relief relief duties, country route duties, and last but by no means least 'blue book specials'. In all but the last case there was a fortnightly changeover system so that if driver Alf relieved off early turn driver George, the following week their situations were reversed. The idea here was to allow each pair to fix their own actual (as opposed to the book) relief times and of course it added another complication. The blue book specials were another Plymouth speciality, and I seem to recall there were then about 98 of them. Each crew booked on around 6.00 am picked up their regular bus from the open air park, and ran out to some suburban terminus. They then worked to the dockyard which was then very active, did a second trip and by 9.30 am, were back at Milehouse. They then re-appeared in the afternoon, ran light to Devonport for the early 'float time' when the first wave of men left the yard, usually ran back light for the later 'float', and by 6.00 pm at the latest had to be back at Milehouse and off duty. All this made the then Halifax duty situation virtual child's play.

The fleet at the time numbered some 300 strong. There were eight pre-war Leyland 'TD5s' that had surprisingly been rebodied by Leyland in 1953, the only such chassis that ever underwent that process in the factories of their birth. A few wartime Guy 'Arabs' survived usually with Roe bodies, out of the 106 utilities once in stock, and six Crossley '42s' made me almost feel at home. All these had lowbridge bodywork as had numerous Leyland 'PD1' with Met-Cam bodies, and the Leyland 'PD2s' with Leyland bodies. As an aside here, there should have been either 20 or 30 Crossleys in total but someone must have got wise to the failings of the type '7' engine at an early date, as a result the relevant file did make interesting reading.

Why Plymouth had standardised on low height double-deckers prior to my arrival I know not, but by 1958 Leyland 'PD2s' with Met-Cam normal height coachwork were either in stock or on order, and whilst these were to lightweight specification they did not seem to suffer as much as their Yorkshire compatriots. But then I was not involved with their operation, in fact my initial association with the buses apart from being carried as a passenger was precisely 'nil' as I was told I was not allowed to drive them, either in or off service.

Fortunately for me there were some saving graces in all this, which began on my first morning when there was a knock on the door which opened to reveal a gentleman, who said, 'Perrin sir, traffic assistant may I welcome you to Plymouth'. Frank Perrin was a long service employee, who had risen up through the ranks, and who from that moment on became a firm friend and supporter. He was located in the traffic office where his staff proved at all times to be both co-operative and very helpful, as indeed were most of the inspectors who again had long service to a man.

My next surprise took place during my first Saturday afternoon, when as it was too far to go home I spent time bus riding, and so boarded a lowbridge Leyland bound for Honicknowle. I sat on the long front upstairs seat, and just before departure another man came to sit beside me. Once on the move the conductor came to collect our fares, only we both produced official passes. We looked at each other with interest, when the stranger asked, 'Would you by any chance be Geoffrey Hilditch?' I replied in the affirmative, when he introduced himself as Ken Wellman the recently appointed divisional superintendent of the Western National Omnibus Company (WNOC). We spent the rest of the day riding round, and so came to be firm friends going subsequently on various transport excursions (both road and rail) together, which in view of the then local situation was very fortuitous.

This situation resulted from wartime happenings in the Plymouth area. When the blitz started many city dwellers moved out into the country for safety's sake, when Western National resources became sorely stretched. At the same time City Transport's loss in traffic produced spare resource, so the sensible thing was done and a joint committee was set up. An area around Plymouth on the Devon side of the River Tamar was designated, this taking in such places as Yelverton, Meavy, Cornwood and Shaugh Prior etc., and within that area all bus service mileage and receipts were apportioned between the partners. Initially Plymouth City Transport (PCT) had sought licences to extend certain services into outside areas. The Commissioner would not agree but he did make certain representations. These bore fruit and the agreement commenced the week ending 1st October, 1942 when PCT's share became 80 per cent of all receipts and mileage worked in the designated area.

The arrangement was thus rather different to that which appertained in Halifax, and at this time was very much in being as so many changes were being made to the city and its environs which had considerable effect on the pattern of the bus services. For example, what had been the heart of Devonport was rapidly disappearing, as Fore St, with its bombed or temporary shops, was finding itself inside the perimeter wall of the dockyard. A new road was being driven across Devonport Park, and extensive housing estates were being built in Plympton, Ernesettle, etc. This meant that if City Bus introduced a new service which added to its mileage proportion then Western National was entitled to run an offsetting balance somewhere, and of course the reverse applied. A flowering of this concerned the 53 City to Mount Batten service. In pre-war days, so it was said,

WNOC vowed that no red City bus would ever cross Laira Bridge and so enter the Plymstock area, another one that was then outside the city but growing also very rapidly. Now the 53 was worked by PCT lowbridge Leylands, and as will be revealed other excursions were to follow. Here PCT was perhaps unlucky in that we had no single-deck vehicles, so some very rural routes, e.g to Cornwood or to Dousland, had of necessity to be worked by Leyland doubles with their attendant higher fuel consumption, and associated operating costs, for no form of one-man-operation then existed. Nor could it, even had Union agreement been reached, thanks to the type of rolling stock in the fleet.

I took all this in as rapidly as I could, having one personal success when after some thought my General Manager agreed that I could attend the Transport Committee meetings that were held in a room set aside for that purpose in the Milehouse offices. But my 'inferior' status had to be emphasised by my having to sit at a small table set aside from the much larger one that housed the dignatories who attended such gatherings. I sat quietly, took notes, listened and learned for this was all useful experience, as at Halifax I had never been so privileged. It was interesting to watch the various personalities involved, from the lady who seemed to come to each meeting wearing a new hat, who was invariably two items behind the one currently being considered on the agenda, to those who could pose some very pertinent questions when least expected.

I was also permitted to attend the Joint Committee meetings that took place either in Exeter or Plymouth. The General Manager, Traffic Manager, and Secretary of that company usually represented the WNOC, and these events were very professionally orientated as was only to be expected. The WNOC then covered with its 'Siamese' Southern National twin a huge geographical area, and add to that the services of Royal Blue supervised by Clem Preece. Keeping abreast with all the happenings in that empire must have taken some doing, PCT by comparison was small beer indeed, but small or not it had an important part to play, being the major provider of service in the designated joint area, with its 80 per cent share.

There was no doubt too in my mind that we had by far the best fleet. At this time most of the Western National double-deckers had Bristol 'K' type chassis with '5LW' Gardner engines and so they had neither the pace nor the smoothness of Plymouth's later Leyland 'PD2s'. Added to this were the almost inevitable lowbridge bodies as relatively few of the much improved 'Lodekka' vehicles were to be seen in the area. There was one exception here as a 'Lodekka' was always allocated to the 22 service that linked West Hoe with Cattedown. This was a very short route so be on the Royal Parade at any time, and you were almost bound to see one of WNOC latest doubles also 'on parade'. The single-deckers were much more 'civilised' and one day I was invited to try the latest manifestation in the form of the first Bristol 'MW' to allocated to Laira. I wished that we could obtain something similar, but specifying new vehicles was not then for me.

This wish became much stronger when the last local private operator went out of business. Heybrook Bay Motor Services ran out to Plymstock and Bovisand and used some Bedford/Duple single-deckers, one of which had a very noisy rear axle that continued to tell one just where it was even if afar, a condition that seemed endless, well at least until WNOC took over.

The transfer of the No. 57 Plymouth-Wembury service from Western National to Plymouth City Transport meant that, as PCT had no saloons, the associated roads had to be cleared for highbridge double-deck operation, a task that provided some interesting times. Success was achieved and here Frank Perrin, the traffic assistant; the author; and the driving instructor pose in front of the first PCT double-decker to reach the terminus on 9th April, 1959.

Thanks to the formula PCT had to take on some additional mileage and, by machinations that took place somewhere unknown to me, we inherited the 57 service from Plymouth bus station to Wembury, which was all very well as this gave us a second service over Laira Bridge but WNOC always worked the route with single-deckers. Indeed it was suggested that it was not possible to take a double to Wembury but we had no single-deckers so I began to find myself doing some prospecting in deepest Devon, which suited me fine as the 57 actually passed my Elburton home. We had fun. There were trees, electric wires, telegraph wires and cottage out-buildings in the way of double-deck progress, but one morning Frank Perrin, our driving inspector and I arrived at Wembury with a complete and unscathed 'PD2' and the photograph reproduced here depicts that memorable scene. Then we had to show drivers over the road and begin operations.

Thanks to the larger buses we began to carry more passengers, especially on Sundays, so we hit on the idea (which received the blessing of the Traffic Commissioner) of providing some special Sunday journeys, over and above the normal timetable. If the morning dawned bright and fair we put out a series of noticeboards at strategic points, advertising the extras, and then ran them even if the weather later turned out to be wet, as it did on one particular afternoon. I was at Wembury with the family around 3.30 pm, when I saw clouds building up in the west, so I went to the phone, rang Milehouse, and asked the inspector in charge to send me some spare buses down to the Wembury terminus. They had just arrived when the heavens broke, with the result that PCT received some very complimentary remarks from the bus riding throng who otherwise could have become very wet indeed. You have to have a bit of luck sometimes. There was an echo of all this years later, when one of the model bus production firms began to sell an 'OO' gauge scale model of a Plymouth 'PD2' carrying the route No. 57, and the destination Wembury. Needless to say I bought one, and it now reposes in my collection of memorabilia.

Ken Wellman and I spent time planning various route alterations or refinements and it is only fair to say that our proposals did not always receive the blessing of our respective superiors, but it was all adding to the daily interest, and as the weeks went by more work came my way. My General Manager indicated one day that it might after all be a good idea if from time to time I did take a bus out, and I was also entrusted with dealing with the more major matters of traffic department staff discipline. This brought me into frequent contact with our Union secretary and chairman, namely Messrs Williams and Watkins. The rule here was that if an appeal was to result from one of my decisions then that appeal would be heard by the General Manager, who would come to the task with 'clean hands', but I made as sure as I could that no appeal ever resulted from my deliberations.

Another friend I made in this period was Douglas Crawford who was then the Managing Director of the Millbrook Steamship Company, a concern that ran the Cremyll Ferry, numerous boat excursions in and around Plymouth Sound, and some buses on routes in the Millbrook area. It all began when I expressed an interest in seeing the Rowe 'Hillmaster' single-decker that had been purchased some time earlier. Rowe set up a small production unit in Cornwall, and built trucks and a handful of buses over a few years but then like other newcomers to the scene faded out. I had a drive with it and was then invited to accompany him on evening boat

A new PCT service that was started in my period with the undertaking was that to Saltram House the former home of Lord Morley. This was a summer-only excursion type operation and here all-Leyland 'PD2' No. 15 stands in the park after working the first trip outwards from Plymouth.

The Rowe 'Hillmaster' was a very rare bus, indeed only two or three were ever put into service. Here WRL 16 new to the Millbay Steam Boat & Trading Co. was caught on film by Roy Marshall on 12th June, 1958. Thanks to my good friend Douglas Crawford the Managing Director of the above concern I did have a drive with it and was favourably impressed, but the Cornwall-based chassis manufacturer was not to have a long life whilst MSB&T later sold its local Millbrook bus operations to the Western National concern.

trips when, if all was quiet, I could try my hand at piloting our craft, which made quite a change from a Plymouth Leyland. We remained friends for years after I left the area, until his untimely death at an all too young age. Living in Plymouth had numerous advantages, even if house prices then were way above those in Halifax, but I cannot say that I really enjoyed my time at Milehouse.

At Manchester, at Halifax, etc., I had had a job that was interesting and involved, but at Plymouth the General Manager not unnaturally was involved in shaping policy and making all the important decisions, whilst the various departmental heads had their own section responsibilities, just as I had before becoming DGM. As Deputy I was neither fish nor fowl, and I was never sure just how I was regarded by my chief, although as we will see later I was to find out in a way that I never expected. As it was I never felt that, Deputy or not, I was close to him, especially as he was in the habit of never asking any member of the staff who might find themselves in his office to take a chair. I solved this problem, not by standing, but by resting myself on the edge of his conference table whenever I was in discussion with him. My previous GMs never failed to point to a chair if there was any likelihood of a prolonged conversation.

I also realised that there was so much about the undertaking that I did not know, and from time to time I did wonder what might happen if my chief, who was not in the best of health at this time, came to be off for a prolonged period. But I must stress in all this that I never had the slightest doubt as to his competence, it was just a case of personal relationships, and methods of working. As it was I was still ambitious and so when in late 1959 the post of General Manager to the Great Yarmouth undertaking was advertised I decided to apply even though there would not be any salary advantage, and it would mean making an expensive household removal if I was successful. Consequently I posted off my application and settled down to await a response.

Chapter Six

Top Job - General Manager, Great Yarmouth

The waiting was broken when a telegram arrived to say that I had been placed on the short list, so would I confirm by return that I would be available for interview the following Tuesday. Needless to say my answer was in the affirmative. As a result I left home early on the Monday, travelled by train to Paddington, crossed London to Liverpool Street, and then boarded a second train for Great Yarmouth having previously booked a room at the Star Hotel. This was most conveniently located, being close to the station (Southtown) and across the road from the Town Hall where the inquisitions were to take place, in the usual Municipal manner.

You arrived at the venue, reported your presence, and were then conducted to a room where all the candidates were concentrated, so if you did not know just who your opposition was beforehand you then speedily found out. On such occasions conversation was to say the least somewhat stilted. If my memory serves me right there were eight of us so gathered, but that number decreased as, one by one in alphabetical order, you were conducted into the Council Chamber. There the Mayor was in his high chair, the Committee chairman sitting on one side of him, the Town Clerk on the other, with the rest of the Committee members located on what were in those days the aldermanic benches. You, the victim, was shown to a seat in the well of the chamber facing these august personalities. There was a brief introduction, and then the questioning began. Initially the questions were taken from a preset list, but one could be sure that these would be exhausted and then various members of the Committee would bowl their own googlies.

The questions as a rule were not over difficult to answer, but one had to beware of traps, so it was a case of sit up, speak up, and then shut up; but you could be certain that someone somewhere had taken soundings, and your pedigree was known in pretty great detail. As for traps, well take this example.

One General Manager gave a paper at a conference on how he had solved the preventative maintenance problem, he did not do any. You let the buses run, and when a failure occurred, carry out the necessary repair. It was, or so he said, cheap and very efficient, only the relevant operating area was as flat as the proverbial pancake. He then applied for a bigger post and was interviewed when he propounded his 'don't do it' theory. Someone, though, goodness knows by whom, had been primed beforehand so this committee member who did not have a technical background asked what was his fleet's size, and what was his peak output, this producing a spare bus figure. Now the local fleet covered some very arduous routes only its spare fleet content was about half that of the applicant's, so how did he explain that? He couldn't! So whilst the pundits beforehand had placed him favourite for the post here was an occasion when the favourite fell at an early hurdle.

When your interview was over you were shown into a second room, where the conversation became rather more lively, as you made a mental note of the time it took the next member of the opposition to join you. I suppose the average was around 20 minutes to half an hour so all present were in for a long afternoon, but at length all of you were once more together, and then came an anxious wait. Who was going to be asked to return, for that person would be the successful one, and on this occasion it happened to be me, and now came some vital minutes.

You were asked if you would accept the post, if you declined then you were not going to be paid your travel and subsistence expenses. If you said you would then, 'When can you start?', and of course had you any questions. Now it so happened that the Great Yarmouth salary was equal to the one in scale terms that I was then receiving at Plymouth and no one would want to move back to the bottom of that scale, so a spot of horse trading followed. Was the Committee prepared to offer one something more? The top of the scale would do very nicely but it was seldom that anyone was so successful, although normally a compromise was possible; but salaries are important so let's dwell on that subject for a moment.

The designated Chief Officers were at that time paid on population-based scales, consequently Town Clerks, Treasurers, Borough Engineers, Medical Officers of Health, Directors of Education, etc., knew just what they could expect, bearing in mind the size of their local authority. But nothing of the sort applied to Transport Managers, it was almost a case of catch what you can, despite the fact that by 1959 such departments were often the biggest in terms of number of staff employed and also the biggest from a trading department turnover point of view. Then someone had a brain wave, 'Let us [they said] pay on mileage run in the boundaries of the borough'. As some 95 per cent of all Great Yarmouth mileage was then so restricted I received, after only a short time in office, a very acceptable increase, but as we will see this arrangement did cause great heartburn in another place. This happy event was for the future; for the present I was able to obtain an advance on my current remuneration, and so I left for Plymouth to submit my notice, receive the congratulations of my General Manager, and to await the day when I too would become a Transport General Manager.

Finally here a word about increments, £60 per annum in this case. They became due each 1st April provided you took up your post before 30th October. If after, as was the case here, your salary stayed put until the year but one after, so start on the 1st November, 1960 and you waited for an advance until 1st April, 1962. For the record, the Great Yarmouth maximum at this time was £1,680 per annum. This figure seems incredibly small now but back in 1959 meant a very acceptable standard of living to the recipient.

Now my predecessor at Great Yarmouth had been Ralph Bennett, now moving to Bolton as GM, who in later years achieved great distinction as the Manchester supremo and finally as the Chairman of London Transport. Yet again history was to repeat itself, as Ralph had moved to Great Yarmouth from Plymouth where I duly succeeded him. He had therefore had as short a time in Yarmouth as I had in Plymouth but in that time he had made a very positive impression, often in ways that were not obvious to the travelling public as a result of re-organisations made within the offices. He had also set about repairing the main Caister Road Depot, for the very attractive brick frontage with its large illustrative panels of transport vehicles was in dire need of attention. Some £5,500 had been earmarked for remedial works but he had not had time to see completion effected.

He had, though, also been active on other fronts, having re-organised the flow of buses along Southtown Road by an ingenious route revision, and had

To operate his new services around Gorleston or from Harbord Crescent to either Vauxhall station or Cobholm Mr Bennett hired five small Guy one-man buses with Eastern Coachworks 26-seat bodies and Perkins 'P6' engines. London Transport purchased 84 of these vehicles in in 1953/54. They ran in Great Yarmouth during 1958/59 being replaced by the Albion 'Nimbus' vehicles. Their career in London was rather varied, withdrawals taking place between 1957 and 1972. Here No. GS 68 stands at Vauxhall station.

One of the six Willowbrook-bodied 31-seat Albion 'Nimbus' machines stands in the depot yard. When 'on song' they had quite a brisk performance plus a tendency to list towards the bows. Troubles lurked below though, both the floor of the vehicle and the yard surface as described fully in the text.

started some new ventures. The most interesting was the Gorleston circular routes, No. 8 in one direction, No. 9 in the other, which ventures attracted hot opposition from the Eastern Counties Company who were more than anxious to protect the revenues on the 19 route to Bradwell. This was outside the borough but was an area that was going to see substantial residential development in the years to come. In the event Great Yarmouth buses did cover a small portion of this contentious area, but were not permitted to stop for passengers on the two sections of highway that lay outside Great Yarmouth. Within Yarmouth itself were innovations in the form of two services, also one-man-operated, that ran as No. 5 from Vauxhall station to Harbord Crescent towards the southern end of the sea front, and No. 6 from Cobholm to the same location, these being co-ordinated, as so much of their routes were common.

To work the latter, Ralph had originally experimented using small Guy buses hired from London Transport, and when the trials were judged to be worthwhile bought what seemed to be much more suitable small underfloor single-deckers in the shape of six 31-seat Willowbrook-bodied Albion 'Nimbus' machines which had an unladen weight of 3-16-2. As fleet numbers 90 to 95 they went into service in July 1959, having cost £3,133 each, and were, on paper at least, the most suitable then available for the work.

At the time of my arrival these were the newest vehicles in the fleet that consisted of:

10 Leyland 'PD1' double-deckers with Massey bodies, Nos. 51-60, new in 1948.
10 Leyland 'PD2' double-deckers with Leyland bodies, Nos. 61-70, new in 1949 or 1950.
4 Leyland 'PD2' double-deckers with Leyland bodies, Nos. 47-50, new in 1953.
5 Leyland 'PD2' double-deckers with Massey bodies, Nos. 71-75, new in 1955, with concealed radiators.
5 Leyland 'PD2' double-deckers, new in 1957, as above also with Massey bodies, Nos. 31-35.
13 AEC 'Mark V' double-deckers with concealed radiators, and 470 cu. in. power units. These came in batches of five in 1956, four in 1958, and four in 1959 Massey-bodied, Nos. 26-30 then Nos. 36-39 and 43-46.

These with the six Albions gave a licensed fleet of 53 vehicles, but in addition standing delicensed in the garage were:

8 Wartime Guy utility double-deckers with Strachan or Park Royal bodies still much as delivered with wooden seats.
5 pre-war Leyland double-deckers with Massey or Weymann bodies one of which, No. 13 of 1939 vintage, had a Massey body that was virtually identical to the 1948 deliveries.

Finally to complete this catalogue Ralph had ordered four Leyland 'Atlantean' double-deckers with MCW bodywork, Nos. 1-4, for early 1960 delivery.

Some of the early 'PD2/1' buses of 1949 still retained their original engines and gearboxes (unlike Halifax) with synchromesh on the three higher gears, but the later ones had the alternative suffix 'H' box which had a constant mesh second with synchromesh only on third and top. These could give you some interesting moments, but at least were an improvement on the 'PD1' variety which had what must have been the slowest post-war gear change of any British-made vehicle. The Guys were worse, though, for their selector layout was the reverse of the

Mr Bennett ordered four Leyland 'Atlantean' of the 'PDR1' type for delivery in early 1960 but sadly the MCW concern fell behind with construction of their bodies and so they were not able to carry the traffic found in the peak weeks on the No. 7 North Denes-South Denes route with its extensive caravan camps at either end. Here No. 1 (fleet Nos. 1 to 4) is outside the racecourse waiting for the punters to emerge. Note the 6d. flat fare boards.

other buses, i.e. second position on a Leyland or AEC equals top on a Guy, etc. As for the AEC buses with their short travel gear sticks, full syncromesh and small power units, they did not drink fuel they only sipped it, at least on Yarmouth's flat terrain, and this was of course something with which I had to acquaint myself. It was also a source of initial wonder.

The wonder came when my wife decided to journey to Great Yarmouth with me over the weekend before I was to take up my appointment on the Monday morning. We duly arrived in the town at about 4 o'clock on a grey and wet winter afternoon, and as we drove down Regent Road she looked at the only visible sign of life, to whit one cat crossing the road, and said, 'Just what have we come to?' Time was soon to change her outlook, but then we were once again faced with all the trauma of moving some 300 miles, after finding a new house, and arranging new schools etc. It is, on occasions like this, if one is ambitious for promotion, that wifely support becomes paramount.

Now a new job can give new surprises and I had one a day or two later when I came to attend my first Council meeting. I was sitting with my fellow senior officers at a table in the well of the chamber where I had previously sat alone for that interview when we arrived at the minutes of the transport committee. The Chairman of the committee said in time honoured fashion, 'Beg leave to move Mr Mayor', the Vice Chairman followed with 'Beg leave to second', and the Mayor began to call out the numbers when one member rose from his chair to pose a question. More comments followed when suddenly the Mayor said: 'Could you please give us some information here Mr Hilditch?' Needless to say I could not, being as it were brand new, and so I had to rise and say so, for it was not usual then for Officers to have to speak at full meetings of the Council, but the practice was not unknown here. One had to be on one's toes on such occasions and what you said could depend upon how brave or foolhardy you were, take for example this case.

One General Manager, in a place not to be identified here, came up with a scheme to re-organise part of his undertaking, and managed to receive Committee approval for his project. Council, though, was a different matter, as some members felt that their wards, and hence their constituents, would be more than inconvenienced, and so the debate became long and, whisper it not, rather heated. Eventually the Mayor who was doubtlessly bored by it all asked the GM if he might be able to enlighten the members in any way, when our hero rose to his feet and said, 'Yes Mr Mayor, I can, so might I advise the Council that it is now five minutes to eleven, and the last buses will be passing the Town Hall very, very shortly'. Few people had cars those days, so his advice was taken, the debate, and the Council, quickly shut down and his scheme passed without any further division. Oh to be so brave!

Some years later in Halifax I came up with a scheme to re-route the No. 32 service. Again in Council this was not popularly received, and a long debate followed. During this one member said, 'Mr Mayor will someone please tell me just what is the route of the 32 service', but no one could. I knew naturally, but in Halifax chief officers, apart that is from the Town Clerk, could not speak on such occasions, so in the event the Mayor suggested that things be moved on and so a wee while later the 32 West End service was duly amended.

To return, though, to my early days. The first thing you need to do is to take stock of your new empire and it is usually wise to make haste slowly so item one was to investigate the financial situation along with Mr Tranyier, a long service staff member who was the administration superintendent. It was quite encouraging, but it did not stay that way as we were entering a period of rapid rises in costs, and so as soon as 19th March, 1960 craftsmen received an advance of 3d. per hour, whilst on the 2nd April platform staff were given an advance of 10s. per week. These rises were compounded when on 11th June the working week was reduced to one of 42 hours without loss of pay, and an extra three days' holiday went to all members of staff with more than 10 years' service. After this, increases came thick and fast on rather more than an annual basis. Add to this rises in everything that one needed to buy, and the steady erosion in passenger traffic through the increased use of private cars, the shorter working week, and the decline in evening entertainment travel as a result of the universal acquisition of television sets, and anyone with the task of keeping a bus undertaking economically sound was scheduled to have a great deal of head scratching to do in the years to come. Only at this date these factors were not entirely apparent, so what else did I find?

My researches extended to the garage where our engineering superintendent, Cyril Tooke by name, reigned being assisted by six fitters, three working shifts, three body builders, three painters, one tyre fitter (at this period there was no mileage contract), one greaser, one electrical man and 17 assorted cleaners and labourers. These gentlemen in total maintained the fleet, with virtually no modern equipment, and repairs from a cost per mile point of view were just

Caister Road garage did have some equipment plus a few elderly machine tools that dated from tramcar days. Here is a view of the fitting/machine shop before a new lathe and radial arm drill were acquired. The partition on the right formed part of Mr Tooke's original base.

A laid-up Guy utility stands in the little used part of the premises that later became the car testing station with a vehicle lift and other essential equipment. In contrast to modernity the ex-tramway horse-drawn tower wagon is on the right and a very reduced pile of redundant equipment remains on the left together with some oil drums and an oil bowser, etc. This picture is one of a series I took on my arrival at Caister Road.

about the lowest of any municipal operator, although I had to shudder at some of the practices that were performed.

For example on the odd occasion when an engine was to be changed, the vehicle concerned was run nose-on to a substantial garage stanchion that carried the arm of a crane jib. All the preparatory work was undertaken and then another bus was run up alongside, and a rope was secured via the jib, one end of the (steel) rope was secured to the affected power unit, the other to the working bus. That machine was put into reverse, and so up and out came the defective piece of motive power.

There was no fuel pump test bed or injector test equipment. Much repair work of necessity had to be carried out on two long pits in a part of the premises that were open to the main parking area. All rather different to what appertained at Halifax, or Plymouth.

There was in one corner of the empire a building that must have been an 'add on'. Enclosed and of reasonable size it housed at the time of my arrival some delicensed buses, and a pile of assorted bus bits which I began to probe. One item that I raised aloft was quite unknown to me, but Cyril advised that it was a gear lever, but not one I had ever known. It had come from an early Great Yarmouth Guy. This pile would have been a treasure trove to anyone involved in *circa* 1960 bus preservation but, I regret to say, I saw the whole lot on its way to the scrap heap, and into that section of the premises went our new annual car testing shop, for the initial 10 year test regulations were coming into effect at this time. Do not think here that I am in anyway being critical of Cyril and his merry men, for it was up to management to see what was really needed and then make sure financial authorisation was given. Here Ralph had made a substantial start, but again had not had enough time to do all that he wished.

Major repairs were undertaken on two long pits open to the rest of the garage so, with a badly fitting door in the near wall, winter working conditions were not ideal. Two Albions are on the left and two Leylands on the right No. 50 was on of 14 'PD2s' with Leyland bodies. Behind is a 'PD1' with a post-war Massey timber-framed body one of a batch of ten.

Cyril was a gem, and I pay due tribute to his memory. He was a truly practical engineer, who was exceedingly conscientious, so much so that he would not take holidays. I virtually had to drive him away from Great Yarmouth to visit the works of the firm that had received our order for all the items needed to set up our new fuel pump test shop. I must here confess that several of my innovations/alterations were by no means blessed by the engineering personnel, and we had some testy times, repainting being one subject that came under close scrutiny. But then I received a lesson in human behaviour, and for what it is worth I will pass it on to my readers.

Harry Blackburn had been the General Manager for a good many years, commencing in Great Yarmouth in 1931 having transferred from Keighley. Prior to that he had been with Karrier Motors of Huddersfield, so knew all about three-axle chassis fiascos, and was worth talking to. He retired as Ralph came on the scene, but was still to be found for several hours each day in the garage. This was because we then had several Artcem machines in operation. These looked for all the world like a television set and were fixed above the windows of the lower saloon front bulkhead in line with the centre gangway. As the bus moved a motor would wind a blind past the screen, and on this blind, which was illuminated, were a series of trade adverts. These passed before the eyes of those facing forwards and, when the blind reached its end, a switch reversed the motion and so it went on. They were quite complex and Harry, wearing an old brown smock and rather battered trilby, acted as their maintenance supremo, changing the adverts, replacing bulbs, and doing all that was needed to keep them fully working. It was in a way unusual, but to his credit never once did he try to interfere in what Ralph or I were about.

On the particular day I had a visit from a representative of a national firm who for some years had been a frequent caller and who, according to rumour, had been a close friend of Mr Blackburn. This particular call had been made at my request, as I had a complaint regarding some product recently supplied. To look at the problem meant taking a walk into the garage, and as we passed down the lines of buses, Harry came across our path at right-angles. When he saw my visitor he moved towards him, put out his hand and said, 'Hello XXXXXX how are you, I have not seen you for ages', when his former associate cut him dead. Then when we were some way off that individual turned to me and said, 'I never could stand that fellow'. It made me realise that there are those who, to paraphrase Shakespeare, will be 'hot' friends for as long as you can sign an order form in their favour, but when the day comes that you no longer have that power then your once 'hot' friend cools very rapidly. I made no comment then as to what had occurred, but later in the day I had the task of explaining to a very hurt Mr Blackburn that I was sure the visitor had failed to recognise him, being arrayed as he was in his old trilby and smock. I did, though, ensure that the number of official orders heading in a particular direction thereafter became considerably less.

The 'one cat' situation in Regent Road continued until Easter when life began to brighten, and Great Yarmouth began to open up like a flower in the sun. For the holiday period the Caister route was extended to the Wellington Pier thus taking three buses instead of two, and thereafter came the fair which in those days completely filled the Market Place as it still might. By this time we were deep in planning for the summer season that was soon to be upon us, when staffing loomed large on the agenda. At the time of my arrival we had 71 drivers and 59 conductors on the books, but some of the drivers were then working on conductor rotas. To maintain the much improved summer services we needed as a minimum 102 drivers, and around 114 conductors, so how did we manage? At the end of each summer a review was made as to how many men would be required for the winter and what vacancies, if any, needed filling. Each inspector was then given a list of temporary staff, and asked to indicate which in his opinion were the best. Those chosen then had the chance, up to the vacancy limit, of staying with the undertaking, and during the winter likely conductors would be given PSV driving training. When the summer season arrived those PSV-qualified conductors became temporary drivers, and the conductor ranks were filled with ladies, university students, many coming from Belfast, and local men who had applied for jobs with us.

The summer services included such seasonal-only routes as the No. 4 from the Racecourse to South Denes, or the No. 7 from North Denes to South Denes that was a true gold mine. A vehicle would fill up at the extensive caravan camp which existed at either end, and returns of 100 pence per mile (pre-decimal of course) were not unknown. So by Easter the 'relics' were dug out of the recesses of the garage, cleaned, fettled up, and prepared for further work; and here I was not appreciative of having to restore wooden-seated wartime utilities to all-day service but sadly we were badly let down.

Ralph's four 'Atlanteans' were scheduled for spring delivery and would have been ideal for the No. 7 service, but they finally came into stock some four months late, something that rather destroyed my faith in the body contractors. Each one cost £6,207 18s. 9d., the chassis accounting for £3,040.

This summer increase brought with it another winter problem that was speedily realised. The only one-man-operation at this time was on the three services covered by the six Albion saloons, but as costs rose and traffic slowly, but surely, fell away one-man-working could and would cut winter costs. But lose conductors, and you lose your summer driver training potential, and it was much easier to recruit students to fill conductor lines than it was to find PSV drivers at very short notice, so how do you solve that one? Only answer, take the overall view and accept what is happening.

In 1960/61 Great Yarmouth buses ran 1,800,939 miles, carried 15,822,624 passengers, and took £245,852 in receipts. Just two years later mileage had fallen to 1,793,713, passengers had fallen to 14,577,070. And receipts were down to £238,145, whilst expenditure had risen appreciably, and this despite certain service improvements and the start of a number of new ventures, plus the purchase of more new vehicles.

One ever-increasing problem that was not to be solved was that of summer traffic congestion, although one measure to reduce this was now put in hand thanks to the closure in February 1959 of the former Midland & Great Northern Railway, and with it the Beach station.

During my first summer in the town the many express and excursion coaches set down or picked up their passengers at the Britannia Pier where a lay-by existed for the purpose, only this was far too small. The presence of lines of coaches, with their often confused passengers, promoted chaos at a major road intersection. I counted, for example, 54 coaches leaving from the spot in 45 minutes during one Sunday evening. Saturdays were much worse. The Council then bought the station site for coaching purposes and we came to the conclusion that the station buildings should remain and serve road passenger needs, as should most of the platforms. In front of the main platform a lower pavement was constructed to form an arrival platform, the rest of the old railway construction being removed. This left the back of the rear bay platform alone, but before it a series of 'saw tooth' pavements formed new departure spaces, conversion work going on during the winter of 1960/61.

At the same time we researched names and addresses of every firm running into the town, and then went into correspondence with them. Meanwhile the Traffic Commissioners drafted new Great Yarmouth conditions to apply to the associated road service licences, and in the early summer of 1961 the Beach Coach station opened for business, and what business! A list of all the then operators is given below with the home areas they served.

Operators using Beach Coach Station, Summer 1963

Operator	Serving
Albanian Coaches Ltd	St Albans, Hatfield
Allenways Ltd	Birmingham
Andy's Coaches	Birmingham
J. Ashmore & Sons Ltd	Birmingham, Smethwick
Charles Banfield Ltd	London
Barton Transport Ltd	Leicester, Loughborough, Nottingham
Bermuda Coaches Ltd	Nuneaton
Blue Belle Coaching Service	Clapham, Fulham, Hammersmith
Blue Bus Service	Halesworth
Bishops Luxury Coaches	Markfield, Coalville
E.J. Bostock & Sons Ltd	Macclesfield, Congleton
Burwell & District	Mildenhall, Soham, Burwell
Chownes Coaches	Banbury
Don Everall Ltd	Wolverhampton
East Midland Motor Services	Chesterfield
Eastern Belle Motor Services	Bow, Canning Town, London (East)
Eastern National Omnibus Co.	Southend, Basildon, Chelmsford
Eatonways	Birmingham
Elseys Coaches	Mappershall
Evergreen Coaches	Oldbury, Blackheath, Cradley Heath
Flights Tours Ltd	Birmingham, Sutton Coldfield
Gillards Tours Ltd	Normanton
Godiva Banton Coaches	Coventry
Greatrex Motor Coaches	Stafford
Granville Tours	Grimsby
Grosvenor Coaches Ltd	Enfield, Edmonton
Hanson Coach Services	Huddersfield
Hazeldine Hire Service	Bilston
Harper Brothers Ltd	Lichfield, Cannock
Hebble Motor Services	Halifax, Todmorden
J.W. Kitchin & Sons Ltd	Castleford, Wakefield, Morley, Bradford
W. King & Sons Ltd	London

Operators using Beach Coach Station, Summer 1963 (continued)

Operator	Serving
Lambert & Sons Ltd	Ditchingham, Norfolk
Leon Motor services	Doncaster
Lincolnshire Road Car Co.	Lincoln, Scunthorpe, Newark
Mansfield & District	Mansfield, Ollerton
Midland Red	Peterborough, Leicester
Midland General	Chesterfield, Mansfield, Southwell
Moseley & Sons	Barnsley
Montys Coaches Ltd	Nuneaton
Mulleys Motorways Ltd	Bury St Edmunds
Norfolk Motor Services	Ipswich, Colchester, London, Skegness
North Western Road Car Co.	Congleton, Macclesfield
N&S Coaches Ltd	Corby, Market Harborough
R.L. Osborn & Son	Kettering
Potteries Motor Traction	The Potteries, Stoke, etc.
Popular Coaches Ltd	Canning Town
Premier Coaches Ltd	St Albans, Watford
Premier Travel	Cambridge, Oxford
Reliance Coaches	Rotherham
C. Riley	Rowmarsh
W. Robinson & Sons Ltd	Lancashire towns, Manchester
A. Rowe & Sons Ltd	Cudworth, Barnsley
Royal Blue Coaches Ltd	Kettering
Seamark Brothers	Luton
Sheffield United Tours	Sheffield, Newark, Worksop
J.R. Street & Sons Ltd	Hertford, Ware, Hoddesdon
A. Towler & Sons	Feltwell, Brandon
Travel House Ltd	Luton, Dunstable
Trent Motor Traction	Nottingham, Derby, Alfreton
A. Timpson & Sons Ltd	London
United Counties	Northampton, Luton, Bedford
United Service Transport Ltd	Dagenham, Barking
Valiant Direct Coaches Ltd	Southall, Ealing, Uxbridge
Venture Coaches Ltd	Hendon
Viking Motors Ltd	Burton-on-Trent
Wallace Arnold Tours Ltd	Wakefield, Castleford
York Brothers Ltd	Northampton

The first Saturday, 23rd June, passed very peacefully everyone coping easily but then, expecting things to warm up, I took a week's holiday, and so missed Saturday No. 2. I returned from Devon on Saturday No. 3 but despite a long drive had to swallow a meal and then head for the coach station to find out how we had fared. The hard-cored main surface looked like a battlefield; on it were about four remaining vehicles and in the distance covered in a brown dust and limping towards me was our traffic superintendent Wilf Beckett.

Now Wilf was one of the nicest of men who was always conscientious and courteous, but not this evening. He saw me and said, 'I don't care if you sack me on the spot GM, but *I will not* come to this place on a Saturday again, it is *too much*'. Now this was not like Wilf, who had started his transport career in Oldham (again), and whose first driving shift in that place saw him piloting a

Beach Coach Station, Yarmouth

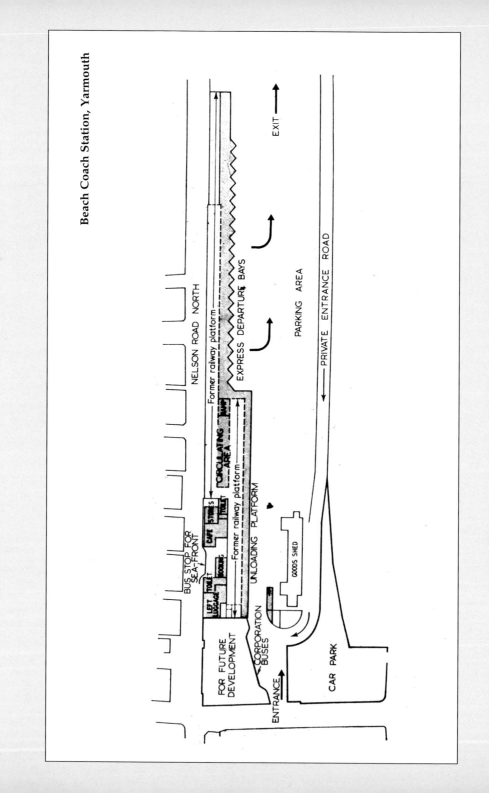

very early Guy six-wheeler, then he gravitated to Karriers so there was stern stuff in his frame. What therefore was the problem?

Well it fell into two parts. Properties in Wellesley Road lay at the rear of the station area, and the Council had reserved a strip of land against their boundaries in case the owners should decide to have a series of rear accesses constructed, at their expense. Along and parallel to this strip was a second strip that formed the entrance to the station for coaches coming from the north. Sadly, however, these two subtractions gave insufficient space for two long coaches to be parked one behind the other and at right-angles to these strips.

This Saturday had seen a great lift in usage, and as the space rapidly filled up, one difficult coach driver had left his machine parked so that it was obstructing the one and only exit then locked the coach and disappeared on a long layover into the town. Net result - coaches pouring in, none going out, and traffic chaos on Southtown Road, Acle Road, and Caister Road or in other words the three main routes. In fact the only ones into the Borough. A cup of tea, and a chat in the station buffet, fortunately restored Wilf to his normal co-operative frame of mind, and so we were all set for the next Saturday, when we were overwhelmed yet again, only this time in a very different manner.

Some coaches came in very early in the morning, but the visitors could not claim their lodgings until around lunch time so it seemed to me that we had scope to start a left luggage service. If only I had known what we were getting into. Consequently I asked our tyre fitter Tommy Rowe, who was a strong man, if he would like a spot of overtime doing the necessary. He said, 'Yes', and so early that Saturday morning we opened up. Tommy came to need all his muscles as in no time at all he was surrounded by a multitude of bags and cases of all sorts and sizes, and desperately needed some help that was brought in, by which time he had almost vanished under the piles of luggage.

During the following week our body makers lined several of the previously disused offices at the south end of the buildings with luggage racks, and in no time at all on Saturday No. 4 these came quickly to be filled. In the end with every possible foot of wall racked we came to the position of having up to eight staff members taking money, labelling, stacking, and handing over to their respective owners piles and piles of luggage, and what luggage. It seemed that the many visitors heading for the numerous caravan or holiday camps in the area felt that there was a great shortage of food in and around Great Yarmouth. So we had cases so packed with tinned goods that if you lifted one by the handle to swing it onto a rack you were left holding the handle or in extreme cases, well they were, found the contents rolling around your feet as the bottom dropped out. It really was incredible as were other happenings.

Opening the station caused confusion to operators and to passengers, not all of the latter really appreciating that the days of picking up their vehicle at the Britannia Pier were now well and truly over. This particular Saturday a rather large lady and her somewhat diminutive husband had an argument. He was sure their coach would be leaving the pier. She said, 'No, it's from the station'. Net result - he took one child and vanished on safari towards the pier. She stayed on the premises with the rest of the brood, but whilst he was absent their homebound transport came in, loaded up and set off for distant parts. She was in a panic, so much so that when he finally reappeared, she, hot, flustered and

A second-hand station. For most of the week the former Great Yarmouth Beach railway station had a quiet life. Closed to trains in February 1959 it was easily adapted to its new use in 1961/2. Here on a peak 1962 Saturday morning homebound passengers stand on the new low departure platform and on the higher former railway facility. Note how a new roof had been provided utilising the original ironwork. There were 21 departure bays laid out on a 'saw tooth' basis, every one clearly signed.

Left: Coaches set passengers down at a low level arrival platform which ran parallel to the main station buildings housing the booking office, waiting room, cafe, toilets and, last but not least, the left luggage facilities. Then they parked up on the areas set aside for the purpose before moving prior to departure time onto the bay (or bays) allocated to their company. As a result, the chaos that had been a feature of the Britannia Pier location previously used became a thing of the past. *Right:* One could never have imagined just how much left luggage would be handled on peak Saturdays. Here is just a part of the queue waiting to leave their cases around 7.00 am on a Saturday morning after experiencing overnight journeys from many parts of the country. Work in that office was certainly a way to develop one's muscles.

very upset, went up to him, shook him as a dog would shake a rabbit, and exclaimed to all those around as the shaking continued, 'You great steaming nit'. It was a memorable scene, but then in despair she burst into tears.

Having had a week's holiday they now had little, if any, money left, and their seasonal service ran only on Saturdays. Now a Great Yarmouth Transport service with a difference swung into action. We determined that at the end of the day we would have no items of left luggage or any passengers left over, so we took the family into the booking office, gave them some tea, and discovered where home was. We then went through all listed subsequent departures to find which ones ran to their town or somewhere nearby, and then inquiried as to which coaches, if any, had some spare seats. Invariably a driver would, with a little coaxing, agree to accept some additional bodies, as happened here, so one family left us with grateful thanks. Often the reverse occurred, when a coach company had too many passengers for the seating capacity then available and we were asked if we could provide some additional duplication. Our drivers would usually volunteer for some quite long distance trips, trips that did on occasions provide us with some amusement. Here we normally provided a Daimler 'Freeline', their Roe bodies having parcel racks, luggage boots and semi-luxury seating.

On one such Saturday morning a well known firm in the Midlands made an urgent request for a duplicate, so the garage turned out bus No. 17, as spare 'Freelines' were otherwise engaged. Now No. 17 had started life on 23rd May, 1950 with Hebble Motor Services of Halifax, a company that will receive a more substantial mention later in these pages. It consisted of a Leyland 'PS2' chassis and a front-doored Willowbrook body. We had bought it for use as a one-man reserve vehicle, but Hebble had originally specified dual purpose bodywork so it could be employed on the Halifax to Blackpool and Scarborough express services. When new as fleet No. 42, BCP 829, it was a powerful performer, and despite its now advanced years there was still plenty of urge under the bonnet. When it arrived on the stand to load up, the host company drivers made numerous ribald comments about its old-fashioned appearance compared to their smart new Bedfords. Indicating that it would take hours to reach its destination they told our man he could leave in advance of their convoy, and they would doubtlessly see him, i.e. catch him up at the recognised midway refreshment stop. So it came to pass, only now the biters were well and truly bitten when, at that same stop, after more pithy comments, our man gently indicated that he had already dropped his passengers off at their destination, and was now halfway home, so what price their Bedfords now?

It all made one wonder just what problems must have occurred before the coach station came into being and now the old railway booking office came into its own, as we became agents for some 15 companies.

Over the next two years we managed to improve the facilities in so far as the Civic purse would allow, and by the start of the second season our north access road had moved onto the land held back against Wellesley Road properties, they never having back entries, and so a former parking problem was solved. We also engaged additional supervision, so that Wilf's locked and badly parked coach problem should not happen again. Despite his early protestations he was after the third Saturday restored to his normal self, and taking a considerable interest in what went on at 'The Beach' as did all the staff.

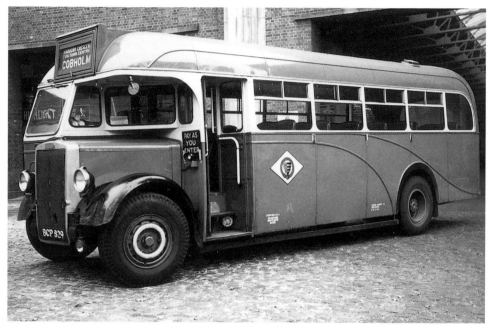

Roy Marshall tells me we first met when he called at Caister Road depot, asked to see me and then wondered if I would have Leyland 'PS2' No. 17 brought into the yard so he could take its picture. I did, and here is the result, 40 years later. A bus with 'urge'.

Next came five Daimler 'Freelines' again with Roe (dual purpose) bodies, Gardner '6HLW' engines and semi-automatic gear boxes. These as fleet Nos. 21 to 25 were very substantial vehicles as almost all the running gear was identical to that in the double-deckers. Another three came later these having one piece windscreens.

As traffic superintendent he and his team were never short of work, as services had to be augmented at least twice as the peak weeks rolled round, and then decreased again until the winter timetables were introduced at the end of September, timetables that began to see increases in one-man-operation with the arrival of the first five Daimler 'Freeline' single-deckers with Roe bodies that were also taken into stock as Nos. 21 to 25, three more came later. These were unusual machines, but there was some sense in their purchase, as the innards of their Gardner engines and most of the running gear was identical to that of the 'CVG6' double-deckers. But mention of seasonal service lifts leads me to mention an almost incredible story, but that is how it was retailed to me.

Whit Saturday was always a crunch point. This was the day when the initial summer services were introduced, and this was the time when the new duty schedules could fail to receive the approbation of the bus crews and rebellion could firmly be in the air, and so it came to pass.

I walked down the Wellington Pier late on the Friday evening in company with the then Mayor, who was also the station master at Gorleston, but who had spent his earlier years signalling on the Woodhead line, thinking that if a union meeting scheduled about that hour went as forecast there could well be no buses in the town the following morning. It did, a vote was taken, and strike action was agreed, but now came the incredible bit. Every night a bus was left on the forecourt of the garage to take staff who lived in the Gorleston area home. It was parked overnight in the old Gorleston tram shed, and was used each early morning as the inward staff bus so, after the meeting in the canteen, the late turn men took their seats, but the bus did not move. Eventually, tired of waiting, inquiries were made when their staff bus driver colleague indicated that the shift fitter on duty would not let him depart, saying that if they were now on strike, and it was after midnight, then obviously he, the driver, could not be covered by insurance and so that bus was staying at Caister Road, period!

The question was asked, 'But what if we were not on strike?'

'Then there is no problem' came the answer, so after a quick chat the strike resolution was rescinded, and that bus duly rolled, as did the whole service the that morning. Well it is a fascinating story but that is how it was told to me when I arrived at the office that Saturday morning.

Now I am sure that many enthusiasts wonder what they would do if only they could run their own local transport concern, but as a new General Manager you soon discovered that you were not the Supremo of your empire. You of necessity had to become immersed in local domestic and not so domestic politics, so let's leave the buses to take care of themselves for several paragraphs and investigate just what might be involved here.

After some years of experience in the field I came to the firm conclusion that a County Borough as it existed pre-1974 was a very good method of local government, especially when such authorities covered rather more fields than was later the case. It followed from this that if as the Transport Manager you wanted the garage roof, or the drains or a wall repaired, or an extension built you needed advice from the Borough Engineer or the Borough Architect, who would then produce an estimate of cost that could be put to Committee. If you became involved in a highways congestion problem, then the Borough Engineer and the local Chief Constable came into the picture, for in the days when I started Great

Massey Brothers body building plant was based in the former Pemberton Wigan steam tram shed and being small in size produced from one to two bodies per week. Arthur Tyldesley who was head of the concern liked to pick his customers and preferred to work for seaside undertakings if possible. Among buses supplied to Great Yarmouth was this Leyland 'PD2' fleet No. 35, one of a batch of five dating from May 1957. With gold anodised window finishers Massey all-metal bodies were built to almost individual standards. Arthur was rather behind when it came to quoting for rear-engined bodywork though.

After the 'Atlanteans' came the first batch of Daimler 'Fleetlines' that also carried Roe bodies with one piece windscreens giving a vastly improved forwards view. No. 51 of the 51 to 54 series is also on racecourse special duties. These vehicles had the Gardner '6LX' engines.

Yarmouth, like other County Boroughs, had its own police force which came under the jurisdiction of the Watch Committee, as did the local fire brigade.

At the head of the municipal structure was the Town Clerk, who was there to ensure the administration worked and who was the chief legal officer. His department serviced every committee, and members of his staff acted as committee clerks, whilst the Town Clerk would usually attend transport committees in person, so his support for a pet project of some magnitude was often invaluable.

Next in importance was the Borough Treasurer as no General Manager usually signed cheques. If the department wanted to buy something routine, say for example a batch of Leyland spares, an official order was made out in triplicate. One copy went to Leyland, one copy to the Borough Treasurer's Department and one copy was retained. When the material came to hand the contents of the order were checked against the delivery note, and a little later against the invoice that Leyland would issue. When this was done a stamp was applied to the document, it was certified as being correct, and then passed to the Treasurer so that a cheque could be sent to the supplier.

All these invoices would be listed and the list placed on the table before the next Transport Committee took place. Members could then inspect the list and ask questions on the contents when the Treasurer, or his representative, would turn up the invoice from the file they brought with them, and the GM would provide an explanation as to the whys and the wherefores. This may all seem cumbersome and it was but public money was being spent, and it was right and proper that the rules were followed. It follows that a Treasurer could take a jaundiced view of some expensive development proposal but on the other hand he could be very helpful, so here were strings that needed to be waxed. I recall at this point the need when in Halifax to replace our crumbling office block; the then Treasurer suddenly produced from some obscure back pocket all the monies needed to provide the replacement premises, money that I did not previously know existed.

I could enlarge this list but what I am trying to show is that you did not operate in isolation, but here came the rub. The costs of all these activities carried out by the other departments were costed out in the treasury by some jealously guarded (or so it seemed) formula and then appeared in your transport accounts as Central Administration Charges. There was usually little or nothing that a General Manager could do to affect the sums so recorded. In later years no invoice list as such came before Committee. Audit pulled out about six invoices at random and did a full investigation, when only if some admin failure was found did any Committee report materialise.

Dealing with the Transport Committee could also have its moments. About a fortnight before the next came due your committee clerk would inquire what items you had for inclusion on the agenda so one gave thought to what would be appropriate, this depending on what could be decided by management and what needed higher approval. Remember here, the rule was that a committee and/or Council would set policy, and Managers would manage but some elasticity here was more than usual. To your list would then be added items originating in other departments, and when the collection was complete the agreed agenda was circulated to all concerned with the required reports. One for each separate subject, clearly describing what was intended and providing a relevant recommendation.

Once this had been done, the GM would meet up with his Chairman to go through the agenda and reports so that the Chairman was not going to be faced with any nasty surprises as the meeting progressed. I well recall my first such occurrence. My new Chairman phoned me and asked me to call at his bungalow. On arrival he told me to seat myself at the table, handed me a glass of sherry and as we went down the list wrote 'yes', 'no' or some other single word against each item. When we reached the end he thanked me for coming, and added, 'Not bad, we should be through in about ten minutes', which proved to be the case. But they were not always that short, and as we have seen Council discussions could become very involved when usually all the General Manager could do was to sit in his seat and take the flack.

When the meeting was over the committee clerk would produce a draft set of minutes and here you just might be able to resort to a spot of gentle editing, but let us not dwell further on this rather delicate aspect of the matter. When agreed those minutes were then printed into the monthly book of Minutes of all the committees and sub-committees of the Council that had met during the associated period, and the contents of this volume came before the full authority for final ratification.

Do not think, though, reader that the proceedings of a Council meeting are totally spontaneous. Some parts when a member asks a question might be, but you can be assured that before the night, the political groups in their private caucus meetings have gone over all the contents within that printed book and decided which to support, which to oppose, and which to let pass without comment. A full Council meeting could be a trying time for any aspiring General Manager, and especially so if a proposed fares increase was up for discussion. So let us digress for a while and consider just what those simple words could imply, and in so doing consider traffic staff wages back in the early 1960s, which I am afraid means talking in pre-decimal currency, namely pounds, shillings and pence, and back-tracking to page 77.

On my very first day in Great Yarmouth a driver was paid a basic wage of £9 8s. 6d. for a 44 hour working week. Then as we have noted on 2nd April, 1960 an extra 10s. 6d. became payable. Not much you may say, but on 10th June the working week was reduced to 42 hours without loss of pay, meaning an appropriate rise in the hourly rate which flowed through into overtime, holiday, sickness and employer's superannuation make-up payments. Added to this every staff member with 10 or more years continuous service received an extra three days holiday per annum with pay.

On 22nd April, 1961 wages were advanced by 11 shillings per week. On 20th May, 1962 there was an an advance of 6s. 6d. per week plus £1 per week holiday bonus. Finally, in my last Great Yarmouth days another 8s. 9d. was added to the then basic rate as from 21st April, 1963. These today seem paltry figures, but they are relative to the times, and to a new manager gave food for thought; so question number one when you received official confirmation of the first award was 'Can the undertaking afford to absorb it in full without further action being called for?' Well, municipal undertakings were not intended to be large profit generators. Council policy most likely required one to break even or make a small surplus. So let's say the answer was in the negative.

What next? Settle down and do some arithmetic. What effect is this going to have on the current year's final accounts? And as far as one can forecast try to ascertain how the picture will look at the end of next year if nothing significant (like another wage award) occurs. Having come to a conclusion then as to how much extra finance is necessary can one foresee any useful economies, if so subtract their effect, and then what have we to do to fares to regain financial equilibrium?

Now in those, and many later, days, the municipal undertakings used five or six line Ultimate ticket machines. So five or six printed tickets had to cover all your fare values, perhaps say a 3d. and a 4d. for a 7d. fare. But how could you accurately discover just how many 7d. tickets had been sold, and during these calculations pay full regard to your fare scale spreads which in Great Yarmouth were then laid out as follows?

Stages travelled	1	2	3	4	5	6	7	8	9	10	11	12	13	14	15	16
Adult fare charged (d.)	2	2½	3	4	5	6	6	7	7	7	8	8	8	9	9	9

Average stage distance = ½ mile

Puzzle reader, you need to cover this fares range with just six ticket values. Which six would you choose? Note how in the upper ranges one can travel the equivalent of three stages for the same fare, so again one has to try to assess what the effect would be on income if that three stage concession was reduced to two stages. I trust you have the idea.

Now when you have finally arrived at some conclusions do a report to the Transport Committee and set down the recommendations in full, showing how you have arrived at the end result, and produce some sample fare tables so that everyone can see what will change and where. You can be sure that there will be a full discussion but in the end the Committee will hopefully accept your proposals, and then you await the full Council meeting when things might hot up somewhat. It may be that the ruling group will accept the inevitable with some understandable reluctance, but the political opposition could well take a very different view, suggesting that either the whole scheme is just ludicrous, or need not happen at all. In later years too, anything involving an upwards review of concessionary fare travel was just pure dynamite.

As I have remarked earlier, municipal undertakings were not normally regarded as profit makers, they were intended to serve the best interests of the ratepayers, and fares were not raised without good reason. But as busmen's pay represented such a high proportion of operating costs, as it still does, any significant variation inevitably meant raising more cash. In due course acceptance in whole, or part, would be forthcoming, although before that happy stage was reached in very contentious cases there could be either a rejection of the report, or a reference back for further consideration which meant some GM was going to suffer a lot more heartburn.

Let me make one thing very clear. I make no comment whatsoever on the desirability, or otherwise, of the social implications involved. I am just trying to pursue the main theme behind this book, 'What was it really like then to be a General Manager?'

The next hurdle comes once Council confirmation has been forthcoming, for one cannot act without it. Do a letter to your local traffic office and ask for a supply of essential official forms. These were designed so that when the Traffic Commissioners come to review the case before them they are able to study what your figures mean laid out in standard format, to make it all clearer to them. They are filled in and returned whilst you, who will doubtlessly have to act as the undertaking's principal witness, prepare your brief and it is always useful to send off a copy of this as well so that the Commissioners will know what you are going to say. Some time later in an early issue of that well known fortnightly publication *Notices and Proceedings* a public inquiry hearing will be listed, and this might just take place in your own town hall rather than in the area traffic office so one awaits the day.

Now in pre-war days fares, in that era of no inflation, just did not normally rise, in fact they often went down. There will be those around who then could recall those palmy days and wonder, if your predecessors could do that, why cannot you? Opposition is therefore likely to be the name of the game and that opposition could come from passenger groups, other local authorities, trade unions whose members are going to be called upon to pay your higher fares, and/or other interested parties. Often those various parties will be legally represented, so you could be in for a lot of hard questioning and the Commissioners could well throw in some of their own, especially if they feel that your final proposals involve a degree of unfairness. For example is the undertaking intending as a matter of policy to leave fares to a remote housing estate alone whilst every other one goes up?

Coping with a fares increases represented a lot of work, as it still does except that public inquiries are a thing of the past. Before the proceedings came to a close the Commissioners usually made a grant, either in whole or with minor modifications, and a date was agreed as to when the new charges might be introduced. You reeled out, perchance battered and bruised, to start doing all that was necessary, producing new fare scale books and publicity and usually some new pre-printed tickets, but here came a normal municipal snag. By the time one had been through all the committee and council cycles, and had had to wait for the inquiry to take place, several weeks could have passed by which time the extra wages had become payable, so here was a provision one needed to make in those early estimates.

Then comes the big question, 'Will the extra money sought come in as you hoped?'

Now this is only one facet of managerial involvement with Traffic Commissioners; there was then that other heady subject of road service licence applications, but fear not we will come to this matter later in these pages. In the mean time let us turn to the affairs of the Association and Federation.

Puzzle answer

Did you forget to allow for child's travel at half fare? Try 1*d*., 1½*d*., 2*d*., 3*d*., 4*d*. and 5*d*. Issue double tickets or two in combination so 6*d*. = 2 x 3*d*., 7*d*. = 3*d*. + 4*d*., 9*d*. = 4*d*. + 5*d*. There was a button on every Ultimate machine individual ticket line which, when pressed, issued two tickets but the ticket counter only advanced by one. Compare the ticket numbers sold to counter readings to ascertain how many double tickets were issued. Present day electronic ticket machines provide all the answers without the arithmetic - but are far more costly and readers and modules are also needed.

Chapter Seven

Association and Federation

At the time of my arrival in the ranks of the General Managers, there were 96 municipal undertakings, this number having been reduced by one a little while earlier when the Grimsby and Cleethorpes concerns elected to merge. They ranged in size from the giant - Birmingham, Glasgow and Manchester undertakings with their fleet strengths of around 1,600, 1,550 and 1,100 vehicles respectively - to the tiny Llandudno or Colwyn Bay concerns with their seasonal operations, or the seven vehicle fleet of Bedwas & Machen which was the smallest having all-year-round services. To increase the total of 96 one could add Hartlepool which had just four double-deck buses, but as these were operated by a contractor, on behalf of the Council, and so not directly, it came into a different category. There were also some overseas members.

Irrespective of size, however, each and every one was in membership of the Municipal Passenger Transport Association, or MPTA, which in later years was to change its name to the Association of Public Passenger Transport Operators, something that was deemed desirable when the PTE organisations came into being.

Now it can be assumed that there were within the local authorities forming the membership some 90-plus committees that covered transport affairs, and with these came a similar number of Committee Chairmen and Vice Chairmen. There were not, however, a like number of Chief Transport Officers, General Managers, or whatever one might choose to call such officers as Len Merrall of Rawtenstall who had the unique distinction of being responsible also for transport happenings in both Haslingden and Ramsbottom. He had only taken up office in Rawtenstall in 1943, whereas Ronald Fearnley of Coventry had moved there in 1933 from Southend where he had been appointed transport manager back in 1929. He therefore was the senior in service of the fraternity.

The MPTA had begun life as an association of tramway managers back in the early 1900s, as a forum in which the professionals might exchange views and news, but in no time at all its scope was widened to include both Chairmen and Vice Chairmen. In this regard it was quite unique in that both officers and laymen had equal voting rights, the President of the MPTA being elected annually on an alternate manager/layman basis.

The country was split into areas, and in each a full area meeting was held normally every two months, when the three representatives from each unit could be expected to attend. Each undertaking acted in turn as host and, in view of the travelling distances that were often involved, providing lunch, a meal that was normally graced by the presence of the Mayor and other members of the municipal hierarchy. Such affairs were decidedly formal, with one or two speeches the order of the day, unlike the meetings of area managers that took place also every two months but on an alternate monthly basis to the formal meeting.

Consequently everyone had the chance to find out what was going on elsewhere in the area and in the country, but the latter aspect of the matter was reinforced by the two annual gatherings. These consisted of a springtime managers' get-together usually at some inland venue, whilst the national conference took place in the autumn normally at the seaside after the last of the national political party gatherings had taken place. Here it was usual for a seaside town to be chosen, provided it had a municipal transport undertaking (Torquay was an exception), because of the number of persons attending (wives were invited, as were numerous members of the trades fraternity) and so adequate hotel accommodation of a suitable standard was essential.

Alas, this desired standard was not always attained, and there was one notable occasion when the annual and very formal dinner did not go as it should. The first course arrived more or less on time, the next two or three became ever slower, and then the service just dried up. Our wine waiter too gave up and took a seat on the floor behind me, but was bribed with the promise of a glass or two if only he would look after us. This he did, but the glass or two generated into rather more, so if no one else had a happy evening he certainly did. The following morning those staying in the headquarters hotel had another surprise as the staff were conspicuous by their absence so a posse of wives invaded the kitchens, and proceeded to cook and serve numerous breakfasts. Usually, however, decorum was preserved and the night saw the Vice President elected to the top office when he would normally announce the date and location of the next annual gathering.

Shortly before the commencement of each national conference those attending received a pack of the relevant documents. These included tickets for the various functions, a list of those scheduled to attend which gave details of their undertaking or firm, and the hotel at which they would be staying. Also included were the annual reports of the association and federation, a conference programme, and copies of the papers which were to be presented. There were usually two of these or occasionally three.

The two annual general meetings were formal affairs when the President or Chairman of those bodies went through the report which covered the years working, and presented the annual financial statement, when the contents where open to debate and acceptance or otherwise by the membership. There were a few occasions when those debates did become rather contentious.

The authors of the papers ranged from members of the government, through senior civil servants, members of the manufacturing industry, overseas operators, outside experts, and members of the MPTA itself. On the front of each printed copy of the papers was a tear off slip, and if you wished to take part in the discussion that was scheduled to occur after the author had delivered his words of wisdom to the multitude, you filled it in, and handed it before the event to the secretariat. Then you waited to be called before putting forward your observations on what you had heard. Each paper was embargoed and could not be published before the speaker had delivered his oration.

Papers needless to say varied from absolutely excellent to decidedly abstract, and at this point watch out for there might be a President about. One momentous year I duly received my pack, and scanned through the enclosed papers. One of these was far too technical for me, so I decided there and then that here was something that I knew nothing about, and did not want to know, but here I was in grave error.

At about half after midnight on the day which would see that paper delivered, my wife and I were about to leave the Town Hall after the annual dinner dance when there waiting in the foyer was the President.

> I have been looking for you [said he] because no one is down to take part in the discussion after Mr X has given his paper, so will you please do me a favour and start it, and rope in a few of your pals to follow you thereafter. We cannot have a flop on our hands.

One could not ignore such a request from the President so 3 am saw me sitting up in my twin bed trying to decide what I could sensibly say and in the process congratulate the author on a very profound presentation. Whilst I so pondered my wife gently slumbered on, to remark when we came to rise, that from the look of me I had obviously had a bad night so was everything alright with me?

This was bad, but giving a paper yourself . . . more conscription . . . was far worse. First came the problem of what subject to choose. It really needed to be pertinent, topical, not very political, if you were an officer, and something that would stimulate a debate yet not to the extent that the views that you expressed were subject to almost universal ridicule. Then of course came the presentation itself. Was it possible to do the necessary without having to read each line of your script, and at the same time inject some humour into the proceedings. I did it just once at a National event, but was never brave enough to repeat the venture. Additionally as we have seen earlier what you had said as the speaker could rebound on you later, witness the 'Routine maintenance saga' (*see page 72*).

Still this was all a part of municipal managerial life, and if you were lucky and became the longest serving professional member of the Executive Committee of the MPTA or APPTO then you too would find yourself elected to the Presidential chair. In the event I never did make it, only reaching the vice presidential position, thanks to local government re-organisation occurring 12 months too soon.

Now if you did not know beforehand just how someone from (say) Aberdeen could find out the pedigree of an applicant from Brighton you need search no further. Everyone knew everyone else in the industry, and a great many quite close friendships came into being as a result.

At the time of my arrival the head office of the MPTA was in London, where I went for my first ever meeting, but soon afterwards it was moved to the rather remote, for most members, location of Chelmsford. So it was many years before I ever paid a visit to Friars House in that town. Great Yarmouth was in what was certainly the largest geographical area, which included the undertakings of Lowestoft, Ipswich, Colchester, Southend, Luton, Maidstone, Brighton, Bournemouth, Portsmouth, Southampton, Eastbourne, Swindon and Reading, together with Exeter and Plymouth. These two latter technically were in an area of their own, but could not be left to exist in isolation, so formed a part of this much larger group. From the area membership were elected an appropriate number of managers or laymen to sit on the Council of the MPTA for a set term and the same general rules applied in the case of the Federation, so what did that do?

The MPTA in its assorted gatherings discussed such things as government pronouncements, transport field developments, and anything else that was germain to its interests. To assist there were a number of committees, dealing with engineering affairs, the motor bus committee, the claims committee, the traffic committee, the finance and accounting committee, and the training committee, etc., for the MPTA sponsored a small number of juniors who spent time away from their own concern for a period of some two years. For example young engineers would find themselves elsewhere gaining experience in traffic operations or finance and administration departments, and often such trainees would in due course aspire to senior positions. But to become a trainee you needed to be already employed in the industry as a junior, and as we have seen (*in Volume One*) obtaining a start in the industry was far from easy, so some of us were never so lucky. Once again the members of these committees were nominated by their areas, and whilst my old engineering chiefs at Manchester and Leeds sat on the motor bus committee so did men from much smaller concerns. I was a member and later Chairman of this body.

One thing the MPTA did not do was to act as an employers association, and it was for this precise purpose that the Federation came into being. Once again there was an executive committee whose members came from the various areas, and from these also came the three recognised officers of the Federation, namely the Chairman, Vice Chairman and the Treasurer. This committee considered anything that had to do with pay and conditions (apart from administrative staff) of those working in the industry, and with the appropriate unions carried out all the national negotiations, being a party to the national agreements which resulted from deliberations which took place either in the National Joint Industrial Council (NJIC), or the National Council for Craftsman. The title of the latter was indicative of its scope, the former covered platform staff and semi-skilled or unskilled personnel, e.g. cleaners, labourers, etc. Area meetings as a result were in two parts, and had two agendas, one covering MPTA matters, the other dealing with Federation business.

All this could, and did, generate a goodly amount of paper work which was handled at headquarters by the General Secretary, who covered both MPTA and Federation affairs, being, along with his union counterparts, the joint secretary of the two national negotiating bodies. Each area also had its secretary, but he was always one of the General Managers, who either volunteered or was conscripted to fill that office when the facilities available within his undertaking were used for the purpose. This was not a job I was ever desirous of filling.

Sitting on the Federation executive committee was by no means a bundle of fun, but someone had to do it, and this comment particularly applied whenever pay negotiations were in the air. The trade union side would put in a claim, and a full meeting of the NJIC would be convened. This would take place in the large top floor room at Transport House in London, a room containing two very large tables connected across their tops by another not so large.

At this sat the Chairman and Vice Chairman, who were elected annually on an alternate basis from each side, these sides each occupying one of the large tables. At the top facing each other would be the respective spokesmen for each party, namely the Trade Group Secretary from the union and usually the Federation General Secretary or the Federation Chairman, these three doing virtually all the talking.

On presenting their case the TU side would retail numerous figures designed to indicate how busmen's pay was lagging behind what could be earned elsewhere, and, but very politely, what a stingy lot the employers were as a result. The employers would listen to this pronouncement, usually ask for a division, and then the TU people would leave for some other part of the building whilst the Federation reps discussed what they had heard. The parties would join up again when usually the employers would say that the application would receive due consideration, and a reply would be forthcoming at a later, but not too late, meeting. This was when the hard bargaining began, often with division after division until eventually agreement was reached and such meetings could be long and very tedious. I know from experience as a member, later treasurer, Vice Chairman and employers-side spokesman/negotiator!

A set of joint minutes would then be agreed and circulated after which what had been decided was obligatory and was implemented on the due date that was also fixed within the NJIC, or its parallel craftsmen's body. It can be said that the national agreement became different things to different people, and so what took place within one undertaking could in some respects differ from what applied in the undertaking next door, and sometimes substantial problems became manifest. If the temperature became very hot, another piece of Federation machinery could swing into action in the shape of a Visiting Emergency Committee (VEC).

This would be made up of a very limited number of people representing both employer and union interests, who would go to the place where trouble had brewed and see the local parties to the dispute, when each would be asked if they would abide by VEC's decision. Needless to say the answer would invariably be in the affirmative, and the members of the VEC would listen to the arguments, and after going into private discussion would try come up with some form of solution. Here something akin to the wisdom of Solomon could be required, but I doubt if we ever attained such high levels of thought, but peace to a greater or lesser extent would be restored. Now this is all very technical stuff, but it could be quite intimidating to a brand new General Manager, who would never previously have been involved in area meetings or attending conferences, etc.

When I made the grade there were only two other managers in my age group, namely Ralph Bennett, who as we have seen was at Bolton, and my old friend and Halifax engineering predecessor, Geoff Harding, then at Aberdare. Almost all the others were up to 20 years older, and had years of experience so they could be expected to be rather off-hand with any new and young member of the flock. Invariably too you would have a Chairman and Vice Chairman who had held their respective offices over a number of years and were quite well versed in procedures, which did not make life automatically easier. You put a foot in these waters very tentatively if you were wise.

As I have said everyone soon came to know everyone else, and I found that my older colleagues were in the main kindly, and would go out of their way to

Managers meet - and are shown the first post-war Halifax AEC 'Mk III' Roe double-decker. Chairman Alderman Edgar Bower is on the left with Sheffield's Mr R.C. Moore on his left. I don't know who is wearing the light mac, but next are Mr Tatham of Bradford and Mr G.F. Craven of Halifax, by the radiator are Mr Vane Morland of Leeds, another unknown, Mr Ivor Grey of Hebble and finally on the extreme right Frank Calvert the AEC Yorkshire area manager. It must have been a proud day for him. The batch of eight vehicles went into service on 1st December, 1946.

Managers meeting. This photograph was taken in Halifax Town Hall and shows from left to right: John Rostron, GM Huddersfield; Alderman M. Jagger, Chairman Halifax; Alderman A. Berry, Mayor Halifax; the author; Thomas Lord, GM Leeds; Edward Deakin, GM Bradford; Ted Metcalfe, GM Todmorden.

chat and be friendly. As I came to write this chapter I looked over my list of then current (May 1964) managers, and find that of the 90 then in office there were only around four who never had any early conversation with me, and of these one was sick, retiring soon after, one never seemed to come to such gatherings, and the other two, one heading a large undertaking, never came into my orbit in my early years but did so later. Here, as an example, I well remember at my very first such assembly (1960) Norman Morton then of Sunderland coming up to me, putting out his hand and saying, 'The name's Morton of Sunderland, Norman to you, how are you finding things?' Such an approach often repeated certainly helped.

In this period, though, life was perhaps rather freer in many ways than it is now and not every minute passed in serious discussion. A spot of amusement could liven the day, or night, and as the parties have now long departed the transport scene I might perhaps offer you some light entertainment as you read these pages.

There stood in the foyer of one conference hotel a large bronze statue of a lady wearing next to nothing, a lady who had one arm raised towards the sky. There were those who saw this bronze, and managed unnoticed to borrow it, carry it upstairs, dress it in a rather flimsy piece of ladies nightwear, and place it in the bed of one member who at the time was not being accompanied by his spouse. To add to the overall effect, a cigarette was placed in the raised hand, and so the miscreants departed, with sundry giggles.

The occupier of the room returning thereto after a rather heavy night was not amused when he saw what was occupying his bed, and came to the conclusion that he knew, nay was certain, who had done the deed. Consequently next day he procured numerous articles of pottery that were to be found in bedrooms in those days when *en suite* was not a description frequently heard, and in the dead of night piled these up outside a certain door knocking on it and fleeing into the night. The person roused from slumber opened the door to find himself noisily inundated by the aforesaid objects, but he was not the originator of the initial prank, in fact he was not even a conference delegate, having nothing to do with the transport industry, so some skilled diplomacy was then called for! Sometimes, though, one's quiet chuckles arose in other ways.

At one such meeting the hall where the main events took place had the usual stage at one end, and behind this stage were windows looking onto a large rear parking area. On this area were several buses, all new, which had been brought to the venue so that they could be seen and hopefully admired by those taking part in the conference. But one wag early that morn spotted a possibility as in prime position was a bus from the host undertaking. Unseen by anyone else, he took this out of its pole position, and put in another that had a similar but not identical colour scheme, but having his name on it.

In due course the gathering assembled, and the Mayor came in to deliver the usual civic welcome when including a paen of praise for his local transport concern, pointing to the vehicle outside and remarking that there was one of the finest, if not the finest, passenger transport vehicles in the country. Worse, however, was to follow, for as he came to sit in his chair whilst the President made his response, the Mayor slowly but surely began to vanish from view as the flooring of the stage gave way beneath him.

Right: Great Yarmouth purchased ten wartime Guy 'Utilities'. Spartan wooden-seated bodies of two builders - no interior lining panels and unseasoned timber. The chassis had a Gardner '5LW' engine, constant mesh gear box and substantial rear axle well nigh indestructible, with a 28 mph flat out top speed. Guy went on to produce more sophisticated 'Arabs' up to the 'Mark V' version with its dropped frame to provide a two-step entrance forward passenger door. Good! The 'Mark V' was then replaced by the 'Wulfrunian' only then to reappear when 'Wulfrunian' sales failed to prosper. It was sadly all too late. Guy finances became critical and so a bankrupt concern became a Jaguar take-over. Goodbye Guy!

Below left: There arrived one day in Great Yarmouth a Guy 'Wulfrunian', painted in Wolverhampton Wanderers team colours. Here was 'modernity' with a vengeance. Front-mounted Gardner '6LX' engine semi-automatic gear box and dropped centre rear axle, *plus* air suspension independent at the front and disc brakes. No bonnets, were provided, these being left to the body builder. To add to the complexity the Cave-Brown-Cave heating system was included. After a careful assessment we came to the firm conclusion that this was 'a bus to far'. My, how they could corner, and in the process produce heavy front tyre wear. Here is a 'Wulfrunian' chassis. Note the temporary front wheel arch bracing to be replaced in due couse by some additional body builder strengthening.

Below: It must be said that the Guy 'Wulfrunian' was some engineering project. Note here how the main frames are reversed from the conventional, and the substantial rear axle carrier pressing, plus the attendant air suspension bellows. It formed in all, a brave attempt to take bus technology forward whilst maintaining the advantages of a front-mounted engine. Time, expense and lack of development were against it. Sad!

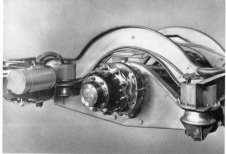

Those in the audience watched enthralled as the Mayor sank as the sun sinks below the horizon, only in this case the horizon was formed by the surface of the table until he vanished from view completely, a vanishing that concluded with an almighty 'crash'. Fortunately he was unhurt, and took it all in good part, but it certainly was an occasion to remember. There were, though, occasions when things went wrong, and everyone suffered. One conference was held in Liverpool and an evening reception and dance was held on one of the Mersey ferries. The delegates did not realise that the boat was to take them for a short cruise, until the floor upon which quite a number were dancing seemed to drop down beneath their feet. The resulting sensation was weird.

This was only a gentle promise of what was to follow for the next day a cruise to see the docks, and have lunch on board, was on the agenda. No one, before boarding, appreciated just how rough the Mersey can get, so very few lunches were eaten and some very sorry looking conference delegates were more than thankful when in the late afternoon it was possible to bring the boat back into dock. As one survivor then said, 'There is a lot to be said for land-based double-deck transport'. A conference really could provide one with some interesting, and also boring, times.

The nadir was reached at one conference annual dinner when the principal speaker was a national politician who, unlike most of the breed, had a rather soft voice. Now it might have been possible to hear what he was saying if you were sitting within a few places of him, but for the assembled throng this was simply not possible, so as he droned on, the sounds of quiet private conversations began to rise until no one was taking any notice of him. He, quite unperturbed, continued until he came to the end of his script. On such occasions, which thank goodness were very few, one had to have sympathy with the President who had to cope with it all, and offer a gracious reply. Sadly, this gentleman did not receive the sort of advice one of his successors came to enjoy.

One professional member of the Association was in the little boy's room and began to chat amiably to the stranger sharing the facilities, when our colleague expressed the hope that this particular night's VIP would cut it short and so not bore the pants off his listeners. He was consequently somewhat shocked to find that the recipient of his observations was indeed the night's 'Top of the Bill', but at least some positive good came from his endeavours.

It was usual for those sitting at the various tables to run a sweep on how long the speaker would actually speak. You paid your money, say a 'fiver', and put your estimate on the sheet held by the organiser, when the winner usually paid for a round of drinks. It so happened that our man had told me of his *faux pax* before the dinner began so I took a chance and put forward a rather reduced estimate, an estimate that duly scooped the pool. It was for me, at least, a lucrative evening.

Enough of this frivolity, let us return to more serious matters. As you will have already noted, at least half the MPTA/Federation delegates at either a national or area meeting of either one or both of these bodies would consist of members of local authorities. As in the main they would also be senior members with years of service it followed automatically that they were very well versed in the niceties of debate procedures, and knew when to raise points of order or other like interruptions. Despite this in my early years pure politics seldom came into debates, in fact in more than one place whilst the Chairman of the Transport Committee would be chosen by the majority party, the Vice Chairman would often be from the opposition, all in marked contrast to the situation in later years. Finally, whilst there was no compulsion as to whether one attended an area meeting or not, you became less than popular if you failed to put in a goodly number of appearances, and this comment applied particularly when it came to gatherings of managers.

Life at the local level continued to be of absorbing interest, and especially so in the summer, when I came to the conclusion that the introduction of a circular tour of the Borough might go down well. Application was made for an excursion licence, and this is a good place in which to throw some light on bus service regulation as then practised.

Three types of licence then existed. Excursion and tours . . . but few municipal concerns held any of these. Express licences, only this did not mean that services so covered travelled at high speed. It meant that no adult fare on any such service would be less than one shilling. Finally there was the good old stage carriage licence when fares could be at any level (with the consent of the Commissioners) starting at the halfpenny. It seems incredible these days that such a small amount could purchase quite a long bus ride, but ½d. was what I used to pay pre-war or wartime when I travelled in an Oldham Corporation 'A' bus from Star Inn to Hulme Grammar School or return, this service running from Greenacres to Chapel Road. Now I have already mentioned that fortnightly publication *Notices and Proceedings*, so you carefully read the contents for it would list every application received to vary the conditions attached to a road service licence or to seek a completely new grant. A perusal would tell you about any neat piece of piracy that one of your competitors might be planning. They, without doubt, would be doing likewise.

Now some applications would be very minor, say to put back a service time by five minutes to meet a factory output, but others could be of a greater magnitude, covering a route variation or even some brand new facility. In this latter connection a municipal undertaking would in earlier times have to jump not one hurdle but two, and this sad state of affairs applied when it came to projecting services beyond the boundaries of the owning municipality. At such times one usually had to apply for 'consent' and consent meant securing permission to run your buses over the necessary lengths of the foreign highway. Application would be made to the traffic office, appropriate notices had to be printed in newspapers circulating in the associated district(s), and a further insertion had to be posted in the *London Gazette*. Anyone with a relevant interest, other bus operators, local authorities, and local residents, could and would object, and then the inevitable public inquiry would follow, when achieving success was far from easy as objectors usually came legally represented and the applicant would do likewise. If one was successful the service could not begin until yet another application had been made to cover the intended timetable, fare scale and stopping place list. Here was the reason why so many municipal undertakings in the past did little running outside their territory. If one was lucky and did gain a consent, one could find that your opposition could prevent the grant of a road service licence, or have quite a few onerous conditions imposed on it.

ASSOCIATION AND FEDERATION

At this period any matters relating to road service licences in Great Yarmouth had to be put through the Town Clerk's office, but in due course a little administrative smoothing took place and the transport department began to deal direct with the Eastern Area Traffic Office in Cambridge, to which city we repaired on the day that our excursion and tour licence application was down for hearing. Needless to say the Eastern Counties Omnibus Company and all the local operators put in objections, which was unfortunate from a Great Yarmouth point of view because the ruling theme in these times was - Can you establish a need? - with the accent being on need. It was to say the least difficult but we did our best, and then lost hands down, despite our Town Clerk's very best endeavours as he fought the case. But when the Chairman of the Commissioners had handed down this adverse judgement he added a very worthwhile postscript.

He thought that the situation would be resolved if only GYPT would apply for an express licence, and this was something I must confess to never having thought about. It meant in essence that we could offer a circular ride by running a circular service several times a day in one direction only on that minimum fare of 1s. or more. As a result, except on the very last trip of the day, passengers could be picked up at any recognised stopping point, and not just at the Britannia Pier which came to be regarded as the focal point but through Gorlestone as well for example.

Eventually the need to apply for consent was abolished and this certainly made life a lot easier when it came to outside borough activities. But the need to prove 'need' continued until Norman Fowler became Secretary of State for Transport and introduced the 1980 Transport Act, for this turned things completely on their head.

Now the inference became that every application ought to be granted automatically - *unless such a grant was against the public interest.* This in many ways made life even harder. If, for example, you are running a 10 minute service along a road, and seem to be meeting all the transport need that there is, how can you say that the arrival of competitors' buses also running every 10 minutes is against the public interest, as passengers are now going to enjoy a frequency of 12 buses per hour as against the original six? Some forms of possible defence were available, but as all this is beyond the years being covered here let us leave that subject for another possible day.

The original concept of road service licensing did give holders of such documents a degree of security, but it did at the same time lead to possible stagnation, so some of us viewed the whole business with mixed feelings, until the passing of the 1985 Transport Act ended the effects of what then became totally redundant legislation. Under the 1985 regime *Notices and Proceedings* continues to be published every 14 days, but the scope of the contents is now rather different.

Finally I should qualify what I have said about consent to go outside the boundaries of one's authority, for in some places a local act was in existence that did allow some latitude. For example, there might be a clause in it that allowed the operation of buses within a 10 mile radius of the Town Hall, or in the area of another adjacent and specified local authority. Birkenhead Transport had powers to run in Bebbington, but when the undertaking wanted to use the Mersey Tunnel 'consent' was required before a road service licence could be sought.

To return now to our new circular service. As the Chairman of the Commissioners had spoken our express licence application was granted without any other objections being received. So we set the round trip fare at 2s. for a 19 mile ride and commenced operations to carry rather more passengers than had ever been imagined, as I found for myself one summer evening.

I watched the scheduled tour buses depart full, and was about to head for the town centre when a stranger approached to ask if this was the circular loading point. I said that it was but the last buses had already gone when. He replied what a shame it was, as his party had been intending to have a ride all week only as this was their last night they would have to forego the pleasure. I asked how many persons were involved and when told 14 asked him to collect his people and bring them over. I then told him that if they would stay on the stop I would streak back to the garage in the car, and have a bus run for them. I duly returned to Caister Road where there were plenty of buses but not a single spare driver. I consequently drove a Daimler 'Freeline' down to Britannia Pier, but no spare man there either. Consequently I had a conductor off a service bus collect all fares, as by this time there was an almost full load. There was only one thing to do, and that was to drive the Daimler round myself which I duly did to receive the thanks of those on board for my trouble.

Shortage of capacity became paramount in Great Yarmouth on race days when the undertaking, plus Eastern Counties, plus the local coach operators, ran a series of special services from points along the seafront to the racecourse. Here GYPT really had the pole position being the established operator. There was a desire to put every available vehicle on the road and the pinnacle of this policy was reached during a September 1962 race day when, for the first and only time in my professional life, I saw a bus garage that did not contain a single stopped vehicle. In fact it did not contain any vehicle at all, a circumstance that lasted for about 30 minutes. Even the last of the wartime utilities complete with wooden seats were plodding up and down, only after seeing No. 22 actually bending under a full load I had it withdrawn on the spot bringing the 100 per cent availability figure to an abrupt end.

Now taking the punters to the course was a task that was spread over around two hours but when the last race finished everyone tried to leave at once. The net result was complete chaos, especially in the town centre, and schedules went completely to pieces and all one could do was to wait until all the race traffic had finally dispersed, but a wet summer day could also have a similarly adverse effect on operations.

The fact that there was only one road - Southtown Road - linking Great Yarmouth with Gorleston and that was the only major route to the south did not help. To make matters worse the highway was interrupted by the Haven bridge which was often lifted to allow shipping to pass, thus timetable reliability could be a problem.

General overall reliability was not being helped by the vagaries of our six Albion 'Nimbus' vehicles. Chassis bracketry was somewhat 'tishy', with the result that bits and pieces tended to fall off, these faults being exacerbated by the vibrations coming from the four-cylindered horizontal engine, itself far from being a world beater. Sadly here the vacuum braking power was obtained not from an exhauster but from a butterfly valve attached to the induction manifold. Smooth out the vibrations and the effect of that valve is reduced, set it to give a good brake and the engine does its best to leave the frame. Add to this a proprietary gear box, that from time to time lets a driver engage two gears at once, plus a gear selector mechanism that can become so loose that to engage reverse a driver has to open the half-cab door, and swing the lever so that it passes outside the cab area altogether, added up to a decision to replace all six by a like number of AEC 'Reliance' chassis with Seddon or Pennine Coachcraft bodies. On the face of it this was an unusual choice but that concern was desirous at the time of breaking into the municipal bus business, so the price tendered at £2,250 per body was one that just could not be ignored. The complete vehicle cost £4,480.

In later years Seddon's under Redmond family direction did just that on quite a substantial scale, and gave the established chassis and body suppliers quite a few shocks in the process as we will see. The replacement decision was taken on 14th February, 1963 and I began to look forward to the ending of my Albion saga, only I little knew.

At about the same time I read in the trade press that Gorton Tank was to be closed, so I wrote to the works manager asking if, before it did, I might be given the chance to visit the works for a last look round. Permission was speedily forthcoming, and so on Thursday 28th March, 1963 I spent what could have been a very melancholy afternoon visiting all the areas I had known so well in my apprenticeship days. Many of the men that I had worked with were still in post, and like me wondering after what Gorton had been how a complete closure had come to be possible? What also once seemed totally impossible was to find myself sitting in the machine shop office, drinking tea with foremen Fred Mitchell and Tommy Hagan, where Fred reminded me how he had chased lazy apprentices round the shop. This was after a visit to section four in the erecting shops where most of my old playmates were just completing overhauls on their last two locomotives, one being a '9F' 2-10-0 the other an '8F' class 2-8-0, not the sort of motive power that was ever to be seen in my time.

Being in the area, or at least almost so, I also called in to see my old Halifax chief, and, whilst we were chatting in his office over another dish of tea, he told me of the latest Halifax innovations. The Joint Committee had decided to order 10 Albion 'Nimbus' chassis, to be fitted with 31-seat Weymann bodies, the idea being, or so it seemed, to use these to work shuttles from the main Calder Valley Halifax to Hebden Bridge route to those upland places, such as Cragg Vale, Midgeley, Booth and Heptonstall. Needless to say access to such locations involved negotiating considerable climbs, or by Halifax standards not such ferocious gradients.

I gently suggested that a review of this policy might not come amiss, but if a posse of 'Nimbus' had to be contemplated why not experiment and buy our six for starters at a bargain price. Dick, though, had done his 'Nimbus' homework, and so told me that these would be updated examples with an Albion six-speed overdrive gearbox, an exhauster, and other modifications that should prevent most of the troubles we had experienced; however, the same engine was to be incorporated. I left Halifax wondering, as I could not see passengers taking kindly to the loss of their existing through services, even if the problem of making transfer tickets available with an Ultimate ticket system could be solved. Still it had nothing to do with me, Great Yarmouth was where my transport problems lay and it was back to that Borough I drove the following day, never for one moment realising that the coming summer would be my last in the town.

It proved to be both interesting and hectic. Fourteen new Daimler buses with semi-automatic transmission had entered service, with five more on order together with some Leylands, and as a result the last of the pre-war fleet, plus the utilities, had made their last journeys. We had made several changes to the regular services in an attempt to boost patronage, extending the Gorleston Cliffs summer service from the town centre to the Wellington Pier being one example, whilst we had also improved Saturday connections into the coach station where we were, if anything, busier than ever. The circular tour was also making money, but there was one area of concern and this lay in the Gorleston circulars.

These were no longer actually circular in shape, but followed a figure eight layout, this being done to give more frequent runs into the centre of Gorleston. Quite a lot of house building was now taking place in the area, so it was worth persevering with the operation. We also had a neat timetable leaflet available for free issue, and had improved bus stop timetabling and information displays. The offices too had been improved and extended.

According to folklore whilst the main entrance to the offices was quite attractive it had seen little use in earlier days. Apparently if one did enter, it was to be faced with a wooden screen into which was inserted a convent-like aperture. Here, so it was said, Mr Blackburn had met and chatted to sundry callers, few being sufficiently privileged to be allowed to gain access to his office.

Ralph had speedily removed the screen or partition, now I had the whole area revamped, and the once stone staircase covered with a non-slip material. The office extension was at ground floor level, and involved driving a doorway through that elaborate garage frontage. Part of the extension came to house the administration staff, thus releasing space on the upper floor to provide an improved traffic office, and our traffic superintendent with a more private room, his old quarters being taken over by the chief inspector.

His staff too were considered. Previously the early turn inspector when booking crews on had to stand with his paperwork in a corner of the garage, hard by the canteen. Now he had, just inside that newly-driven doorway, a small office designed for the purpose.

Finally at the rear of the garage, below what was now the fuel pump shop, an office had been formed where Mr Tooke could keep his maintenance records and have some more satisfactory space for himself, but I was never able to finish my planned set of improvements. The next item on the agenda would have been to have formed an enclosed workshop in the north-east corner of the premises with some improved pits offering better access to rear- and underfloor-engined buses, but change was in the air, this process starting in Halifax where my old chief, suddenly it seemed, elected to retire.

Now the family had settled down well in Great Yarmouth a town which according to my fellow chief officers represented 'The death of ambition', but in my case could it be at my then age of 37?

I think that Dick was rather miffed by the fact that his salary was strictly controlled by that 'Mileage within the Borough' formula whereas, whilst the 'A' or Corporation buses might be so restricted, those of the Joint Committee covered many miles per year in such outer areas as the Calder Valley, Brighouse, Queensbury and Ripponden. So much so that if only the GM's pay was based on the overall total a 100 per cent increase was not impossible - but far from likely, as Dick obviously well understood.

Still as the advertised salary was over £1,000 per annum more than the one I was then receiving that was an aspect of the matter that I might choose to ignore, so the question I had to answer was, 'Should I apply?' I pondered the matter, having in the process a practical demonstration of the way in which Great Yarmouth Transport was in actual fact built on shifting sand, this being due to the opening of the Beach coach station.

As well as booking tickets for various operators coming into the town, we also began to do vehicle servicing, when providing refuelling facilities proved to be quite profitable. This service could, however, only extend to vehicles with diesel engines, as we had no petrol storage tanks, so one thing was obvious . . . put one in.

The order was duly given to a reputable contractor, who arrived with his men and equipment one Saturday morning, and in no time at all the cobbles in the indicated section of the forecourt were lifted, and several long-disused tram rails were cut out. Then it was necessary to dig down around 10 to 12 feet, put in a concrete base, build on that the surrounding brick bund walls, lower the awaiting tank in, strap it down, fill the voids round it with sand, pipe up, and then restore the yard surface only - SNAG.

The excavation went well for the first four to five feet, and then the digger struck sand and water. As the water oozed into the hole, so did the areas of the yard round the hole begin to slip away, and fall into the ever-increasing in size excavation, only now the digger was not digging any more.

What should have been a fairly simple job turned into a very difficult one, when the sides had to be shored with sheet metal piling, and the base work needed quick-drying cement, and a pump, but in due course the contractor won, and our petrol installation came into use.

I, too, came to a conclusion.

Great Yarmouth was a small undertaking with some 70 buses at the time, several of which were kept in stock for summer use. Halifax on the other hand was over twice as big in vehicle terms and three times as much if one compared their respective mileages, whilst there was that salary differential, so on the very last morning possible I finally asked my secretary to post my application for the job. Then once again it was a question of waiting to see what might transpire, but I was not over hopeful. I had previously applied for the post of General Manager at Oldham, a job I would really liked to have had, but although I did make the short list after a very few minutes into the interview it became all too obvious that I would *not* be returning to my old haunts. Could history be repeated? The answer was soon forthcoming.

One for the Federation? No, Crossfields bus station was not usually so busy, but on this occasion the staff had left their vehicles to attend a union meeting. Two Yorkshire Woollen District vehicles and two Hebble buses occupy the bays in the foreground. I counted 27 Halifax machines in this picture.

At the same time another 22 stand on the old Alhambra site or in adjacent streets. These were *Halifax Courier* photographs but its editor maintained later that his man had missed a unique shot - namely that of a certain GM sitting on a bus station wall reading all about it in the evening paper - not something I now recall.

Chapter Eight

A Rover's Return - GM Halifax

The closing date for the receipt of applications was 27th July, 1963, and a few days thereafter I received a letter telling me that my name had been placed on the short list, and so would I appear for interview on Tuesday 19th August, only on this occasion this was to take place in the evening. Consequently having spent the previous night in Oldham, I drove my car over some long familiar roads, and then parked it in Sowerby Bridge and took a bus into Halifax. The bus needless to say was a Park Royal-bodied AEC 'Regent' that had received those strengthening modifications.

I seem to recall that there were six candidates assembled to be put through the sort of municipal interview already described, and this one was in no way different, but in due course we had all been processed, and assembled together to wait anxiously for the decision of the Committee. Once again I was fortunate, and on being invited back into the Committee room was told by the Chairman that my selection was virtually unanimous, there being a single vote against me. I was then quickly left in no doubt as to who had cast that vote, when the long serving member of the Council concerned came to me, said that it would be churlish not to congratulate me on my success, but had felt he had to take the view that I was too young to fill the job. As an aside here Mr MacKenzie must have been around 10 years older than I then was when he obtained the post, and Mr Le Fevre some 20 years older. I countered the Councillor's remark by saying that if that was all he had against me then every day that I held the office would see his reservations reduced accordingly. With that he promptly agreed and we shook hands. Now this particular member certainly had an inquiring mind, and had caused at least one of my immediate predecessors much 'heartburn' at times, and so I did wonder how I would find him. In the event he left the Council shortly afterwards, to re-appear some years later when he proved to be very helpful on more than one occasion. Now all this gave me food for thought, but my return journey to Sowerby Bridge gave me some more. By chance the bus that returned me to my car was the one by which I had travelled inwards earlier in the evening. The same crew were in charge, and they by 'jungle telegraph' already knew who their new General Manager was going to be, and so also offered me their congratulations. The conductor in an unguarded moment expressed the view that there were going to be interesting times ahead, as the traffic superintendent and I had never really seen eye-to-eye in my earlier period with the undertaking.

Now it was often the case, and still might be, that traffic and engineering departments did not agree. Traffic took the view that if only the black gang would stop playing with their charges, and get them on the road, traffic could make money, whilst the engineers were known to express the view that traffic staff represented a bunch of professional 'Bus busters' who should not be trusted with prams let alone their PSV beauties. This reminded me of the time when, as engineer, I was in Elmwood garage when a fully overhauled 'Regent III', complete with Park Royal body of course, was awaiting its first call to duty after spending several weeks in the shops. The garage foreman marked it up for a short working, and allocated the vehicle to the driver who was rostered for that turn.

That worthy climbed into the cab, started the engine and revved up to to build the air pressure up to the desired level, but failed to notice that the pre-selector box was still in reverse gear. Suddenly as the pressure was sufficiently high the bus took off backwards, and as luck would have it one of the few roof supports that Elmwood possessed was right behind the bus. Had anyone been passing behind serious injury or death would have resulted, as it was there was an ear splitting crash, clouds of dust fell from the roof girders, and the staircase was now in the lower saloon where no staircase was ever intended. I marched a shaken driver into the office of the traffic superintendent, and being in a very positive frame of mind made a few pithy observations that did little to improve traffic/engineering relationships.

Now I had to return to Great Yarmouth the following day, so was not able to call in at Skircoat Road to see my old chief or the staff, but there followed a period when Dick had gone into retirement and the traffic superintendent was appointed acting manager as I had to work out my notice. During this time the latter would write me various letters asking for my observations or decisions on a variety of subjects, such missives beginning with the words 'Dear Sir' and always ending 'I am, yours faithfully'. This did not augur well for the future, and so needed addressing as soon as possible.

The opportunity came on the morning of the 5th November when for the first time I entered the old office building via the door at the Huddersfield end of premises that was usually used by the GM and took my seat in the chair previously occupied by my illustrious forebears. I asked the TS to come and see me, thinking, as I did, that this was Guy Fawkes day after all and so seemed very appropriate.

Now traffic superintendent Frank Murray had had quite a remarkable career, starting in the 1920s as a junior bus conductor and working his way up to his present post, being both competent and hard working. Our chat soon produced the result that we obviously both wanted to see the undertaking progress, and we were both of the same mind as to how this might be done. Consequently there were no fireworks then, or on any other day over the 11 years that we were together, and I could not have wished for a more loyal and supportive assistant than he proved to be. It is now over 40 years since that association began, but we have kept in touch over the years, and I am more than pleased to regard him as a tried and trusted friend.

Once that little matter had been dealt with, what was the immediate outlook like? Needless to say finance was the immediate problem. Dick Le Fevre before he finally retired had told me that he would try to give me an easy start, by putting in fares increases on both the Corporation and Joint Committee services, and was as good as his word. Only it was becoming obvious already that the forecast levels of income were not going to be reached, so what were we going to do about that little matter?

Next in order of priority was the staff situation. It bordered on the dire. There was a full time conductor school. Each new starter began on a Monday, and spent each day until Friday in the school room. Then on the Friday they were put with an experienced conductor who showed them the ropes, and so continued until the next Thursday. Then on the second Friday they were brought back into the school room and given a test. If they passed, then the following Monday, or even earlier, saw them marked up on the output sheets for a duty of their own, and it was usual to have around 10 persons forming each weekly intake. But as 10 came in at one end rather more went out at the other, and as a result we could split the platform staff members that we had into three categories.

Number one consisted of the men who had been with us for years, were committed bus workers (together with certain remaining conductresses) and so had no intention of leaving. Group number two was made up of employees who seemed to quite like buswork, but who oft-times found themselves under domestic pressure. Their wives did not appreciate the shift patterns that had to be involved, and especially so if they wanted to go out with their spouses on Saturday evenings only hubby was then out on the road in charge of a bus. As a result resignations for domestic reasons were all too common. Some men left of course after several years with us because more lucrative opportunities seemed on offer, but would seek to return, especially if they had taken up goods vehicle driving. They quickly found that whilst a bus by its very nature is 'self loading', a wagon can represent very hard work in that connection, and in those days tail gate lifts, if ever seen, were certainly very few in number.

Category three were the products of this era of over-employment. They came and went from job to job, seldom settling anywhere, and represented a floating and far from reliable staffing element. Let me stress here that this state of affairs appertained basically to the platform staff. Works personnel came into a very different group, as the craftsmen, many apprentices trained in the undertaking, continued year after year.

Then there was the bus fleet, 168 strong at the time of my arrival. Here was an increase dictated by the building of several schools in the Holmfield area, an area which came to be known as the school base. As a result very many pupils were picked up by special buses at the Crossfields bus station every morning and transported to Holmfield. But this was not lucrative business as in effect those extra buses carried just two single loads at half fares each weekday, or in the case of contract holders at discounted fares, but Holmfield lay within the Borough and we were offering in part a Municipal service.

Now in my engineering days the then Borough Treasurer was a man who kept a very tight rein on each department's financial affairs. In the case of Passenger Transport this was to the extent of having two members of the Treasurer's staff actually working full time in the Skircoat Road Commercial office. But with his retirement things had eased, they were no longer *in situ* and by some good work Dick Le Fevre had managed to have a complete set of punch card machinery installed in the offices. A very few ladies under chief clerk Miss Turner produced all the necessary financial figures quickly and accurately, providing management every four weeks with a set of financial and statistical returns that indicated just how we were faring. Here we came to administrative complications.

Joint Committee buses ran on virtually every road into Halifax, picking up and setting down passengers at all the relevant stops. So it had been agreed that as from the 1st April, 1951 the takings of every service coming into the Borough should be multiplied by the figure of 33.262, and then divided by 184.960. These two figures represented the average takings on those routes, both as a gross total, and of fares taken in the Borough over the three previous years, and whilst either party could have challenged the basis of the calculation after the 1st April, 1959 no one ever did. The net result was worked out, and then 21 per cent of the answer was paid by the JOC to the Corporation in consideration for JOC buses having passenger picking up and setting down rights in Halifax.

Then the Hebble Company was required to identify all fares taken within the whole of the JOC or 'red' area and of the amount so produced 25 per cent was split off. Of the resulting figure 20 per cent was allocated to the Corporation side of the undertaking and 80 per cent to the JOC. The Yorkshire Woollen District Company also came into the picture. It paid £600 per annum to the JOC, and 25 per cent of all fares its buses took from passengers both picked up and set down within the Borough to the Corporation side although later this was also compounded to the fixed sum of £330. Finally the Huddersfield JOC paid £85 per annum to the Corporation in respect of similar borough area passengers.

Now you may think that this was complex, but here we have only touched the tip of the iceberg for then there were the 'internal' arrangements. Every Corporation or 'A' bus was owned and licensed by the Corporation. In the JOC fleet half were covered similarly by the Corporation the other half held by the British Railways Board, but all the staff were employed effectively by Halifax Corporation so time spent on JOC work had to be charged by the hour to that side of the business. The costs of some items, e.g. works plant or washing machines, etc., were allocated on the basis of buses owned by the two parties, whilst other headings were assessed on the principle of mileage worked; so if one was not careful, there was plenty of scope for error.

The situation was made even more complicated in 1958 when on 3rd March, with the consent of the ruling bodies, three new major cross-Halifax services which joined Corporation and Joint Committee services together were introduced these being:

Illingworth-Halifax-Rishworth
Causeway Foot-Halifax-Sowerby Steep Lane or Hubberton
Ovenden/Beechwood Road-Halifax-Stainland

Designing the bus workings, timetables and duty schedules, etc., was no real problem, and these and other changes made in the same period saved six buses and their attendant crews, but let us look a little further at the end result.

Take the former for example, and remember that the Ultimate ticket system was in use, with pre-printed and individually numbered tickets. A conductor might have started his shift in Halifax, so his waybill would show all the starting ticket numbers. At Rishworth he would book up, and again when back in the town centre loading point. The process would then be repeated on arrival at Illingworth, again when back in Halifax, and so on throughout his shift.

In due course he would pay in, and tickets sold would be priced out against cash received to produce a balance, shorts or overs figure, but now came the added complications. One of Miss Turner's lady assistants had to analyse each line of that waybill, and price out what monies were received on each Rishworth return trip and again on each Illingworth return working. Those monies had then to be posted to the relevant part of the undertaking. The 'A' service revenue went into the Corporation coffers, and that for the JOC was allocated accordingly being also subject to the Borough Area receipts formula.

Note again had to be taken of man hours worked on each separate section and so charged, and the same went for mileage, when if, say, Corporation buses ran more miles on the 'B' part of the exercise than JOC vehicles did on the 'A' then in due course that balance had to be worked off. When the out of balance mileage over the whole undertaking had reached a significant figure, Miss Turner would advise me of the figure and I then had to ensure that offsetting steps were quickly taken to restore *status quo*.

Things continued thus until 26th April, 1965, a day which saw these links broken and the most dramatic change in the pattern of service that had occurred for years introduced. From that date onwards care was taken to keep main line bus workings and duties completely on one section of the undertaking or the other when the total ticket sales value shown on a waybill simply was posted to where it belonged, mileage fell similarly and a huge amount of in-office administration time was saved as a result. Pricing out individual waybill lines must have been a very tedious task, but it was done and very accurate those unsung 'doers' were. Their essential part in the operation never did receive the praise that was their due and I am in consequence delighted to have the chance here to pay a little tribute to their now long-past efforts. Now to continue with the main theme.

One average week in each four-weekly period, where no bank holiday or other special event occurred, was taken as a base, and all the figures for those seven days were calculated out, the percentages thus derived being applied to the various gross totals, and the speed with which the information became available beat the time taken by a subsequent computer installation. But even when these were to hand, working out just what a fares increase might bring in when five or six line Ultimate ticket machines were in general use over the longer distance services did give one food for much arithmetical exercise as Halifax routes were quite lengthy even in 1963/4. Dick's fares increase was not producing results so what was the answer? The subject was given a lot of thought. In the end a restaging exercise was undertaken placing them at significant locations, or at ⅓ mile intervals. This proved successful and despite ever-rising costs fares were kept stable for some three years thereafter.

As for the bus fleet this consisted of the 168 vehicles we already had made up of the following varieties:

15 quite new AEC 'Mark V' machines with 'new look' fronts, synchromesh gearboxes, and MCW group 72-seat front entrance double-deck bodies.
41 AEC 'Regent III' double-deckers with rear platforms, and either Roe (just a few) or Park Royal bodies all but six of which were of the famous composite, narrow pillar design.

The last 'Regent III' double-deckers were ordered by General Manager Freddie Cooke being a batch of six for the Corporation as fleet numbers 355 to 360 (later 75 to 80). New in December 1951 all had Park Royal metal-framed bodies that were much more satisfactory and a revised indication layout. When new No. 360 (80) was fitted in the lower saloon with Siddalls 'Moreseat' seat frames. These had top rails and seat backs offset, ostensibly to give more shoulder space but were not appreciated by the customers.

A centrifugal clutch was fitted into a Halifax Daimler 'CD650' in an attempt to improve fuel consumption. This it did but spoiled the smoothness of the transmission so its life *in situ* was not of long duration.

47 Leyland double-deckers all with synchromesh gearboxes. Eight of these were the survivors of the nine with Leyland bodies well known from my engineering days. The other 39 were much more modern 'PD2' or 'PD3' machines, again with MCW group forward entrance bodies.

26 Leyland underfloor single-deckers all again having MCW bodies arranged for one-man-operation. Nine of these were based on those 'Worldmaster' chassis having semi-automatic gearboxes, the remainder were 'Leopards' with synchromesh gearboxes. The first of these, bus No. 231, was delivered with a two-door layout, but this was very unpopular, so it was quickly altered to a single front entrance/exit, the others coming out similarly.

27 Daimler 'CVG6' vehicles. Seventeen of these had Roe bodies consisting of the first 12 that now sported those Leyland 0.600 power units and the last five having the combined lighter teak/alloy framing and retaining Gardner '6LW' engines. The series was completed by the 10 MCW-bodied buses nine still with Gardner '6LWs', the tenth with the 'CVD6' turbocharged unit, but all with bodywork that had been suitably strengthened to stop the water leaks and panel loss as previously mentioned.

Two AEC 'Mark III' single-deckers with unmodified rear door Roe bodies, these being the survivors of the once 22-strong post-war fleet.

Last but not least were the 10 Albion 'Nimbus' lightweights with Weymann 31-seat bodies, the six-speed gearbox and vacuum brake exhauster. These dated from June 1963 and as the valleys shuttle idea was by now fully forgotten were to be found on sundry one-man services such as those to Millbank and Heptonstall. I truly wondered about these but my wondering was not to be of long duration.

This was not by any means the end of the story, for shortly before he retired on 8th October, 1963, and rather to my annoyance, my former chief had placed orders for another 30 buses, thus adding to the eight Leyland 'PD3' MCW double-deckers that came into 'A' fleet stock as bus Nos. 51 to 58 in December 1963 or January 1964. These replaced several Park Royal 'Regents'.

The 30, needless to say, were to be based on Leyland 'PD2' chassis again with synchromesh gearboxes and were to carry MCW group bodies scheduled for completion at the Weymann Addlestone factory. These were to form two groups of 15, for delivery in 1964/5 and 1965/6. Of the 15 eight each year were to become 'A' fleet buses, the other seven becoming part of the JOC or 'B' side establishment.

I had, however, to give Dick full marks in one purchasing respect, as he had persuaded the Committees to buy buses out of revenue by setting up a renewals funds, something that was going to save hefty interest payments in the days to come. For the record a 'PD2' chassis was then quoted at £2,256 16s. 8d. and a Weymann body at £3,213 18s. 0d.

On the face of things there was nothing I could do about this forward ordering, but then fate took a hand and the staff at Addlestone went on strike so it is convenient here to to discuss what was the end result. It soon became very obvious that the stoppage was going to last for quite a time, and as some of those timber-framed Park Royal/AEC 'Mark IIIs' were beyond redemption some second-hand purchases were acquired. Five of these were again AEC 'Regent IIIs' with Roe bodies formerly of the Leeds fleet. They kept their original green livery but to lighten the overall effect the window frames to the lower deck were now painted cream. Next came two ex-Sheffield AEC/Park Royal 'Monocoaches' but those used for one man work did receive full fleet colours.

The turbo-charged Daimler 'CVD6' 'Mark VII' engine fitted easily into 'CVG6' vehicle No. 93, after a later engine change, displacing the Leyland 0.600 unit which in turn had displaced the original Gardner '6LW'. It proved to be a very reliable unit. Note this 'CVG6' was now in my favoured original Halifax livery.

Thanks to the Weymann strike the fleet updating programme went by the board, so to offset the need to rectify some Park Royal-bodied buses several AEC/Roe double-deckers were purchased from Leeds. They kept the basic green livery but the lower saloon window frames were painted cream. One stands here at Highroad Well. The old tram shed lies behind the wall where father joined the army in 1915 to find himself posted to the West Yorkshire Regiment - and the Leeds pals. Bob Mack took this picture on an enthusiasts tour along with their LCT transport.

It was not possible to extract from Addlestone chassis already delivered to that works, but 10 of the later ones were diverted to the plant of C.H. Roe, eight becoming 'A' fleet Nos. 59 to 66, the other two JOC buses Nos. 278 and 279. These arrived late in 1965.

Two 'PD2' chassis were then dropped and two 'Leopards' obtained instead. These received Willowbrook dual-purpose single-deck bodies and arrived in September 1965 to be described further. Eventually the Weymann workforce returned to bus building and so the 18 outstanding buses started to be delivered from December 1965 as JOC Nos. 280 to 289 or 'A' fleet Nos. 67 to 74, the latter being the last bus to be turned out by Addlestone and entering service on 31st January, 1966. It was all a very sorry story.

In the meantime I asked the question. 'What in the light of current circumstances is the best bus for Halifax?' There was one way to find out, test every possible double-deck variety, and at this time Britain actually had a bus building industry whose members kindly began to co-operate. Halifax passengers began to see all sorts of vehicles in different hues performing on their local routes, but before all this began some high-powered diplomacy had been called for. The previous Gardner and Daimler problems were still in the minds of various Committee members, whilst Mr Hugh Gardner, whom I had upset as assistant engineer back in 1955, was still very much a power in Patricroft. He was finally persuaded to supply us with a new '6LX' engine at a bargain price and this was then fitted into Daimler No. 95 thus replacing its 0.600 power unit. This '6LX' unit could deliver 135 bhp, and proved to be a most excellent product, so bus No. 95 along with a new Leyland 'PD3' and an AEC 'Regent V' formed the home team against which the performances of the 'invaders' were monitored. In the event all the front-engined buses we tried had their good points, and were well developed, but looking ahead led to the inevitable conclusion that the rear-engined model with its facility to be one-man-operated, when the trade unions and the law had come to such a conclusion also, was going to take the pole position, but which one?

The full list of our trial vehicles consisted of:

Daimler 'Fleetline' demonstrator 565 CRW with Alexander body.
Leyland 'Atlantean' demonstrator SGD 669 with Alexander body.
Wallasey 'Atlantean' with MCW body.
AEC 'Renown' 7552 MX with Park Royal body.
Guy 'Arab V' 888 DUK with Strachan body.
LTE front entrance 'Routemaster' 254 CLT with Park Royal body.
Dennis 'Loline' EPG 179B with Northern Counties body originally built for service in Hong Kong.

We also looked carefully at, but never ran in service, a Leyland/Albion 'Lowlander'.

All were 30 ft long, and we endeavoured to ensure that all the engines were on full power settings. These trials were designed to assess complete suitability, so whilst fuel consumption and performance were important we also wanted to obtain some indication as to just how easy - or difficult - long term maintenance was going to be. The results of the tests will be found as *Appendix One* at the end of this volume.

Thanks to the 'Old Pals Act' my Roe friends took 10 of the Leyland 'PD2' chassis and fitted then with 65-seat teak/alloy framed bodies. Two entered the JOC fleet as numbers 278 and 279, the other eight became 'A' fleet numbers 59 to 66. Here No. 278 stands in Skircoat Road yard on 3rd September, 1965 before entering service for the first time on the No. 43 Huddersfield service. Sadly no more buses were supplied by Roe to Halifax - the reason comes later.

The outstanding Weymann-bodied Leyland 'PD2s' were a long time coming but at last in December 1965 JOC vehicles Nos. 280, 281 and 282 were available for use. Nos. 283 to 289 then followed. The 'A' fleet series Nos. 67 to 74 arrived with a rush in January, No. 74 the very last bus to come out of the Addlestone factory entering Halifax service on 31st January, 1966.

The whole exercise produced a good deal of interest, with a repercussion years later when the author of an article that appeared in *Classic Bus* No. 39, after commenting on these trials, put in a paragraph which read: 'And what did Halifax then buy? It continued to buy Leyland 'PD2s' and 'PD3s' then in 1966 switched to Daimler 'Fleetlines' and then even five Dennis 'Lolines' in 1967.' He obviously did not know of my new vehicle order inheritance. As it was thanks to the Weymann strike it was possible to switch some of the body contracts, but that was not possible with the chassis except for the deletion of those two 'PD2s' units, and their replacement by a like number of 'Leopards', again fitted with clutches and synchromesh gear boxes. Coming as has been noted into JOC stock as bus Nos. 269 and 270, the chassis cost £2,278 each; but here comes another new note, as semi-luxury/dual purpose bodies with 41 seats came from the Willowbrook factory, when the bodies were painted in revised livery, as the photograph clearly shows. These were priced at £3,208.

As an aside a 'PD2' chassis then was invoiced at £2,293 3s. 2d. Goodness knows why they were priced to the odd 2d. but my records show that such was certainly the case. Note here the effect of the application of a rise and fall clause on the figures originally quoted.

Now back to that all important question, what purchase recommendation do I make? Let us therefore follow my thinking at the time through, when reader you can decide for yourself if you agree with my reasoning. For a start I was in no doubt that driving a vehicle with a conventional gear box was much more labour

Two intended Leyland double-deck chassis were cancelled and two 'Leopards' obtained instead. These were then fitted with Willowbrook 41-seat dual purpose bodies which were given a revised livery. Private hire thoughts were now stirring but one had then any idea as to what the future would bring. As JOC vehicles 269 and 270 they went into service in October 1964. In my view the synchromesh gear box fitted spoiled the 'Leopard' hence the move to the semi-automatic AEC 'Reliance' later.

The various vehicle tests were run against what we already had in stock so here is the home team consisting of Daimler 'CVG'/Leyland 0.600 No. 92, AEC 'Regent V' No. 218 and Leyland 'PD3' No. 206, one of the eight JOC buses Nos. 201 to 208 that came into stock shortly after I became General Manager.

Amongst the buses tested was this AEC 'Renown' with a Park Royal body. It was regarded as an improvement on the Halifax MCW-bodied AEC 'Regent' Mark Vs, but really failed to impress.

intensive than one with a fluid flywheel and semi-automatic gear box. True, the fuel consumption of the latter was rather higher than that of the former, but on the other hand maintenance costs were somewhat less. Coping with a Leyland synchromesh gear box (still far better than the old 'PD1' unit) on Halifax hills could be trying, and here engaging that very low crash bottom gear could give a driver a few nasty moments. Now we had two-pedal control so when it came to vehicles intended to perform on heavy stage carriage services that was surely the way to go.

Then it was a choice of front or rear engine. To some extent the latter were still something of an unknown quantity, Halifax had never run any up to that time, but there were two obvious advantages in that, firstly, Great Yarmouth had shown me that with a front door right by the driver platform accidents were almost a thing of the past. Secondly, an underfloor single-deck vehicle made one-man-operation much easier than it ever was on one of those AEC 'Regal Mk III' conversions. A rear-engined double-decker had a similar front end layout, so when in due course double-deck one-man-operation became possible a rear-engined machine would allow easier route conversions. Having reached this stage, did one buy the 'Atlantean' or the 'Fleetline' as there was no other possible choice at that time, so let's think about chassis frames for a moment.

They form the foundation of any vehicle, and in my Halifax engineering days I had seen the problems we had had with the 'Regent IIIs' suffering all too often with frame failures around the area of the front springs rear bracket. The 'PD2' buses were better, but then we only had nine of them. On the other hand Daimler frame trouble was unknown and this was one area where the 'Fleetline' seemed to score. The 'Atlantean' used the 0.600 engine in this period and there was not much wrong with that, and of course Halifax had a goodly number of them running in 1963, but I felt that the '6LX' was going to do everything that our original '6LWs' never could and so my once quite strong anti-Gardner attitudes melted slowly but surely away. Then the 'Fleetline' had that ingenious gear box that meant one could fit a low height body without having to have the rearmost upper saloon seats accessible by the old low bridge side gangway configuration, which the 'Atlantean' as then marketed required until sometime later when Coventry began to supply Leyland with its unique gear box.

Well we did not have many low bridges in the area but there was one in Brighouse on the Field Lane route then worked only by single-deckers but an area where large scale housing development was taking place, so follow the Boy Scout motto and 'Be prepared'. There was one last consideration that loomed largely in my mind. Leyland was the big producer, and its vehicle prices were often lower than those of its competitors, and Leylands were the choice of so many of my contemporaries. But Leyland had by this time obtained control over AEC and here was the hint, or more than a hint, of an emerging monopoly, and this I saw then without the benefit of hindsight. I considered that two or more competing design teams would do far more to improve the breed than ever a single unit, no matter how large, would, and so surely Daimler had to be the choice.

Then it came to bodies. One could negotiate that bridge with a body that was not a true low height but one which was built down so as to give both clearance and reasonable headroom in both saloons at 13 ft 10 in. and this was something that Northern Counties were offering. Accepting the Wigan quotation meant

The first Halifax 'Fleetline' No. 105 of September 1966 stands brand new at the Hebden Bridge 'frontier' terminus. By sheer good fortune the Northern Counties bodies were ordered to a reduced height to pass under a Brighouse railway bridge. Only the Wigan-based firm would at that time offer this type of body. Roe's and MCW could provide standard high or lowbridge bodies but no intermediate dimension. Masseys would not quote at all having yet to body a rear-engined chassis. 'Millwood Garage here we come!'

'Queenie'. On 1st March, 1934 bus No. 7 entered Corporation service. 'She' had a 59-seat English Electric body and cost £1,613. However, the petrol engine shrouded by the body often became over hot whilst thanks to the absence of passenger doors they and the crew became over cold in winter whilst little weight on the rear axle plus single tyres meant a lack of directional stability on wet or icy cobblestones - and Halifax had its share. As a result 'Queenie' was taken out of service on 30th June, 1938, it was then sold back to AEC Ltd. Note the tramway-style life guard below the front panel.

cutting out the Roe company after Crossgates had helped to offset the delays occasioned by the Weymann debacle, but sadly my old friends said that they could not at the time produce an interim height model. And so the Daimler/Northern Counties combination came into being and what a blessing that turned out to be as happenings in 1971 will show. There was, by the way, some weight saving adopting such a design. The first seven 'Fleetlines' for the 'A' fleet duly arrived in 1966 as buses Nos. 99 to 105. The chassis cost £3,144, and the bodies £3,780, but thanks to the on-going effects of inflation by 1974 these prices had risen to £5,465 and £6,450 without any major specification change being called for.

Bus No. 105 was the first to enter service on 1st September but this was not the first Halifax bus to have a passenger door in front of the front wheels. Way back in 1934 Mr G.F. Craven, the then General Manager, had inspired the purchase of 'Queenie', a revolutionary AEC side-engined double-decker. Consequently a picture of this remarkable machine is included in these pages.

The Dennis 'Loline' purchase was quite another matter, and perhaps here I let my heart rule my head, but again that anti-monopoly feeling still nagged, and there were some involved technical aspects.

Back in 1954 when contesting that 22 'CVG6' purchase, Dennis submitted a double-deck 'Lance' chassis quotation that from a documentation point of view

In early 1967 five Dennis 'Lolines' with Northern Counties bodies came into stock as JOC fleet numbers 300 to 304. These had Gardner '6LX' engines and five-speed overdrive semi-automatic gear boxes. The complete bus cost just £7,000. The last 'Lolines' built they were sold to West Riding Automobile Co. of Wakefield in the summer of 1970 but this would not have happened had we then known of the Millwood Garage problem that would face us in 1971. They would have been ideal for the Halifax-Todmorden-Burnley service.

was just about as scrappy as it could have been; also their price for a machine with a conventional gear box was way above that for a 'CVG6'. Now Dennis almost went overboard, for my secretary staggered into my office carrying a parcel of sizeable proportions. In it was a most exhaustive quotation that covered a host of possible specification permutations, plus so many drawings that had we had the plant and intention we could almost have started our own 'Loline' manufacturing. There was of course the Gardner '6LX' engine, a four- or five-speed overdrive semi-automatic gear box, and air suspension at the rear, and air suspension was at the time quite outside my experience. The price seemed almost too good to be true so we took a chance and placed an order for five, asking for that five-speed overdrive box that certainly gave these buses a useful turn of speed, and note here the word useful.

Northern Counties bodies were again specified to be fitted with rather better seating than that to be found in the 'Fleetlines', but sad to say we did not reach the heights of luxury which I had found as a schoolboy in those pre-war North Western Bristol 'K5Gs'. As it was the complete vehicle cost exactly £7,000 (chassis £3,650, body £3,350) delivered to Halifax.

Here was another vehicle that had promise but really needed further development to cope with Halifax operating conditions but the air suspension proved to be no problem. The engines surprisingly were, and it took us some time to appreciate why the tappet assemblies would disintegrate. These sad occurrences were due to drivers charging along in overdrive coming to a downwards gradient and then engaging a lower gear to provide some braking effect; instead we had 'breaking' as the momentum of the vehicle carried through the transmission and so over-speeded the engine to its profound detriment. The high gearing also had an adverse effect on fluid flywheel seals but later the fitting of a combined fluid flywheel/centrifugal clutch went some way to eliminating that nuisance.

Later on, 'Lolines' began to appear on certain South Yorkshire works contracts and reports started to come in of double-deckers travelling rather faster than any other similar vehicle. Management shook its head in pure disbelief maintaining that there was obviously a high degree of exaggeration within those reports, but a 'Loline' was fast, 55 mph was possible, and very stable too.

As 'B' fleet buses Nos. 300 to 304 they entered service in February or March 1967 to be sold *en bloc* to the West Riding Automobile Company in late 1970. These 'Lolines' turned out to be the last of the breed, and so could not be multiplied, but had we known at the time of the sale just what another 12 months would bring they would never have departed as they did for Wakefield, for they would have been ideal performers on the Halifax, Todmorden, Burnley through service.

In the event the association with Guildford led me to discover that Dennis at the time possessed a wealth of engineering talent. This in turn led to developments in later years, the effects of which are still with us today, so in retrospect from an industry point of view these five buses formed a very fortuitous purchase.

Now I did not realise in these early days that my 11 years in Halifax were to fall into three categories, these being firstly the traditional times, traditional because the undertaking had existed in its two part form from April 1929, and it seemed in November 1963 that this would continue for years to come. The second period came after the passing of the 1968 Transport Act and the third and final era really started in the late summer of 1971 when we discovered that Local Government Reorganisation was going to occur as from 1st April, 1974 - a date that surely sticks all too prominently in the minds of those engaged in municipal administration around that time.

We were now in that first period, and having to cope with the very differing attitudes of our two governing bodies was proving to be an interesting experience. The Municipal Committee was typical of every such body. Made up of Council members drawn from each of the three political parties, there was something of a parochial outlook. Fares, service frequencies, the provision of bus shelters, passenger (or constituent) complaints and like matters were the basis of committee discussions. Finance was of course important but it seemed in general that the members were quite happy if the undertaking could at least break even each year, when one could invariably obtain what one wanted provided that it could be paid for. Getting into debt, or asking for support from the civic purse, would not be popularly received.

The Joint Committee outlook was rather different, as the five railway members, all officers of the then Eastern Region, wanted to see a financial return coming their way at the end of each year. The timetables, location of stops, and provision of bus shelters basically concerned them not at all, but financial health certainly did. In this connection I remember telling the Committee about our first ever continental private hire operation. One railway member from an accountancy background asked, 'Who had authorised the purchase of the necessary GB plates for the vehicle', and I never was sure if he was joking or not. I must say that I found JOC meetings to be quite exhilarating and I enjoyed meeting up with these York- or Leeds-based executives.

As for bus stops, though . . . I had not been back at Halifax long before I received an urgent message to meet up with the Municipal Committee Vice Chairman at a precise time, at a precise spot to find him awaiting me at a bus stop hard by a fish and chip shop. The Vice Chairman proceeded to give me a 'verbal thumping'. He did not like the position of that recently planted stop, and wanted it moving PDQ. Whilst we had been discussing the matter, the proprietor of the shop had been watching the proceedings through his window, and then joined us on the pavement, asking, 'Is this young man from Transport Jack?', only Jack was not our Vice Chairman's Christian name. When my companion replied in the affirmative, the shopkeeper surprised me greatly by saying, in local parlance of course,

What art tha going to do abaat my fishyeds? I've three bins of em int back that are reet ripe. I rang up thy office to ask for em to be shifted this morn, and a snotty-nosed girl asked 'Art tha making a complaint'. I bloody well am ah said when she replied, 'Sorry, we are not taking any more complaints until after the holidays', I were furious.

I politely pointed out that I came from the Passenger Transport Department, whilst dustbin and rubbish matters came into the province of Transport and

Cleansing, but as the gentleman with me happened also to be on that Committee he was the best person to deal with the shopkeeper's problem. An interesting discussion then ensued during which time I entered into a form of diplomatic retreat. That ex-Vice Chairman and I met up last summer when I looked at him as we shook hands with a smile and said, 'What art tha going to do abaat my fishyeds?' I won't repeat his answer but we chuckled over that and various other incidents that occurred now almost 40 years earlier. The stop continues *in situ* still.

Details of this incident needless to say never appeared in one of my annual reports, but I quickly came to the conclusion that I ought to expand these into something of an historical document, and as I prudently kept copies they now form the basis of much of the detail in these pages from this time onwards. I have also kept a daily personal diary from 1945 right up to this time which has also been very useful in this connection.

There were, though, numerous bright spots after one nasty problem had been solved, this relating to our sinking offices. These consisted of a single-storey building that had been erected after the earlier completion of the Skircoat Road tram shed extension along the side wall of that building which fronted Skircoat Road itself. This building was perhaps some 20 feet wide, and its roof trusses were supported partly by the then new front wall of the office, and the masonry of the car shed, but by 1965 it was all too obvious that the frontage wall was both sinking and beginning to lean outwards, with unfortunate internal effects. One did not expect to see the young lady carrying a tea tray with one hand, holding up an umbrella with the other to prevent rain water coming in through the roof causing 'beverage dilution' but it did happen and so the Borough Architect was called in to advise. His comments were succinct: 'Get out quickly, as the roof trusses are now close to coming away from their end supporting pad stones', but as finding a new home was not going to be easy we had the front wall propped up at a cost of £422 to give us time to decide just what to do.

The answer was to demolish the building that had once been erected to house some of the early buses, and was later used to house the Skircoat washing machine, and erect a permanent but prefabricated two-storey building on the site. Prefabrication here was decided upon to reduce the weight of the structure, as the whole area consisted of built-up ground, and we did not want to be faced with a repetition of what had gone before.

The new offices were formally opened by the Mayor, Alderman Eric Whitehead, on 14th June, 1968. This gave us the opportunity to celebrate this event and the 70th anniversary of the running of the first tramcar in the town (on 19th June, 1898) with a dinner, dance, and on the next day a parade of old vehicles as a section of the Halifax Carnival. The total building cost was £33,940.

Now amongst the old vehicles we had borrowed to take part in the procession were the horse bus from Manchester, and the AEC 'K' type double-decker from the then Museum of Transport at Clapham. Transporting these two priceless relics to Halifax gave the home team some very worrying moments, whilst unloading the 'K' bus from the articulated low-loader kindly provided by the AEC concern resulted in unexpected repercussions. We had no suitable equipment to get it off the trailer, and whilst there was a lift in the Transport

Management had a plan to improve the premises as funds permitted. Consequently the old washing shed was demolished to make way for the new office whilst a new one was erected at the rear of the premises and a more efficient washing machine installed. At the same time the end of the garage entrance was walled and roofed to eliminate its previous wind tunnel propensities. Sadly time ran out and the scheme which also saw developments at Elmwood had not been completed by 31st March, 1974. The single left-hand outside tank no longer took Coalene deliveries.

and Cleansing Department that could have been of use, the building in which it was housed was so low that entrance was simply not possible. We were completely stuck until our engineering superintendent, Harold Clarke, remembered that in his young days some chassis had been sent to Halifax by rail, and were unloaded in the Shaw Syke goods yard via a track that ended at a sloping stone-built ramp.

We proceeded to Shaw Syke to find the premises firmly closed, but from the top deck of the 'K' we could see that the ramp still existed. It took no time at all to open the gates, drive in, shunt a few trucks . . . 'Matadors' are very handy vehicles . . . and drive the 'K' across some very precarious planking to gain the surface of the ramp. Whilst we were so engaged the guardian of the goods yard hove on the scene, and demanded to know what we were doing in his domain, only to be assured by Mr Clarke that as semi-JOC staff with its railway associations we were 'part of the same team'. We then, under his suspicious gaze, carefully restored the railway rolling stock to its rightful position, and departed for base. But then came the evening of the dinner, when during a witty speech Eric Dalton, then the Railway Chairman of the JOC, accused an innocent General Manager and his equally innocent staff of breaking and entry, false pretences, interference with railway equipment and numerous other crimes.

It was obvious that reports had been submitted but the 'K' was to see Shaw Syke for a second time when it was returned to its homeward-bound transport.

Putting the horse bus on the road was another problem, as finding the right sort of harness was much more difficult than obtaining the services of a pair of animals. We were on the point of giving up, when we found that our mason's assistant had in earlier years been a carter, and still had a set of 'hain chains' at home. So I had my first ride in a horse bus and could not help noticing that the ride was surprisingly smooth but also surprisingly noisy.

Eric Dalton, despite his remarks at the dinner, was a real friend to the undertaking as the next few lines will show. I had been doing some research to discover that the British Railways Board had powers to run contract carriages if their journeys started or ended within the City of Sheffield, the County Boroughs of Halifax and Huddersfield, or the Borough of Todmorden, hence the reason behind the appearance of bus Nos. 269 and 270. We then began to run some private hire operations as the staff situation came to permit, but this innovation was not popularly regarded in other quarters, and there was no prize for guessing who was most vociferous in expressing opposition. Mr Dalton later told me of the approaches that had been made to him as Chairman to stop our activities, but he was firm in saying that he was not there to prevent our endeavouring to do more than just balance the books. And so the scope of the department's activities began to widen, and in ways that were quite unexpected.

There was in Halifax at this time a firm of considerable size involved in the confectionery business, and by virtue of its product line employed a high proportion of female staff. It had found that the South Yorkshire mining areas were places where a goodly supply of such labour existed, and so the company went into the coach hire basis and every morning several vehicles laden with its employees left various mining villages, at quite an early hour, for the Halifax plant.

These morning and evening excursions were the source of much passenger complaint, cold vehicles forming but one, and matters came to a head one day when a coach was turned out, or so I was told, with a broken accelerator spring. A piece of string was secured to the pedal, and the free end then given to the young lady sitting right behind the driver who was asked to provide the necessary tension as the journey proceeded. The Manager of the firm then made contact, came to see me, and asked if we might provide his firm's transport requirements.

I had to point out that we could if we purchased some appropriate vehicles, specially for the operation, but that would not be the end of the matter. It was quite a way from Halifax to sundry beyond-Barnsley villages, and in view of the hourly span that morning and evening journeys would demand, two drivers per vehicle would be necessary with, at our hourly rates, all the attendant costs. As the works closed at lunchtime on Fridays, we could possibly only need the services of one driver on that day.

Our visitor was determined. We were asked to quote, did so, and our price was promptly accepted so we purchased several second-hand coaches to supplement the one we already had, and went into business.

To supplement Nos. 269 and 270 a couple of the 'Nimbus' machines had been fitted with improved seating, and to expand this programme an AEC Park Royal-bodied coach that had been in an accident and had a badly damaged front end was purchased very cheaply to provide some more seats. On examination it was found to be in much better condition than could have been expected so it was repaired and put into service as fleet No. 200. It and our additional purchases now consisted of:

AEC 'Reliances' with 470 engine and synchromesh gearbox

Fleet No.	Reg. No.	Body	In service
200	MBV 347	Park Royal, 41 seat	19th June, 1965
261	NRK 356	Park Royal, 41 seat	22nd February, 1966
262	PXO 994	Park Royal, 41 seat	10th March, 1966
263	TCJ 486	Burlingham	25th February, 1966
264	TGJ 485	Burlingham	3rd March, 1966

Later in 1967 Nos. 200 and 262 were fitted with new Plaxton bodies, Nos. 261 and 264 were also rebodied in 1968. All were renumbered as Nos. 256 to 259 inclusive.

As a result, dawn, or some time earlier depending on the season, saw a convoy of Halifax vehicles departing from Elmwood garage for the deep recesses of South Yorkshire, and then returning to Halifax with their loads of young (or not so young) ladies delivering them in time for their 8.00 am start. By the time we were making the first pick-ups, our coaches had covered some 30 miles minimum, everything was well warmed up, and complaints of cold buses became a thing of the past. Subsequently two or three of our 'high speed' Dennis 'Lolines' were also allocated to the work having fortuitously been fitted with that high back seating. It can be truthfully said that our enthusiastic contract drivers became involved in various new experiences as their passengers often proved to be very lively ladies.

Our first coach was an 'accident damage' purchased to provide a set of luxury seats but was too good to dismantle. Here rebuilt, it stands as AEC 'Reliance' Park Royal fleet number 200. Next to it another ex-Timpson AEC/Park Royal awaits rehabilitation as fleet number 262 (PXO 994) and life from March 1966 on our South Yorkshire works contract excursions.

The useful expansion of our afternoon and evening tours took us to new areas and here three of the numerous "Fleetlines' used that night invade the village of Delph where four closely situated public houses provided useful refreshment stop facilities in later days.

There was also a dramatic increase in the number of square cardboard boxes to be found around the premises containing sub-standard biscuits that were sold off cheaply by the firm. Here was a business which in total certainly did liven the old place up. Sadly, as a result of an industrial dispute in 1973 when all our vehicles came off the road I had to tell our client that we could not provide the service that was so essential to his company and had to recommend that he sought another contractor as a matter of urgency. This he did and so our South Yorkshire excursions came to an abrupt end, never to be resumed.

Other excursions, though, did materialise. For quite a number of years the undertaking had been running two afternoon or evening local tours that have been mentioned previously in these pages, and Frank and I concluded that we ought to expand the number. Application was duly made to the Commissioners to introduce a third and a fourth such operation taking in new territory, which would cover the soon to be built Dean Head dam, and the M62 motorway, which represented a sizeable civil engineering project. Then we had a spot of luck.

We had of necessity to have legal representation at Traffic Court hearings where we were always at a disadvantage, in that the transport opposition represented by Hebble and partners would use a solicitor who was a professional traffic court advocate. Our representative would come from the Town Hall, and who, whilst being well versed on planning appeals, etc., had had little or no experience in Traffic Court. On this occasion, however, our Town Clerk was apologetic. All his staff were heavily engaged on various civic matters, so we would have to help ourselves. Then Frank remembered a name, and we made an appointment to see the person concerned in his Leeds office. He listened to what we had to say, and sadly shook his head. He had done little work of the sort we were suggesting in recent years, and was in any event far too busy to assist.

However, he had a nephew in the business, who was quickly ushered into our presence, introduced, and really before we could say, 'Yay or nay', this young man said he would certainly take the case for us, as it would be a new experience for him, never having appeared previously in the Traffic Court. Frank and I looked at each other and wondered. We then had a new experience. The nephew went over our intended application chapter and verse and then did a great deal of homework. He took fully on board the need to establish 'need' and so asked us to bring some of our long established tour customers with us to Leeds on the day of our application hearing by coach, 'as many as possible, park up in the bus station . . . by courtesy of Leeds City Transport . . . and have them there an hour or so before starting time when I will be with you'.

He was as good as his word, boarding the vehicle, talking to our supporters and rehearsing them, as to the questions he would ask, and the answers he would then prefer to hear. Under his guidance all went totally according to plan, and a full grant was made by a positively beaming Commissioner.

On conclusion of the hearing and before we left for home, one local coach proprietor who had been vehement in his opposition came to me and said, 'I don't know where you got that fellow from and I don't know what you have paid him, but whatever it was he was worth a bxxxxy lot more'. I privately had to agree with him and so from that time on, for as long as Halifax Passenger Transport continued to exist we employed him as our traffic court advocate, and never lost another case.

The net result of this endeavour was that on 30th May, 1967 tour No. 3 was finally introduced. Well before departure time from Commercial Street the queue stretched right round the block, and no less than 18 vehicles came to be used. Tour No. 4 followed on 15th April, 1968, and this too proved to be very popular. I will add at this point that later we acquired all the short trips of this nature that had been licensed to Hebble which continued in either original or slightly modified form, so by 1972 we were able to offer our very faithful patrons a good variety of afternoon or evening drives.

This touring success brought with it a problem, passengers wanting a mid-way refreshment/comfort stop, but only a very limited number of licensees were prepared initially to open their establishments to us. Consequently putting the contents of three or four well laden 'Fleetlines' through a single village pub gave rise to some hilarious circular tour occasions. I can honestly say that in all my years I have *never* drunk a pint of beer, but back then I certainly pulled a few!

Life in this period was never dull, but one had at times to wonder about decisions one had previously made, and now came one such instance. . . needless to say there were others. We were entering the age of the computer, and presumably no self-respecting Borough Treasurer wanted to confess at a gathering of his compatriots that his department did not house such a wonder of the age, and so one came to inhabit a building that was not all that far away from a certain transport undertaking.

Once it was in full working order the next question to be asked was, 'What can it do, and where can it do it?', or am I being unfair here to a brother chief officer? Doubtlessly that first question came first, but the immediate answer seemed to be stores, so a posse of experts descended on each such establishment within the authority, and began to lay down how from 'computer day' material ordering, stock maintaining and issues were to be recorded.

This was something from which I gracefully withdrew, not being fully up to date as it were, but I did show some interest in what then transpired, wondering as I did so (a very bad habit) just what all this was costing, and thinking all the while about those central administration charges. The machine naturally began to do its stuff, and whereas our old BC (before computer) punch cards had produced holes, this investment began to produce reams and reams of paper.

Some time later I chanced to venture into our stores to be greeted by a rather woebegone stores chief who showed me the mound of paper by which he was currently surrounded. He then went on to confess that as none of it really gave him the information he needed he had not discarded the old system, but continued to keep it up to date, and in the process simply filed all the bumph that was reaching him from that other place.

Now, though, his filing cabinets were full to overflowing, there was no more space, so what should he do? I looked over his evidence that seemed very compelling, and indicated that he should keep what came in for say a couple of months and then quietly bin it, carrying on with his worthwhile efforts making sure in the process that his old style records were as up to date and fully accurate as possible, against the day when questions would be asked. Now came the tender moments, as those questions arose a lot sooner than ever expected.

The council recruited an outside expert to investigate just what was happening in those various stores, so he duly arrived in our parish and began to probe rather too deeply for comfort. I should add here that once his investigation had been concluded he was charged with submitting a report to the appropriate committee. Stormy waters appeared to be very much in the offing as we had simply dumped the expensive output from a very expensive machine, and even Chief Officers can, under this type of circumstance , feel very much at risk. The report duly declared that there was indeed one very well run stores department within the council's empire and guess where that was? Our treasurer was a gentleman, though, grinning all the while as he discussed those contents with me, when I am sure I heard him mutter something to the effect that the devil looks after his own, but maybe I was wrong. Now, although it was not then apparent, the end of my period number one was just around the corner.

Years later when I was the then Government's Bus Operations Adviser and working in Whitehall, several civil servants and I were discussing the merits, and perceived demerits, of those politicians who in living memory had been the political head of the Department of Transport, to use just one of its titles. I put forward the name of Mr Tom Fraser as the best ever, when my companions looked very surprised and said, 'But he didn't do anything'. I countered by pointing out that in doing nothing he had left the industry alone to get on with the job of running transport undertakings without interference and what a blessing that was, but then perhaps I was biased.

The new incumbent of the post, Mrs Barbara Castle, was not from the same mould and so we reached the prelude to the passing of the 1968 Transport Act which saw the setting up of the first four Passenger Transport Executives and, after the sell out of the British Electric Traction group, the National Bus Company.

Thus commenced a period of changes that were to continue through the next two decades, when its effects were to have initially surprisingly beneficial results locally, and then others that were most definitely in my view the very opposite.

Before this Act really took effect one interesting development took place on 1st April, 1968 when the first Halifax bus left Crossfield bus station for Sheffield on new services worked jointly with Huddersfield JC, Yorkshire Traction and Sheffield JC. One of these, the X68, ran as an express via Huddersfield and Penistone and then direct to Sheffield. The other, the 68, was slower using the same route to Penistone to enter Sheffield via Chapeltown. If a bus ran out on the X68 service it returned on the 69 or vice versa.

The 18 ft 6 in. wheel base 'Fleetline' chassis could easily accept a 45-seat single-deck body with an easier entrance than that on an underfloor-engined vehicle at the time. Here two such examples await delivery from the Seddon/Pennine Oldham body factory. they went into service as numbers 109 and 110 during the first week of February 1969. They were built to accept the same window glasses as fitted to the contemporary Willowbrook-bodied examples. Two more British builders that are no longer with us.

I met my wife to be (a Halifax girl) in 1947 and so frequent journeys from Oldham to that town came to be made often via the Hebble Rochdale to Leeds service then usually worked by one of the 1946/7 vintage AEC/Weymann saloons. Hebble also had a few similar bodies mounted on Leyland 'PS1' chassis but these vehicles never impressed me. Here one of the AEC's was snapped by Bob Mack on the No. 19 Bradford to Bingley service that later passed to West Yorkshire Road Car Company.

Much more to my liking were the AEC/Roe front entrance single-deckers of similar vintage that also took their turns on the Leeds-Halifax-Rochdale or Burnley hourly services. Roy Marshall took this shot of one in Bradford's Chester Street bus station again on the No. 19 service to Bingley on 17th March, 1956.

Chapter Nine

Expansion - The Hebble Take-Over

It would not be unfair to say that several of my managerial Halifax predecessors had little time for the Hebble Company, indeed it was often said to me that one such office holder when he met his Walnut Street opposite number was wont to say to him, 'Tell me just what XXXXXX good are you?' Now such words were never uttered in my presence so I cannot confirm this, but . . .

What was certain was that Hebble had been founded by two local entrepreneurs, namely the brothers Charles and Oliver Holdsworth, whose business empire came to include building, haulage, and fuel supply activities amongst quite a few others.

Bus operations began on 1st December, 1924 when routes to Brighouse via Southowram and to Bingley via Illingworth were introduced. The Halifax Council initially refused to grant any in-Borough licences to this upstart interloper, but Hebble buses began to take off from a piece of convenient town centre private land. Once it became known that holding a return ticket from a point outside the Borough made Hebble travel easy, business began to boom. Assisted no doubt by the activities of the nephew of the brothers, a certain Norman Dean, who in later years became well known as the General Manager of the Yorkshire Traction Barnsley-based concern.

The breakthrough really came when the 1926 General Strike began. All the big undertakings saw their buses coming off the road as the staffs followed the calls of their unions, but Hebble was a non-union concern and not only kept running but opened new services to Bradford and Leeds, etc., and managed to retain some of these when normal operations were resumed. Consequently in around two years the initial fleet of six Hebble buses had grown to over 30 and this rate of expansion continued until, by 1929, the fleet total had reached 72. In the April of that year the Holdsworth brothers sold out to the London Midland & Scottish Railway (LMS) which was already running a bus service into Halifax, but this was only a prelude to what came next.

Needless to say Halifax Corporation, and certain others too, decided to fight fire with fire, so Oldham Corporation began a service from that town to Halifax on 15th April, 1927. Halifax had begun to run to Rochdale on 28th August, 1926 but was forced off on 29th June, 1927 when Rochdale Corporation took over but fared no better; so when the latter undertaking vanished from the scene on 3rd December, 1928, the LMS took over running from Halifax station to Rochdale station and keeping its three Leyland vehicles in the station yard. This lack of success municipally also saw the end of Oldham's cross-pennine adventure on 28th July, 1928, all this being due to opposition from the West Riding County Council that feared Local Authority buses could be the prelude to some Municipal territory take-overs.

It was all very sad, and must have caused a lot of resentment in Skircoat Road to mention just one transport office. It must, though, be said that the founding of Hebble and its subsequent expansion would have been much more difficult, if not indeed impossible, if only the Yorkshire Local Authorities had done what their Lancashire counterparts had done and chosen a common gauge for their tramway tracks. As it was whilst Bradford and Halifax cars met head to head at Queensbury and at Shelf, no through running was possible, whilst a tramway journey from Huddersfield to Bradford meant taking three cars and seeing three different tramway gauges. Again although Huddersfield and Halifax trams met at West Vale the 3 ft 6 in. Halifax lines could not be linked to the wider ones employed in Huddersfield, 4 ft 7¾ in.

As I remarked above, however, the sale of the original Hebble concern to the LMS was only a taste of what was to come. For at the same time, by previous agreement, the Halifax Joint Omnibus Committee was about to be brought into being, and this was to have an operating area defined as being within the boundaries shown in red on a map affixed to each copy of that agreement. I never saw any explanation as to why the boundaries had been so drawn but perhaps we had here an echo of that West Riding County Council's earlier objections. Now each Hebble route that started and stopped within those boundaries was transferred to the JOC along with 13 buses (two Leylands, two Karriers and nine Albions), but Hebble continued to run the longer services . . . and the lucrative ones, to Leeds and Bradford etc.

This state of affairs lasted until 22nd February, 1932 when the LMS sold 50 per cent of the shares in Hebble to the British Electric Traction group, and with that sale the LMS Rochdale route also passed to Hebble on 10th December, 1933. But there was a little clause in the deal that obliged the railway side of the JOC to ensure the JOC did not in the future expand to the detriment of Hebble. The Halifax Corporation members remained quite unaware of this undertaking for a considerable number of years, and when it did the boot by quite a coincidence was very much on the other foot.

In 1955 British Railways withdrew the former Great Northern Railway services from Halifax to Queensbury, and thence to either Bradford or Keighley, plus the companion rail link from Bradford to Keighley. It was felt that this gave scope for the Halifax JOC to provide some replacements, but in the end this would-be endeavour was restricted to a rather infrequent operation from Halifax through Ovenden and Holmfield, where GNR stations had been situated, to Queensbury this, for much of its way, paralleling the Corporation service from Halifax to Bradshaw. So whilst 'Bradford' did begin to feature on Halifax destination blinds no green, cream and orange vehicle reached that City.

By this time a certain Charles Holdsworth had become a member of the Halifax Town Council and an Alderman of that body, and also had a seat on the JOC. He was now a poacher turned gamekeeper and (so I was told) had, on hearing of a certain clause within a certain agreement, thundered to the other half of the JOC partnership, 'We will buy you out'. But of course no such sale took place, let me stress this was what I was told. I was not at that meeting although I did as GM see some interesting correspondence that might well still exist in the Town Hall archives.

All this was, of course, history by 1963 when I took up office, but not that many years later Mrs Castle's 1968 Transport Act became law, and things began to happen. The National Bus Company was set up, the BET selling out, and then NBC people came to sit on the Halifax JOC with effect from 1st January, 1969 although one former railway member was retained for liaison purposes.

Needless to say the new men were much more bus-orientated than their forebears and I began to wonder what the future was going to bring as rather more searching questions were being posed, but I need not have been worried. Although, in the short term, things for Hebble looked very promising as between September 1969 and June 1970 the Walnut Street-based fleet expanded to a total of 136 machines, thanks to the take-over of certain ex-Yorkshire Woollen District services, both local, e.g. to Leeds via Cleckheaton, or longer distance such as Bradford-Halifax-Oldham-Manchester, the well known X12 operation.

In view of all this reader you will appreciate my surprise one morning after a JOC meeting at the Town Hall when walking to our lunch venue the Chairman and leader of the NBC side fell into step besides me and said, 'By the way you can have Hebble'. I thought for a moment that he was joking, but such was not the case, so I asked quietly for further details which were promptly forthcoming.

Thereafter formal talks began, Borough Council agreement was given, a notice was placed in the local paper announcing the impending merger, and I began to take a few bus rides into foreign parts to see just what we might be receiving. The results were not exactly encouraging. For example, one evening I decided to have a run to Bradford; so boarded a Hebble 36 ft-long coach in the Halifax bus station that was heading for that City via the mountainous route through Queensbury. On boarding the driver apologised to me for the seemingly bad driving that I would experience but indicated in self defence that this would be due to his vehicle having only two working gears. Despite this handicap he managed very well , and we reached Bradford, Chester St on time. There I boarded another Hebble vehicle bound for Hipperholme, this being a second-hand import that struggled up the steep St Enoch's Road and deposited me at Shelf, where a Hebble double-decker stood in darkness about 50 yards down the road from the stop.

After a short wait a service bus arrived, another AEC 'Regent', and I ensconced myself on the long nearside wheel arch seat, only to be advised by the conductress, 'I would not sit there if I were you Mr Hilditch, as we think the wheel is coming loose and have asked for a change-over'. She had scarcely spoken when the standing 'Regent' burst into life and was indeed the replacement, but this too was not in the best of health, and so I returned to Halifax in a dubious frame of mind. I was soon to wonder more, but in the meantime various Halifax buses were loaned to Hebble.

At 10.35 pm on Sunday 28th February, 1971 Hebble bus No. 618, another 'Regent', left Halifax for Bradford as the last ever working, and I was on it. This marked the end of 47 years of Hebble operations, and could well have ended in spectacular fashion, as the return to Halifax was made via Queensbury with its spectacular descent from that township via a hillside road with quite a drop on the right-hand side as you travel from Catherine Slack to Boothtown. That bus was then run to Skircoat Garage on completion of the trip but was not a vehicle I had elected to keep.

The following morning it was still in our yard and it was snowing, my car was clean and to keep it that way, but wanting to go up to Walnut Street to see how we were faring with vehicle transfers, I jumped into the cab, started the engine and began to turn onto Skircoat Road. As I did the steering wheel began to march across the cab. I promptly ran it onto an empty brake pit and had our fitter check the steering gear. We found that of the three bolts that should have been holding the steering box firmly

The AEC single-deck 'Regals' and their Leyland 'PS1' counterparts gave an adequate performance but in this regard they were eclipsed by the Hebble AEC 'Regent IIIs' with Roe bodies. Several small batches were purchased in the early post-war years, and were then regular performers on the Halifax to Bradford services. Alas at this period Walnut Street garage roof was of low construction, so every double-decker then had to carry lowbridge upper saloon side-gangwayed bodywork.

GCP 5, fleet number 276 was one of the last two AEC/Weymann lowbridge double-deckers to be purchased in 1956, the other was GCP 4 , No. 275. Bob Mack took this picture of the former vehicle heading out of Leeds and the 'squashed up' appearance of the upper deck is all to apparent. Douglas Cane the then new Chief Engineer had been pressing hard for some garage alterations with some success.

to the chassis one was missing, one had no nut, and the other was loose. There was no doubt that Hebble engineering in its latter days was certainly not what should have been desired, nor up to the standards of the now retired Douglas Cane, who had been the company Chief Engineer and a good friend in my earlier Halifax days.

According to fleet lists still in my possession Hebble, just prior to the time of take-over, had 33 coaches, 26 single-deck buses, and 18 double-deckers. The latter were, with a single exception, AEC 'Regents', the odd one being a Daimler 'Fleetline' with Northern Counties body, new in 1966.

Now it had been my plan to dispense with all the Halifax 'Regents' plus the remaining open rear platform machines as quickly as possible. This idea was set back by the Hebble acquisition when several of both varieties had to be kept in stock. They were joined by five Leyland 'Leopard'/Burlingham and three AEC 'Reliance'/Park Royal single-deckers and three AEC 'Regent' double-deckers these having 590 engines, whereas the infamous '618' and several other Hebble 'Regents' had the smaller 470 engine but better looking Northern Counties bodies. Two more 'Regents' and two more 'Reliances' were also obtained on a temporary basis but were later also purchased. As a result of these transfers the JOC fleet strength rose from 90 in 1970 to 106 on the 31st March, 1971 but was not to stay long at this level.

The financial year 1970/71 was one of change. As from 9th March, 1970, the services between Halifax and Huddersfield were fully co-ordinated with alternate buses travelling via West Vale. Then as a direct result of the then new drivers' hours regulations, plus our current staff shortages, cuts had to be made on the 27th May and the 24th August to no less than 26 different routes. Then came 22nd February, 1971.

On that date Halifax buses began to work to Burnley, Leeds and, after so many years, to Rochdale. I gave myself the task of piloting bus No. 262 to mark our re-appearance in that Lancashire town. The following day the orange, green and cream livery was seen for the first time in the Spen Valley with workings to Cleckheaton, and from Cleckheaton to Scholes.

Then on Monday 1st March joint operation with Bradford City Transport began running via both Shelf and Queensbury. The old Hebble Bradford to Hipperholme service was extended to Brighouse, and Halifax buses began to work to both Keighley and Bingley, whilst changes were made of greater or lesser degree to around 20 former local workings. The most significant of these was the bursting of Corporation 'A' service bounds, when, with the consent of the JOC, its former No. 26 Newlands-Halifax-Bradshaw service was extended from Bradshaw through Queensbury to Hungerhill Estate.

The merger went quite a way to solve the staff shortage as much better use could be made of all available hours, but it imposed a tremendous amount of work on the office staff, who had to prepare all the schedules and timetables plus new fare charts. Just to make it all more difficult, this took place at the precise time when the country changed over to decimal currency and who then could tell just how this monumental change might effect future takings. If ever management needed the services of a fully working crystal ball this was the time!

To add to all this, 1970/71 was noteworthy for another and very different event. Some optimists, there could be no other word for them, elected to organise a pop concert at a Pennine location at Krumlin that just happened to be about 1,000 feet above sea level.

Hebble was Halifax area's largest coach operator buying in post-war days bodies by Leyland, Harrington, Plaxton, etc., but to my mind the most distinctive were the four Leylands with Bellhouse Hartwell coachwork. This was one of those small concerns that flourished in that period in the 1940s when demand was strong and supply far from easy, but then seemed to fade away. Fortunately for us Bob Mack was on hand with his ever ready camera to take this shot.

The year 1951 saw the arrival of Hebble's first underfloor-engined buses - six Leyland 'Royal Tigers' with Willowbrook bodies. Here No. 47 (the first of the batch) waits time at the then Burnley/Rochdale stand, which was located at the top of Horton Street until Crossfield bus station was opened in 1954/5. Roy Marshall took this view on 24th March, 1954.

The faithful began to arrive during the afternoon of Friday 14th August, 1970, when we ran various extras. The fare of 4s. was the cause of some early resentment, but in view of what was to follow was just as well. A very large number of people began to gather, and it was noticeable that the majority were attired as one might expect for a pleasant August day, as indeed it was in Halifax. At Krumlin it was a mite cooler, but as I stood by the bus stop looking down on the scene at around midnight on the Saturday all was peaceful and serene, with the stage with its grand piano floodlit, and music echoing around the valley. I had to think (and still do) that things have considerably worsened in that direction since the untimely passing of Major Glenn Miller. He was of course lost in bad weather, and so was the Krumlin Pop Festival!

I awoke on Sunday morning, and looked out of my bedroom window to see some very bedraggled bodies shambling past, so I rushed into Elmwood and asked anyone who was there and had a PSV licence to join me in taking one each of our largest seating capacity vehicles to Krumlin. My choice was a 'Fleetline', and I wondered what was the matter with it as it climbed so slowly up Saddleworth Road from West Vale. On arrival at Krumlin I knew, for the climb had been made in the teeth of a howling gale, and sheltering under the lea of the wall by the bus stop were scores of youngsters who were soaked to the skin, and very, very cold. Krumlin is not the place to be in that sort of weather. Immediate evacuation was very necessary so for the first and last time in my professional life I instructed the Town inspector to stop all early morning Halifax services for at least one trip, and send every double-decker up to me. The crews on arrival were told to take just what money they could. I should add here that once again conditions weatherwise in Halifax were almost balmy, and numerous intending passengers, not knowing just how bad things were only a few miles away, were loud in their complaints when no buses were to be seen. Normal services as I recall were restored from around 10.00 am and on the following day I wrote a letter to the Traffic Commissioners reporting the action I had taken. As it was, the Committee and Council members kindly accepted what had been done and there were few adverse repercussions, at least in the Transport Undertaking. There must have been others in other places, as the staging was damaged and grand pianos are not improved by a very considerable soaking.

Those readers who have some knowledge of the area around Halifax will appreciate at this point that virtually all the route expansion that had taken place in the early months of 1971 had occurred on the eastern side of the town, there being only two ex-Hebble routes that ran out to the west. These were the service via Ripponden to Rochdale, and the one to Burnley that took in the Calder Valley before climbing to Heptonstall and Blackshaw Head. Both of these provided an interesting Pennine ride in summer, but travel in winter could be a very different matter, as I found out for myself one New Year's day. I was sitting at home early that afternoon toasting my toes by a very hot fire when the phone rang, and on picking up the receiver it was to find Douglas Cane, the Hebble engineer, on the line asking if he might have the services of our two 'Matadors' as he was having a spot of trouble on the Burnley route at what was virtually its highest point. I issued the necessary instruction to our garage foremen, and then decided to see just what his problem was.

The Hebble double-deck choice rested on AEC chassis latterly of the 'Mark V' form but thanks to some garage alterations 'highbridge' bodies came to be purchased from 1957. Most were built by MCW but Northern Counties produced the best looking ones as typified by No. 277 shown here at the Leeds King Street terminus. There were four of them new in 1962. Needless to say PCP 403 did not proceed beyond Halifax. If it had the climb from Hebden Bridge to Blackshaw Head would have given its 505 engine plenty to think about.

Hebble's last two AEC 'Regent'/MCW double-deckers were new in 1964. Both were transferred in 1971 to the Halifax JOC to be repainted and renumbered. Here AJX 410 B has undergone the process and is now JOC number 310 whilst sister AJX 409 B, Hebble No. 620, awaits its turn.

On Sunday 22nd February, 1971 Halifax buses began to run to Rochdale after an absence of many years. Here bus No. 262, an AEC 'Reliance' Willowbrook dual purpose single-decker, stands in the now demolished Halifax Crossfield bus station before leaving on the very first cross-Pennine journey. From a comfort point of view a big improvement on a 1946/7 vintage Weymann-bodied single-decker of my earlier travels on this route under early post-war Hebble direction.

Douglas could not have had worse luck. Two, brand new that morning, AEC 'Reliance' semi-coaches were working the service, and so came to a place where the inward-bound hourly vehicle would meet its outward opposite number. Alas, here was a place where the road in front of the former was narrow and on a rising gradient so its driver chose to wait until the other vehicle had come down the incline and passed him as he stood where there was a decent width of highway. Well the Burnley-bound bus came down the gradient alright but not in the manner expected, as the road surface was covered in a sheet of black ice. Braking became non-existent, and those two new buses met head on with considerable damage being caused. Bringing the two back to base was not an easy task and here we were not helped by the atmospherics. A freezing gale force wind was blowing with such an intensity that on leaving my car I had to tuck my head into my coat so that I could breathe properly, in fact leaving the shelter of one of the attendant stone walls was not to be recommended.

That afternoon soured my attitude to one Hebble route, with its 75 minutes running time from Halifax. It seemed to me that as so few people lived beyond Blackshaw Head (not many there either) it would be of advantage to all concerned if one could only travel through via Todmorden and the valley floor, but at the time bus service frontiers were such that it just could not happen. Miracles, though, do occasionally happen and later in 1971 one actually did when the Halifax 'Empire' began a drive on the west and both Burnley and Todmorden began to see Halifax buses for the first time ever in considerable numbers. With that came the virtual end to those ex-Hebble above the sky forays as route No. 15, the low level replacement becoming No. 92, using double-deckers and being just three minutes quicker, after an initial single-deck experiment.

Crewing an early Todmorden bus must have given rise to a very spartan existence, all for not more than 6d. per hour. Here two such stalwarts pose by their steed, a 1907 Leyland open-topped vehicle. This was not on a long distance service, the Portsmouth shown here being within the Todmorden borough. Windscreens, enclosed cabs and cab heaters, what are they?

The Todmorden undertaking pinned its faith in Leyland products and almost inevitably Leyland bodywork for as long as it could. Her two pre-war examples stand on the main Todmorden to Hebden Bridge road near the Whiteley arches with the Calder Valley main line and tunnel portal in the background.

Chapter Ten

Wider Horizons - Todmorden Merger

As the previous pages show the early months of 1971 were rather more than hectic with Halifax buses arriving at terminal points they had never previously seen, but 1971 still had some surprises in store for us and by the autumn these had become very apparent.

This part of the story had a beginning at one of those Transport Conferences, this one taking place in Scarborough in 1968 when the Chairman of the Todmorden Joint Omnibus Committee, who then represented the Municipal side of that concern, came up to my Chairman and I and said with a smile, 'Want to buy a bus undertaking?' The manner was jocular but there was obviously some purpose behind the approach. We countered with a few questions of our own and it came to pass thereafter that more serious discussions began in other places.

The Borough of Todmorden was situated in the area where the main valley of the River Calder is joined by that of Walsden Water where, in earlier days, lay the boundary between Lancashire and Yorkshire. But in 1897 that boundary moved westwards placing Todmorden firmly in the West Riding but perchance its heart was more inclined to Lancashire.

Todmorden never had trams and if it had choice of gauge would have been a subject of discussion. Rochdale cars on 4 ft 8½ in. tracks came as far as Littleborough Summit. Burnley cars followed the Todmorden road out of that town to Townley but used the 4 ft spacing, whilst Halifax had a lengthy route to Hebden Bridge but had its rails laid to 3 ft 6 in. A projected extension further along the Todmorden road to the Whiteley Arches failing to materialise. Todmorden's desire for a local transport system must have been strong for on 1st January, 1907 its initial fleet of four motor buses took the road making Todmorden the second Municipal bus operator in the country, these running to Cornholme, Walsden and along the Hebden Bridge road to the borough boundary.

A depot was built to house these vehicles at Millwood on the Hebden Bridge side of the town in 1908 but here came a snag. Although the fleet had three double-deckers these were open-topped and the garage roof was pitched rather lower than it might have been, with consequences that were to be of long duration. Various modifications were made to the structure over the years, it was enlarged in 1926, but the roof problem was never tackled as I was later to discover, for in 1971 the building was not directly owned but was actually leased from the Gas Board, an odd situation!

Once established a policy of expansion followed so buses began to run into Burnley and to Bacup, with a route connecting Bacup directly with Burnley appearing. Extension to Summit gave connections to the Rochdale trams and a joint express service to Rochdale was also begun. In Todmorden itself were local workings to Cross Lee Lumbutts and Mankinholes, whilst two services were centred on Hebden Bridge. These ran to the hillside community in Old Town and also partly along that route to Peckett Well and then continued along the main road to Keighley, with a better service in summer than in winter on the latter.

Somewhat prophetically Calder High School's sports day took place in 1970 at Manor Heath immediately adjacent to Elmwood garage, Halifax and so the Todmorden buses hired for the occasion 'laid over' in the Elmwood yard, something that did not appear to have happened before in living memory.

The low roof of Todmorden's Millwood garage was a deciding factor in the ongoing purchase of lowbridge side-gangwayed double-deckers but the Hungry Wood Arch was very restrictive before rebuilding. Here a demonstrator early 'Titan TD1' shows it could negotiate the structure with inches to spare.

By the time the Halifax trams to Hebden Bridge were replaced by buses in 1936 one would have thought that a joint Halifax to Todmorden service would have materialised. However, the managements of the two undertakings seemed never to involve themselves in useful dialogue, although there were reasons.

Todmorden representatives were members of the Municipal Transport Association but did not attend Area 'D' Yorkshire gatherings, remaining instead in Area 'C' that took in Lancashire and Cheshire. Both Halifax and Todmorden had joint Committees but by post-war days Todmorden's had BR London Midland Region people on it, whilst men from the North Eastern Region sat on the Halifax JOC and here one thought that little interchange of views ever took place.

This meant that to travel by bus between the two towns a change of vehicle in Hebden Bridge (Cheetham Street) was necessary, with convenient connections conspicuous by their absence, Halifax buses latterly appearing four times in the hour against the three times of Todmorden's. There was by then a limited stop Todmorden service to the Halifax hospitals but by February 1971 this only ran on Sunday afternoons so was useless for practical purposes. By this date too, Todmorden had made several significant cutbacks. The Bacup to Burnley route was no more and no Todmorden buses now reached Bacup, that service having been cut back to Sharneyford or Clough Foot on a very reduced timetable. The fleet once consisting of around 40 all-Leyland lowbridge double-deckers (that roof again) was now down to 27, only seven double-deckers remaining, but by this same year the JOC railway influence was no more. The same National Bus Company officers sat on both bodies and a degree of 'togetherness' began to become manifest.

Now it came to pass that the 1968 talks mentioned at the beginning of this chapter were aborted at the request of the Todmorden Borough Council but the NBC side of that body, whilst acquiescing to local feelings, indicated that a merger was really desirable. Then matters rested for the next two or three years.

Prior to this, however, a through Halifax to Todmorden joint service had begun, although this was still not of a full-day all-day nature, so why was this? The answer was to be found some two miles from Hebden Bridge at Mytholmroyd where the large Calder High School was situated and still being developed. A large proportion of its pupils hailed from places on the Todmorden side of Hebden Bridge, the net result causing confusion and congestion twice a day in Cheetham Street as the girls and boys went through the undesirable practice of alighting from a dark green vehicle to board one painted orange, green and cream or vice versa. The obvious thing to do was to forge a positive link so, after the usual preliminary discussions, an application was made to the Traffic Commissioners for the necessary road service licences. This became the source of an immediate objection from the Hebble company that obviously began to wonder just where all this might lead. Well Hebble did have that hourly Burnley service that took in Hebden Bridge, and from time to time it did run the odd double-decker there from Halifax, but had no real locus so grants were forthcoming as the JOC on this occasion had no difficulty in proving 'need'.

Consequently on Monday 15th May, 1967 a Todmorden lowbridge Leyland was to be seen that afternoon in George Street, Halifax, and earlier in the day a Halifax bus arrived in Todmorden. But this new service was designed only to

At the time of take-over the two oldest Todmorden buses were 20-year-old 7 ft 6 in.-wide all Leyland lowbridge 'PD2s', new as fleet Nos. 18 and 5 (JOC Nos. 351 and 352) on 1st November, 1950. Here No. 5 is about to leave Keighley for Hebden Bridge. Their Calderdale JOC lives were very short in view of their age and lowbridge configuration.

The other five Todmorden double-deckers, again all-Leyland 'PD2' lowbridge vehicles, dated from 1st October, 1951 as fleet Nos. 7, 20, 24, 25 and 27. They became JOC Nos. 353 to 357 on amalgamation. Here No. 24 stands in George Street, Halifax on the through service. It was one of two, as No. 355, to be repainted orange, green and cream (the other was No. 25/356) but neither lasted long in Calderdale passenger service.

deal with the pupils' Hebden Bridge transfer problem. Yet again there was no all-day every-day through facility. It was, though, a start.

Needless to say the new arrangements included a mutual assistance pact in the event of a vehicle suffering 'technical' problems whilst in foreign parts. A well maintained fleet never suffers from breakdowns, so a late model MCW-bodied Leyland from Halifax attempted to enter Millwood garage but that was something that did not come to be repeated.

Things finally began to happen when Ted Metcalfe, who had held office as Todmorden General Manager since 1st February, 1946, gave notice that he intended to retire which he duly did on 12th April, 1971. As a result another meeting was held in Halifax Town Hall on Wednesday 17th March, 1971 when the three parties to the discussions agreed that a full merger should take place at the earliest possible date. A new JOC would be styled the Calderdale Joint Omnibus Committee, the Halifax livery should be adopted as standard, and in the interim this author should become the Todmorden acting General Manager. Thus was the stage set for yet more interesting times for expansion of a municipal undertaking on the 1971 scale was by no means usual in this era. The biggest problem was likely to be getting staffs who had been strangers working together on new services covering previously unknown roads, and sorting out all the attendant union tribal customs.

I began to make frequent trips along the Calder Valley from the 12th April, 1971 as acting GM. Five days earlier both the Halifax and Todmorden Borough Councils had ratified the merger proposals and this came into full effect as from 6th September, 1971, a date that saw the Halifax and Todmorden Joint Committees pass into history. Now the replacement JOC had six members nominated by the National Bus Company , two by Todmorden, and five from Halifax, but of these only five, one and four respectively were to have voting rights. Vehicle and financial apportionments were to be on the basis of 68 parts held by the NBC, 55 parts by Halifax and 13 by Todmorden but, as had been the case in the earlier Halifax body, never in my time did any argument come to result in formal voting being called for. Some changes were inevitable and so the Todmorden clerical section was transferred to Halifax and the associated offices closed.

Ted Metcalfe had done a good job in running a tight ship despite what must have been a fairly narrow remit, as I discovered in the case of the cash office floor. This needed some repairs so I suggested to the second in command that he obtain some samples and quotations to cover the work of a complete retiling, and I would look the results over on my next visit. He did as I had bidden and so we looked over his findings together, when I asked him to make out an order to cover the first choice and I would then sign it so that the work could be put in hand. At this he gently demurred saying that such a decision should be put forward for Committee ratification. My reply was to the effect that the Committee was there to decide policy, and cash office floor tiles hardly came into that category. Here we were dealing with what was a purely management matter.

Ted's biggest problem must have been how to offer the most attractive and yet most economical bus workings in what was a decidedly restricted area, and how to fund new bus purchases as no renewals fund existed, although as the table shows some new rolling stock had been acquired:

This shot of the interior of Todmorden's Millwood garage clearly shows the roof cross beams that were the highbridge bus problem. Here members of the home team ponder their future as their acting General Manager surveyed the scene before the Calderdale JOC merger took full effect in only a few days time. As the premises were surprisingly leased from the Gas Board no bus undertaking was going to spend money on very extensive modernisation or roof lifting. Thank goodness for 'Fleetlines'.

Towards the end of its days Todmorden acquired five second-hand single-deckers. Three came from Sheffield's 'C' fleet being dual purpose Leyland 'Leopard'/Eastern Coachworks 41-seaters. The other two, fleet Nos. 11 and 15, later JOC's Nos. 339 and 340, were ex-East Midland Motor Services Leyland 'Tiger Cubs' with MCW group bodies. New to Todmorden in June 1969 they were never really used for one-man-operation and were soon sold by their new owners Calderdale JOC. No. 339 here stands at Todmorden Market Place.

Todmorden JOC Fleet
As taken over

No. Halifax	Todmorden	Chassis	Body	Seats	New
321	2	Leyland Leopard	Eastern Coachworks	41	*31.7.70
322	3	Leyland Leopard	Eastern Coachworks	41	*1.8.70
323	13	Leyland Leopard	Eastern Coachworks	41	*1.8.70
324	4	Leyland Leopard	Willowbrook	45	1.2.67
325	9	Leyland Leopard	Willowbrook	45	1.2.67
326	1	Leyland Leopard	Willowbrook	45	1.2.67
327	10	Leyland Leopard	Willowbrook	45	1.2.67
328	6	Leyland Leopard	Pennine	43	1.12.69
329	8	Leyland Leopard	Pennine	43	1.12.69
330	14	Leyland Leopard	Pennine	43	1.12.69
331	19	Leyland Leopard	Pennine	43	11.11.69
332	22	Leyland Leopard	Pennine	43	11.11.69
333	23	Leyland Leopard	Pennine	43	11.11.69
334	19	Leyland Leopard	East Lancashire	44	1.4.61
335	16	Leyland Leopard	East Lancashire	44	1.9.62
336	31	Leyland Leopard	East Lancashire	44	1.9.62
337	29	Leyland Leopard	East Lancashire	44	1.1.64
338	37	Leyland Leopard	East Lancashire	44	1.1.64
339	11	Leyland Tiger Cub	MCW	44	†27.6.69
340	15	Leyland Tiger Cub	MCW	44	†27.6.69
351	18	Leyland PD2/1	Leyland Lowbridge	26/27	1.1.50
352	5	Leyland PD2/1	Leyland Lowbridge	26/27	1.11.50
353	7	Leyland PD2/12	Leyland Lowbridge	26/27	1.10.51
354	20	Leyland PD2/12	Leyland Lowbridge	26/27	1.10.51
355	24	Leyland PD2/12	Leyland Lowbridge	26/27	1.10.51
356	25	Leyland PD2/12	Leyland Lowbridge	26/27	1.10.51
357	27	Leyland PD2/12	Leyland Lowbridge	26/27	1.10.51

* New to Sheffield '6' Services in April 1961.
† New to East Midland in 1956 and 1958.
Bus Nos. 326 to 329 inclusive have improved seating.

It was a condition of the merger that the Todmorden fleet was brought up to the same average age of that of the Halifax JOC. In order to achieve this the two second-hand 'Tiger Cubs' that had never been fitted for one-man-operation were sold as were four of the Lowbridge 'PD2s', which had they remained in the fleet would have assumed the identities Nos. 351-354 inclusive. These six vehicles were replaced by three Marshall-bodied 'Leopards' that had previously been with Yorkshire Traction, to become Nos. 358, 359 and 360, together with an ex-Yorkshire Woollen District Alexander-bodied 'Fleetline' and the ex-Hebble Daimler with Northern Counties bodywork. This was given the new identity No. 294. At this point a change was effected, the Alexander-bodied 'Fleetline' going in to the 'A' fleet as bus No. 103, whilst the existing Halifax machine that carried that number became No. 293 in the Calderdale part of the undertaking. Here we were back to that low roof again. It was all too obvious that with the merger must come some new through Calder Valley trunk routes when the former 'bus frontier' at Hebden Bridge would be eliminated once and for all. At this point we come to an

Todmorden bought an East Lancs-bodied 'Leopard' in April 1961, its first underfloor-engined bus which became fleet No. 12. Two more followed in September 1962 as Nos. 16 and 31 and then a final pair arrived in January 1964 as Nos. 29 and 37. All five passed to the Calderdale JOC becoming Nos. 334 to 338 in the same order. Here is No. 16 (335 later) at Todmorden Market Place.

Another batch of 'Leopards' followed in February 1967 again with synchromesh gear boxes but as a new feature Willowbrook bodies were fitted. The first two, Nos. 4 and 9, had 45 standard bus seats and had lower green panels. These later became Nos. 324 and 325 in the Calderdale JOC fleet. Here No. 324 stands in Todmorden Market Place bus station.

element of pure luck, for which George Stephenson, and his low railway bridge in Brighouse, must take some of the credit, if credit is to be awarded.

If any such operation was to be economical then it was necessary to retain the former Todmorden depot, with its staff, and then feed these new services from two depots located more or less at either end of the main line. But that early test had shown that no front-engined high bridge Halifax bus could safely enter the Millwood premises. Thanks, however, to that bridge and the 'be prepared' motto, Halifax had 23 reduced height Daimler 'Fleetlines' in stock with 12 more then on order, a number raised to 17 once merger discussions began. So if only the Leyland organisation would deliver the chassis so that Northern Counties could play its part it would be possible to restock Millwood, and equip the planned new facilities with new high capacity vehicles. Unfortunately deliveries were delayed until June or July 1972 so as a temporary measure four more ex-Hebble machines, two 'Regents' and two single-deckers, plus four ex-Maidstone & District 'Regents' with 470 engines were acquired to avoid the expense of recertifying home fleet numbers scheduled for disposal.

There was no doubt that these mergers did upset the Halifax fleet replacement programme and also put quite a strain on the engineering department. But I was not grumbling, for the end result would be a very tidy operating area which would enable us to improve the overall financial situation with a more economic form of service pattern. It also meant that the Todmorden staff members would not lose their important local government superannuation rights, and there was going to be a job for everyone. Had we not had sufficient suitable buses either in stock or in the pipeline the situation would have been very different, but I doubt if this significant fact was really appreciated by the Committees, workforce and passengers.

The new Calder Valley trunk routes were introduced on Monday 27th September, 1971. The previous Hebden Bridge to Brighouse through workings were cut back to run only from Halifax to Brighouse, whilst three buses per hour left Halifax for Todmorden, then being projected further to Portsmouth, Littleborough Summit or Cross Lee respectively. To supplement these an hourly single-deck service from Leeds and Halifax to Todmorden and Burnley was instituted using semi-luxury vehicles with similar Leeds, Halifax, Rochdale through workings providing a 30 minute frequency over the common Leeds to Halifax section.

Other changes affecting the Todmorden area saw the ending of services to Hebden Bridge station; the bringing back of the Hebden Bridge to Keighley service to start or terminate at Todmorden; the partial re-opening of the Sharneyford and Bacup route (No. 93); the linking of the Old Town route to the ex-Halifax JOC Mytholmroyd to Cragg Vale workings; and last but not least the putting of the Saturdays-only Todmorden to Rochdale facility (No. 95) onto a regular hourly timetable, and adding thereto a later return trip from Rochdale for good measure.

There were at the same date some changes on the Halifax side of the undertaking. It seemed very obvious that the transfer of so much of the old Hebble concern to the Halifax JOC had caused some resentment in another camp and so the West Yorkshire company was given one bus working on the Bradford-Hipperholme-Brighouse route, and all service over the Halifax to Bingley road. In such manner honour was at least partially restored.

Just to make life more interesting for our engineers, a wholesale bus stop sign replacement programme was begun. New poles were planted wherever needed

The other two Willowbrook-bodied 'Leopards' had 43 semi-luxury seats becoming Todmorden bus Nos. 1 and 10 or 325 and 327 in the Calderdale JOC series. Here No. 326 lays over in the Todmorden bus station.

Todmorden's last new buses were six Leyland 'Leopards' with fluid transmission and Pennine bodies. New in November/December 1969 four, Nos. 14, 19, 22 and 23 (later JOC buses to 330 to 333), had 45 standard bus type seats. Here about to become 330 stands in Elmwood yard alongside No. 320, an ex-Hebble AEC 'Reliance'. The other two again had semi-luxury seating.

and all fare stages properly identified in an endeavour to make life easier for the traffic staff who were finding themselves going deep into previously uncharted territories. I can here remember all too well the remarks made by our works superintendent, Eric Nicholson, to the effect that he had never previously realised how adept he was at climbing poles and then planting bus stop signs. All the staff accepted what was being done cheerfully and the whole merger process went off with hardly a hitch. Unfortunately JOC fares had to be raised again as from 24th April, 1972, without any traffic court difficulties, when thanks to the fare stage resigning it was possible to reduce some charges in the former Todmorden area.

Before we consider what the rest of 1971 came to bring let me make a little diversion to comment on other pertinent matters. One never knew just what the day would bring, or the evening too for that matter, for that was when the local papers appeared, and it could well be that your activities, or lack of them, came to appear, as it were, in despatches.

One evening there was a letter to the Editor in one local publication that severely criticised a certain inter-town bus route; needless to say the letter bore a signature but not an address. This stopped me from following up my usual practice of sending a letter direct to anyone who gave the full particulars, when they either received an explanation as to the whys and the wherefores, or an invitation to come and see me at the office for a suitable discussion.

The following morning I had occasion to ring the office of that very publication to inquire about a different matter altogether, and then asked for a contact I had made earlier by name. What I did not know was that there were two people of that name in that establishment, and by chance the switchboard operator put me through to the wrong one, or in this case certainly the right one. On my announcing my name he immediately went on the defensive saying, 'Is it about that letter in the paper last night?'

I instantly smelt a rat, so said it was, when some facts began to emerge. He had obviously written the missive but his name was not at its foot, so I asked why the difference. He replied he had used the name of an uncle. I inquired if he (the uncle) was a regular bus user, to be told to my astonishment that sadly the gentleman had passed over some years previously. My contact added that he did not use the service either, but felt a comment was necessary.

After that one could not help wondering just how many 'Letters to the Editor' were written in that very office, but that was a question that was never going to be answered.

Then I had a visit one morning after the peak period from a driver and his conductress who were very upset. They had worked four mornings that week a certain school bus when riot and mayhem had been all too prominent. The girl in particular was almost in tears as she told me she was verbally abused and then spat on, and her uniform did certainly bear very undesirable evidence of such bad behaviour.

I put them in my car, collected our chief inspector, and headed for that same school where the head was very loath to see us. He was about to depart on some school excursion, so just did not have the time. I persisted and in the end with rather bad grace we were invited into his study. After hearing our story he told us that there was absolutely nothing he could do; the incidents over those four mornings

The vehicle situation in late 1971 was not as good as it might have been thanks to late deliveries of Daimler 'Fleetlines'. As a stop gap measure four AEC 'Regent Vs' with 505 engines were obtained from Maidstone & District to become fleet Nos. 361 to 364 from 1st December, 1972. All had Park Royal bodies but two of these were of the low bridge form and so were allocated to Todmorden. They only ran for some seven months to the end of July. These buses were fitted with platform doors.

had occurred outside the school walls. This attitude annoyed me intensely so I told him that if he could not, or would not, put a foot on the necks of about three miscreants I certainly would proceed forthwith to stop the nuisance.

This was now Thursday morning, so at assembly on the Friday he could inform the multitude that there would be no school buses at all as from next Monday, and I would advise all other local operators why we had withdrawn when I would advise them not to accept any replacement contracts that might be forthcoming thereafter.

He told me that this was beyond my powers but I said it was not, adding for good measure that I hoped that on Monday morning it poured down. With that the four of us returned whence we came.

I had barely regained the office when the phone rang and the Chairman of the school governors of that same school came on the line to ask if I would mind returning to meet him in the head's study, a head by the way who now was *not* going on that planned excursion. The Chairman was someone I had met previously and rather admired so I promptly agreed, and our meeting took place when appropriate measures were then agreed.

As a result not only did that particular problem come to be solved, but a little later several parents said how much they appreciated the action taken as some unfortunate bullying that had been occurring on the buses no longer took place.

The moral of the story here is that life can be difficult unless a degree of co-operation between the different authorities can be achieved, as we proved here. What if nothing had been done, would those school buses have ceased? I rather think they would, so there would have been some stories for the local papers to print and comment upon.

Chapter Eleven

The Ultimate - and Extinction

By the end of October 1971 things were beginning to settle down. Our mixed ex-Halifax, Todmorden and Hebble staff had found their way about the new routes, fares and duty schedules and, thanks to all the work done by the traffic officers and the associated negotiations, no troubles at all had been experienced. It had indeed all gone remarkably well although it was obvious that some route 'fine tuning' was going to be desirable before long.

The mergers had also done much to improve what had been a dire staff situation so private hire was flourishing once more, and some new coaches became a gleam in the eye of management. After a more than a full year at work the chance was taken to enjoy a spot of leave so on Wednesday 3rd November we left for our South Devon holiday home, departing from Halifax in rain and mist which might have been prophetic.

The very next day, i.e. Thursday 4th November, the Local Government Bill was published and in it were some very significant words. West and South Yorkshire were to become metropolitan counties, and in each such administrative area a Passenger Transport Executive would come into being if there was not one already in existence. Here was a sentence of death for at midnight on Sunday 31st March, 1974 the Halifax and Calderdale undertakings would cease to exist, and on Monday 1st April the new PTE would take over; but the National Bus Company would not be affected by the proposed changes to any considerable extent so just what was going to happen to Calderdale? A lot of talking was obviously going to be involved in the not too distant future. This news certainly spoiled my holiday, for I did not view the future with eager anticipation. Still work had to continue so on my return we began to do that fine pruning or tuning, and also ran into some new labour problems that came to affect both the traffic and engineering staffs. It all started in September 1971 when the NJIC decided that member undertakings could negotiate basic wage rates but not conditions. Needless to say a similar decision was soon reached in the Craftmen's Council.

On the traffic side an application was made in August 1972 for a £2 per week per man inconvenience allowance, despite the fact that a similar claim had been lodged nationally in the NJIC, in June, for a rise of 15 per cent on basic rates which, if granted, would cost us no less that £186,000 in a full year. Argument followed with our buses going off the road on Sunday 17th September, 1972, and no services were offered for the next two days. Eventually a settlement was reached with a lead in payment of £1 per week plus a bonus of 50p but this was not going to be very costly as the men's side agreed to accept one-man-operation on the double-deck West End, Pellon, Brighouse, Field Lane and Stoneylane services if the bonuses could be included in the basic rate and this for once was not a problem. It was from a management point of view very tiresome but the next spot of trouble was much worse.

Work study schemes were much in vogue at this time and our negotiations on the idea began back in 1969. A team of consultants was engaged but they were

It was a condition of the Todmorden merger that the NBC would equate the age of its half of the JOC fleet with that of the Corporation so five more modern buses were transferred in. Three of these were ex-Yorkshire Traction Leyland 'Leopards' with Marshall bodies. New in April 1968 they joined the Calderdale JOC in August 1971 as fleet Nos. 358 to 360. Initially all side windows were fixed but sliding upper lights were soon fitted by the new owner. Had the Calderdale JOC existed beyond 1974 their lives would not have been overlong.

An ex-Yorkshire Woollen District Alexander-bodied 'Fleetline' registration No. BHD 222 C was also transferred. It was too high to enter Millwood garage so it became 'A' side bus No. 103 whilst the original Corporation vehicle with that identity passed in exchange to the JOC as fleet No. 293. It (No. 103 the second) was new in May 1966.

unable to begin their investigations due to staff opposition. Eventually on 19th September, 1972 they did manage to make a start, but this led to more problems and on 6th October all the mechanics downed tools, the body shop following the next day, and as no bus repair work was then possible it was eventually necessary to take all the vehicles off the road for a full three days.

As usual in the end a settlement was reached but these service withdrawals had a very adverse effect for afterwards takings dropped by at least £2,000 per week. More fares increases were inevitable, and the necessary applications were made but then on 6th November, 1972 the Prime Minister announced the Regulation to Control Inflation with the result that for the next three months no fares increase was permissible and the undertaking had to stand all the additional costs. It was not until 25th April, 1973 that those fares increase applications were listed for hearing in an attempt to raise 'A' side income by £110,000 in a full year and by £119,000 for the JOC. If ever one wanted to experience managerial stress in full measure the years 1971 to 1972 had to be recommended for the purpose, but from my point of view it did not end there, still we did have a few, very few, compensations.

On 4th December, 1972 the contractors began work on the deferred scheme to enlarge Elmwood garage, so that in due course it could be converted into a workshop when all the fleet would be housed at Skircoat. The extension was planned to provide a new stores, and most pressing of all a tyre shop. This was a facility the undertaking had never previously possessed, the three Michelin employees who looked after our tyres, whether of that manufacture or not, had to make do with a room in the ruinous cottage property that then stood in Shaw Hill. Their task was thankless, as they had no cover when doing their wheel-changing work which was undertaken outside the door, a task that in the midst of a Halifax winter was more than grim, but, true heroes, they were never known to complain.

It was going to take a year or two to bring the conversion scheme to full fruition, and in the meantime it had to continue as a bus garage. So the old Hebble washing machine of the drive-through variety was taken out of the now redundant Walnut Street premises, overhauled, and used to replace the life expired Essex machine. For those of you unfamiliar with this design, this consisted of a frame mounted horizontally below the roof which was lowered down over the vehicle as water jetted out from perforated pipes affixed to the frame, which also carried rotating brushes. It did give quite a satisfactory wash, but as each bus had to be positioned before it could be safely lowered, and then raised to allow extraction, washing was a slow and time consuming operation.

By now the future purchasing policy had been refined, and if you wonder at this statement remember that you can only buy what the industry produces. For double-deck operation on heavy stage carriage services the Daimler 'Fleetline' with the Northern Counties body was going to be the first choice, and similarly where the relevant highways permitted, the corresponding 'Fleetline' single-decker was envisaged, only as this had a 33 ft overall length and a longer wheelbase it could not offer a universal operation. Shorter underfloor-engined single-deckers were therefore needed for pure bus work, dual purpose duties and for coaching, and so I turned to the Leyland 'Leopard' as this had a bigger engine than the AEC 'Reliance' which seemed to me to have a rather dubious future, also the 'Leopard' could now be obtained with a semi-automatic gear box. In my view

Before its demise Hebble purchased a single Northern Counties-bodied 'Fleetline' which initially passed to Yorkshire Woollen. Now also transferred to the Calderdale JOC it became No. 294 on the 19th August, 1971. Looking now like an original Halifax vehicle, only the different destination layout betrayed its origin.

Thankfully between May and July 1972 seventeen new Daimler 'Fleetlines' were delivered as numbers 82 to 86 for the 'A' fleet and Nos. 295 to 306 for the JOC. Of these Nos. 298 to 306 were allocated to Todmorden. Their arrival spelt the end of various ex-Hebble vehicles, plus those from Maidstone & District. Now the main Calder Valley trunk routes were largely re-equipped with 75-seat vehicles to the relief of a certain General Manager.

our earlier 'Leopards' with that old synchromesh gear box with its crash bottom gear were far from suitable for one-man-operation. Consequently an initial batch of five were ordered for the 'A' fleet, coming into stock with Plaxton bodies as fleet Nos. 1 to 5 in the October of 1972. Five more were then ordered, becoming Nos. 6 to 10. They took the road in December 1973, being the last Halifax 'A' fleet buses to be acquired. At the time the chassis cost £2,993 each, the bodies £2,930.

In these later years our vehicle testing work had continued but I must confess that some of the models tried could never be regarded as serious contenders. Two such examples were front-engine-mounted single-deck vehicles of Ford and Seddon manufacture. The intrusion of the engine cowling into the entrance area spoiled the layout, but both also had conventional gear boxes, and in the case of the Ford a most peculiar twist and pull handbrake arrangement that seemed far from acceptable.

Three other single deckers also joined the parade. The first was a Leyland 'Panther' with a Strachan body, that did quite well but did not really appeal, the second one of the first Metro Scania single-deckers or rather a brace of them. The first to arrive went like a rocket, with alas a fuel consumption to match, but after only a few days with us the gear box failed which caused us to wonder as this was of surprisingly small proportions. It was then collected by the MCW people who left us with a second so that the trials could be continued. I was later to have a deal of experience with these vehicles and their double-deck counterparts, so if a third volume of this transport life saga should ever see the light of day a much greater reference to these joint Anglo-Swedish productions will be made.

The last test vehicle to be covered here was the prototype Seddon Pennine RU, which came complete with a Seddon single-deck body. This had a rear-mounted Gardner horizontal '6LX' engine coupled to a Self Change semi-automatic gear box that drove onto the rear axle. It was obtainable either in 36 ft or 33 ft forms. Chassis price at £3,375 was very competitive and so three were ordered that to the disappointment of our Oldham friends were fitted with Plaxton dual purpose bodies. They had hoped to secure that order for Woodstock factory, but I wanted something more upmarket. This proved to be fortuitous in the longer run, as RU Pennine bodies were planted straight onto the chassis with no conventional underframe which gave rise to some strengthening work being called for in most places later. As it was this Seddon production came to be ordered by several municipal undertakings who had never previously favoured Oldham such as Huddersfield, Rotherham, Doncaster, Accrington and Southampton to name just a few. But it was not to be trouble free, the electric system was affected by water ingress, 4 in. rather than 3½ in. springs would have been advantageous, and the front axle of a Seddon unit really needed more substantial king pins and bearings.

The Achilles' heel was the absolute minimum distance between the gear box and the rear axle that left insufficient room for a proper drive shaft that could cope with the angularities involved. As it was a patent coupling was to be found in this vital area that was prone to a very short life. A partial cure was later applied to the 36 ft-long chassis by moving back the engine/gear box assembly as far as was practically possible in the frames, but ours were to the shorter dimension and no such palliative could be adopted. This was regrettable so no more came to be obtained, but I suspect that if the Seddon concern had remained under Redmond direction, Woodstock factory would have updated the design in the light of

Amongst the ex-Timpson AEC 'Reliance'-based coaches that came to be rebodied with Plaxton 41-seat coachwork was former accident victim No. 200 or MBY 347, now number 256. We paid just £275 for 'the wreck' on first acquisition whilst the new body with re-trimmed seats came at £3,000. If ever there was a bargain this was it! It is shown here in October 1967 when back from Scarborough.

1972 also saw the arrival of five Leyland 'Leopards' with 680 engines and semi-automatic gear boxes - the latter features that were a long time coming. As fleet Nos. 1 to 5 Plaxton 45-seat bodies were fitted. These were of course for the Corporation fleet. But why, oh why, did it take Leyland so long to do the obvious and make the 'Leopard' more suitable for one-man-operation?

experience and gone on to produce several more design surprises. But it was not to be, and so another British manufacturer faded from the PSV scene, and as we have seen in Volume One from British manufacturing.

As things stood late in 1973 we could perhaps have been excused had we let the undertaking drift, but such was never the case. Understanding clearly that after 1st April, 1974 the same passengers would be wanting transport, orders were placed for still more new buses, consisting of two Leyland/Plaxton coaches for the 'B' fleet together with four similar vehicles having dual purpose bodies, these turning out to be the forerunners of similar new PTE orders. At the same time eight more 'Fleetlines' with the usual Northern Counties bodies for the 'A' side were sought but thanks to Leyland production problems these were a very, very long time in appearing, and it was not until we were well in the PTE era that they finally emerged. From 1971 all 'Fleetlines' were built to 13 ft 8 in., i.e. 2 in. lower than before.

One more comment on the bus fleet. I was well aware that there were places where no 'Fleetline' could ever venture, and some day if loadings continued at the then levels some new short double-deckers would be needed. But that was a problem to be solved eventually as those later Lefevre 'PD2s' had lots of life before them.

By now the fleet was looking rather more uniform than it had since the Hebble merger with the 'Fleetlines' cruising up and down the Calder Valley and now indeed some way beyond. Our last set of route/timetable changes came into being in October 1973 when, by arrangement with our western neighbour, our vehicles ceased to turn at Littleborough Summit, and began to serve a new terminal point in that town . At the same time a new Littleborough to Burnley through service on a co-ordinated timetable, with those to or from Halifax, was introduced. Cutting out the need to change buses (or onto trams) at the bleak Summit was an improvement that had long been wanted.

Finally these changes were marked by the production of a souvenir timetable booklet that included a fleet list, a potted history, and several coloured photographs of typical fleet members. It was a time of very mixed feelings, for I could see that there were still some opportunities left for further expansion but, alas, these were not going to be possible.

Thanks to all the disruption that had occurred the financial results for 1972/73 were by no means as good as they ought to have been but they could have been a good deal worse. As it was the Corporation undertaking made a surplus of £13,924, whilst the JOC suffered a loss of £22,722, but there was a surplus to carry forward of £99,108; a balance of £117,708 in the reserve fund meant we were not yet bankrupt. Here by way of interest 43p in every £1 was spent on driver and conductor wages, 7.9p on fuel oil, and 15.28p on repairs and maintenance, then no less than 12p went in welfare and superannuation costs. Fuel oil at the end of the year was costing 15.82p per gallon. Our buses in running a total of just over eight million miles used 938,000 gallons and we paid no less than £93,880 in fuel duty. Finally the 910 staff on the books at the 31st March, 1972 had by the end of the following financial year been reduced to 795. Conversely there was a small rise in the office staff employed as, due to the impending PTE, the Borough Treasurer was no longer able to provide the former wages service, and so a wages office had to be opened at Skircoat Road when all calculations, packaging, etc., came to be done in-house for the very first time.

By late 1968 the private hire business had developed sufficiently to make it possible to suggest to the JOC that the time was ripe to invest in some new luxury coaches. Permission was forthcoming and as a result AEC 'Reliance'/Plaxton 43-seat vehicles, fleet Nos. 273, 274 and 275, entered service on 1st April, 1969 in time for the summer traffic. Here the two pose brand new on Scarborough seafront before starting their journey home. At the rear is the Mercedes integral coach (used as staff transport this day) that was on trial during March 1969.

At the end of the 1960s the Seddon company began to really explore the PSV markets heavier end so produced the Gardner '6HLX'-powered Pennine RU with semi-automatic gear box. Available in 33 ft or 36 ft lengths at a very competitive price it made quite an impact on the municipal scene, Doncaster, Huddersfield, Rotherham, Southampton and Accrington being just some of the undertakings that placed orders. Again that 'old pals act' took effect and so we were enabled to see the very first chassis in build and then test it when Pennine-bodied in April 1969.

Change was now very much in the air, and two thoughts loomed large in my mind, namely what would really happen to the undertaking and more important from a personal point of view what would happen to me, for as midnight struck on 31st March, 1974 my job would come to an end. Had I been 50 by that date there was a lifeboat available, as anyone in such a situation having reached that age had the option to retire on full pension, but that was something not open to me, and so I decided to look for something suitable elsewhere. Then I contracted food poisoning and for the next few weeks was most decidedly unwell. This could not have come at a worse time as I was invited to appear on a managerial shortlist in a place where no PTE was on the horizon, but I was much too ill to make the journey. Then the positions for the PTE Director General and the Directors of Operations and Engineering were advertised, so I had no option but to apply for each one. My choices would have been in that order, but I missed out on the first and it was put to me that as I had suitable engineering qualifications I should concentrate on the latter.

Somehow on the day I managed to drag myself to Wakefield for interview when the members of the panel could not have been kinder. I was offered the post at a salary still to be specified and told after being congratulated to go home, and get well just as soon as possible. There was, though, a condition. If I took up the offer it would be on the firm understanding that I would stay for at least two years, and so I shook hands on the deal and went back to bed.

There I stayed for the next three weeks and then feeling somewhat improved told my wife that a trip to our holiday home in Devon would restore me to full working order. If she and my daughter would drive the car the 305 miles that separated one front door from another I would make myself as comfortable as I could in the back. A few days later we made the journey and on the following morning I was ensconced on the terrace in the sun, when I heard the phone next door ringing. Seconds later our neighbour put her head over the hedge and said the call I had heard was for me. The first time that had ever occurred. I made my way slowly to her house, picked up the phone and was amazed to hear a once familiar voice saying, 'Can you guess who this is I?' I could, and we exchanged a few words before my old Plymouth boss took over to say he had been intending to ring me for some weeks, and what a job he had had finding a phone number near to the address Halifax had given him. The object of his call was to tell me that he was about to retire, and then ask if I would be interested in following him at Milehouse? The only answer to that question would normally have been, 'Yes', but I had given my word in Wakefield when I accepted what then was my only alternative to a dubious future. Now I could not go back on my word much as I would have wished, and here let me stress the fact that as a PTE Director I could enjoy a much higher salary than that offered at Plymouth was not a consideration that weighed with me in the slightest. If only he had phoned earlier! But there was little point in dwelling on what might have been.

One had to concentrate on the future, and this concentration meant that much less working time had to be spent on purely Halifax affairs. There were two distinct strands involved here, the first of which involved deciding the future of the Calderdale Joint Omnibus Committee. Something that was formally discussed at a meeting that took place in Wakefield on 19th January, 1973, when the NBC

The Pennine RU showed promise so a trial batch of three were ordered and entered JOC service in October and November 1970 as fleet Nos. 315, 316 and 317. However, rather to Seddon's disappointment, as Plaxton semi-luxury bodies were supplied. In service they ran fairly well but - the electric system was not fully weatherproof, a more substantial front axle and 4 in. wide springs rather than 3½ in. would have been advantageous. The Achilles' heel was the coupling between the gear box and the rear axle, where shortage of space meant that a normal propellor shaft could not be fitted. These buses were 33 ft long, the chassis cost £3,375 and the bodies a further £3,780.

The Daimler 'Fleetline' certainly saved Radford bus production. Under development by its BSA owners at the time of the Jaguar takeover, the first prototype had Daimler engines plus the cleverly designed semi-automatic gear box, power input and output taking place at the same end. Jaguar's engineers quickly realised what a treasure they had but decided that the Gardner '6LX' engine was to be the standard fitting. One never knew for sure but I suspect that price as well as reputation was a factor in this final decision.

side suggested that the lead set sometime earlier in Huddersfield be followed, and the municipalities buy out the NBC assets. Now I have little doubt that if local government reorganisation had not involved the setting up of a PTE this is what would have occurred. Our operating area took in the whole of what became the Calderdale Metropolitan Borough, so restricting pure 'A' side municipal operations to the former Halifax Borough boundaries plus the Queensbury extension would not have been very practical, but on this Wakefield occasion the Council representatives said the idea was a non-starter. They could not justify spending a large sum of money to buy a business that was going to pass 'free of charge' into other hands in just over a year's time and here was a cause of considerable resentment, as municipal assets that had been carefully nurtured over the years were by Act of Parliament going to be appropriated.

To many involved it seemed very unfair and would also see the loss of local control. A further meeting took place in Halifax on 7th March but thoughts then raised did not appeal to the National Bus Company people so on 27th March that body gave formal notice (it had to be of 12 months' duration) to terminate the 1929 Agreement so bringing the JOC to an early end as from midnight on 31st March, 1974. The second strand to my 1973/74 activities meant that as one of the initial three PTE Directors one became much involved with setting up the new organisational structure and recruiting staff. Our first such activity involved the appointment of a Secretary/solicitor, and finding a home for head office personnel. As it seemed desirable at the time that this should be near County Hall, a new building in Wakefield then under construction which became known as 'Metro House' was purchased, this despite the fact that no PTE vehicle would be seen in the City from 1st April.

We also as a Board began to pay visits to the undertakings that were to form the core of the PTE, and it was on one such occasion that we first found just what the new Bradford interchange was going to mean.

On the day the three of us had lunch after some discussion in the office of our shortly to retire Bradford colleague who told us that there was an architect's model of the facility now available, and no doubt we would wish to see it. I was especially interested, as we had joint and own account services running into Bradford. Whilst I had heard about the intention to provide a new bus station in the city I had never seen any of the associated details.

The model was duly brought in and placed on a handy table. The cover was then removed and our lunch host proceeded with the air of a conjurer to demonstrate its many facets, ending with a description of the new office block which was to have a couple of floors added to provide space to house the head office of the PTE. At this stage our Director General designate nearly blew a fuse. At a later stage and at a more formal meeting I asked if no PTE was on the horizon would it have been paid for as a city development project, or would the bill have been placed on the shoulders of Bradford City Transport? I was told as an officer I had no right to ask such a question but could not help thinking that if the latter had been the case then some General Manager would have had a lot of thinking to do. Now came a very different and most unusual financial exercise that was much closer to home.

Having taken the decision to pull out of the Calderdale JOC the NBC side wanted to know how much it could expect from the sale of its half-share. They suggested that as I should know as much about it as anyone I might undertake a spot of investigation and come up with a possible figure. Meanwhile my co-Directors, now knowing that the NBC half of the JOC would be coming their way, also suggested that I might do likewise on their behalf as the PTE would have to fund the purchase price.

I consequently found myself in the odd situation of selling myself a bus undertaking, looking at each bus in turn and trying to assess in 1974 terms its fair value. This exercise also covered every item of plant or other objects of possible value. I finally came up with a figure that will not be revealed here when, to my considerable astonishment, my fellow Directors said they thought they had been given a very good deal whilst our NBC friends professed themselves very satisfied with the sum thus agreed. As I have remarked before, miracles do sometimes happen.

As the weeks sped by municipal operations wound down , more PTE staff members were taken on, and as we as yet had no premises in Wakefield we Directors found a temporary home in the Swinegate offices of Leeds City Transport. I was in the room where some quarter of a century earlier my municipal career interview had taken place. So I *did* sit in a certain chair - but with a different job, and once there I could not help thinking of the remark made to me by the then Leeds Chief Engineer when he had it in mind to send me to the Kirkstall tramway works.

Now as Director of Engineering and Development I would have well over 1,000 buses to look over, with not a tramcar in sight. It was in many ways a sad time. Something that was reflected at the speeches made at the last meeting of area 'D' of the Association of Public Passenger Transport that took place in Halifax on 19th February, 1974. On that occasion representatives from Hull, Grimsby/Cleethorpes, Lincoln and Chesterfield joined those from Doncaster, Rotherham, Sheffield, Leeds, Huddersfield, Bradford and Halifax, only now the last seven of these had only some six weeks to live. The APPTO was also with its unique Lay/Professional representation scheduled for extinction after some 70 years of life. Its prime functions would be taken over by the Association of District Councils, but the Employers Federation was destined to continue for a few more years.

Thus did my stint as a Municipal General Manager come to an end, with of all things a threat. For Halifax in bygone years was famous for its gibbet. An early form of guillotine that was used to behead anyone convicted of stealing any article with a value of more than one shilling within the Manor of Halifax. The site of this contraption had been lost years earlier, but then after my return to the town workmen digging a trench came across the low stone platform that formed its base, and this was suitably restored.

Now on the night of the last formal meeting of the Halifax Borough Council the Chairman of the responsible Committee rose to his feet to announce that work on the re-erection of the gibbet had been completed. Members of the Authority might like to go and see the end result, only a plastic blade had been substituted for the original one which by some amazing chance was still in existence.

The then Mayor, Councillor Raymond Talbot, on receiving this news looked across at me, mentioned my impending move a few days later to the Passenger Transport Executive, and smiling indicated that, 'If the bus fares in Halifax are increased again after the first of April, then we know who will be first'. Sad to say fares in Halifax , and every other place too, have risen since that night to levels that would have been undreamed of back in 1974, but then so have the cost of vehicles, labour, and every other necessary commodity. So whilst in 1975 my association with West Yorkshire transport services came to an end, just to be on the safe side I have never since paid a visit to a location that is clearly marked on the tourists maps.

The Bit at the End

One day when out on 'safari' I took a seat on the top deck of a Leyland double-decker bound for foreign parts, ensconcing myself in front of an elderly gentleman who was then in solitary splendour. Two stops along the road he was joined by a companion also of senior years when the conversation went as follows.

'E na then then how art tha?'
'I'm nown sa bad misen, but hows tha?'
'I'm reet champion but ast heard abaat Fred?'
'Fred?'
'Aye tha knows Fred Higginbottam?' [Only that was not the name.]
'What abaat him?'
'He's gone deed?'
'He asna.'
'Aye has that'.
'What were up wi him?'
'I don't rightly knowt name, but it weren't owt serious.'

If there was one thing I was to miss about living in Halifax it was the humour, conscious or subconscious, that was all around one, nor was the Transport Department immune as I so often found.

The Bigger Bit at the End

A departmental head for whom I worked would often refer to his then General Manager as 'The postman', saying all he did was to read incoming mail, and then pass it out for others to action. I do not know if such was really the case but I did find as a General Manager that often a considerable portion of my day was spent dealing with mail, so perhaps a few words on the subject are appropriate here.

It was not good practice to arrive at one's office too early, as it was truly essential to give the secretary time to open all the envelopes, stamp every document with its arrival date, and enter all the relevant details in the correspondence book, so that a complete record of what came in was maintained. Once she had completed these tasks all the letters were placed in a folder which in turn were placed on 'Sir's' desk but if, when she entered with that folder, there was a little secret smile on her face beware for in that folder would be lurking something that was, shall we say, unusual.

'Follow that bus.' Fleet No. 291, new in October 1968, was released to the Daimler company who provided a new and identical replacement in exchange. Bound for demonstration in Capetown it was a condition of the agreement that it kept its Halifax livery as long as it was in Daimler ownership. Here it is being loaded onto the ship taking it to South Africa. A second vehicle also nearly went overseas later - but domestic requirements had to take priority. Hong Kong was the suggested destination as also still later was Singapore.

Now most of the mail could be regarded as routine. You read through it, and marked out a proportion to one's departmental heads when there might be added the cryptic comment 'speak' or draft a 'reply' or 'deal with this'. But there were always some communications that *you* had to deal with directly and this is where that secret smile would come in , and on such occasions the contents of the associated missives could be so momentous as to be retained in your mind for years.

Let me give you two away and home examples of what I mean here.

One from away.

South Africa

Dear Mr Hilditch,

I had to write to you to tell you of the so very nostalgic time we had the other morning whilst on holiday in Capetown. We normally live up country at the above address, but came here for the week last Saturday. This morning we were in a shop my husband being at the counter whilst I was looking around when I said to him, 'You won't believe this but a Halifax bus has just gone past'. He thought I was joking but when he realised I was serious he joined me in a rush to the door. An orange, green and cream double-decker was running down the street so we hailed a passing taxi and told the driver to follow that bus.

We did so to the terminus and there found the vehicle complete with the Halifax coat of arms on the side, together with your name and address. We wondered what on earth it was doing here, but you can hardly imagine our delight at seeing it for we emigrated to South Africa from Halifax quite a number of years ago, and have never been back home since, so I felt I had to write to you to say how emotional we felt on seeing it.

The reason was simple. The Daimler company was trying to sell some 'Fleetlines' to Capetown but that authority, whilst being interested, wanted to try a demonstrator as quickly as possible. Daimler had nothing available so we agreed to release one of ours for the purpose provided Daimler replaced it with a brand new one to our specification. We also added that whilst in Daimler ownership it should retain our livery, etc., and continue to display adverts for the seat frames, and the seating moquette both of which were made by Halifax-based firms. More details are given in the accompanying photograph caption.

One from home.

Skircoat Road, Halifax

Dear Sir,

I wish to complain about the running of the 8.20 am bus to Huddersfield. I try to catch this every morning but all too frequently it is full when it arrives at my Free School Lane stop, and so I have to wait for the next which makes me very late for school. This is very annoying, so I would be grateful if a duplicate could be provided. I should add that I have mentioned my problem to my father on numerous occasions, but all he says is 'write to the transport manager', so this I now do.

    Yours faithfully

    Diane M. Hilditch

Needless to say a check on loadings followed and Diane did get her duplicate.

At the end of the day all the outgoing letters arrived for either signature or looking over before dispatch although in the smaller undertakings it was normal for the GM to sign all such mail. In the larger ones such as Manchester it was usual for departmental heads to initial all those they were authorised to answer against a facsimile stamp of the boss' signature. Some General Managers I knew took the easy way out and used such a stamp on all letters except those of major importance that came over the desk. I always had such a stamp by me, but I took the view that it was only courteous to append a personal signature in ink to all replies that bore my own reference.

Finally the most acceptable documents I ever came to sign were my own monthly pay cheques as I later came to do, but do you know I was never allowed to write in the associated amounts . . . If only.

Epilogue

At about 6.30 pm on Sunday 31st March, 1974 I took a walk around Skircoat Road Garage, looked over the orange, green and cream buses standing silent therein and sadly began to wonder just what advantages the travelling public would see when the new regime came into being in about 5½ hours time. Was this all a device to ensure that local, as opposed to National, Government came to pay the costs of supporting the local rail network, or would it bring better services, better vehicles and more advantageous fares?

I had to admit to myself that our 1971 mergers had in the main provided opportunities to do some of these things, so it seemed only fair to expect that the same basic principle when applied on a larger (much larger) scale should be able to do likewise. On the other hand, what had been done up to that time had taken place in what was a recognisable traffic generating area, as indeed were those centred on Huddersfield, Bradford and Leeds and one impinged not at all on any other. Perhaps here some day someone with more knowledge of the subject will produce a fully reasoned analysis as to just what the end result was up to the time of privatisation.

As it was through no fault of my own I was losing a job that I had wanted from a very early age, a job that to me over the previous 15 years or so had been basically fun. Certainly one did also have traumatic times, one was not infallible, and one did make mistakes, whilst having to be on one's toes in Committee, or having to sit through a long and often boring Council meeting, was not the stuff of which dreams are made.

General Managership gave you the chance to view local operations as a whole from all the operational, engineering and financial aspects and perhaps stamp some part of your own personality on the end result. This was something that I was going to miss so I could not help wondering how I would fare in the changes that were to come.

As it turned out I was over the following 28 years to have involvements in the transport industry that I never could have anticipated. That, as they say, is another story that might some day be the subject of more printed pages, but by 31st March, 1974 there was one considerable omission. I had not yet found my name on the side of a municipal tramcar. However . . ?

The Halifax Bus Test Results

Maintenance Marks

Maximum of 10 points for each heading

	Leyland Titan PD3	AEC Regent Mk V	Daimler CVG6	Daimler Fleetline	Leyland Atlantean *	Leyland Atlantean †	AEC Renown	Guy Arab	AEC Routemaster #	Dennis Loline	Albion Lowlander
Rear brake adjustment	9	9	9	5	9		9	9	10	9	9
Front brake adjustment	9	9	9	8	9		9	6	10	9	9
Oil changes (all units)	10	10	9	9	9		7	9	10	9	8
Fuel pump change	7	8	8	6	10		6	6	8	6	7
Injector change	5	9	8	6	4		10	6	9	6	7
Flywheel topping-up	-	-	8	10	3		-	9	10	6	-
Clutch or fluid fly wheel replacement	8	8	8	4	4		2	8	9	8	5
Filters (fuel and lubricating oil)	8	9	9	10	10		9	9	8	8	8
Engine change	7	7	7	6	6		7	5	8	8	6
Water pump change	6	7	7	1	8		8	6	6	8	7
Compressor change	6	8	6	9	8	No check made	3	8	6	8	6
Radiator change	8	8	8	8	8		8	8	8	5	8
Gear box change	7	8	8	3	6		2	8	8	4	5
Differential change	8	8	8	3	8		3	8	8	6	5
Front axle change	8	8	8	8	6		8	8	-	8	8
Rear axle change	8	8	8	8	6		8	8	8	7	6
Front spring change	8	8	8	4	6		8	5	8	8	8
Rear spring change	8	8	8	8	6		8	8	8	8	8
Prop shaft change	8	8	8	8	10		7	7	9	7	8
Steering box change	7	7	7	8	8		7	6	7	8	7
Flexible exhaust pipe	7	8	7	2	6		2	8	8	9	5
Cylinder head gasket change	6	7	7	3	8		6	5	7	6	5
Starter change	9	9	9	2	8		8	4	9	5	3
Dynamo change	9	9	8	8	8		8	6	9	7	5
Totals	176	188	190	147	174		153	173	191	173	153

Notes
* *Demonstrator.*
† *Wallasey Corporation.*
# *This bus was built for London Transport; production models for other operators are marketed by Park Royal Vehicles Ltd.*

Fuel consumption figures

Vehicle and date of test	Route (a) inter-urban		Route (b) inter-urban/ local		Route (c) Intensive local		Overall results	
	miles	mpg	miles	mpg	miles	mpg	miles	mpg
Leyland Titan PD3/4 April 1964	1,560.0	9.87	1,183.0	8.64	1,260.0	7.93	4,003.9	8.82
AEC Regent Mk V August 1964	1,494.7	9.40	1,096.0	8.77	1,132.0	8.14	3,722.8	8.77
Daimler CVG6 August 1964	1,463.2	10.60	1,186.4	9.57	800.9	8.90	3,450.0	9.80
Leyland Atlantean (Demonstrator) May 1964	1,535.4	10.39	1,126.8	9.01	877.0	8.61	3,540.0	9.45
Leyland Atlantean (Wallasey Corporation) September/October 1964	1,519.4	9.10	1,058.0	8.53	875.1	7.17	3,452.7	8.36
AEC Renown †	*935.0	*8.99	1,087.6	10.07	1,150.0	8.58	13,162.6	9.15
Guy Arab Mk July 1964	1,508.0	8.52	1,297.0	9.08	905.7	7.19	3,711.9	8.32
AEC Routemaster # October 1964	700.9	10.78	689	9.06	636.0	8.15	2,238.0	9.25
Dennis Loline February/March 1965	1,244.0	9.08	998	8.68	1,085.0	8.16	3,326.0	8.59
Daimler Fleetline April 1964	1,345.7	9.89	1,159.6	9.35	1,211.31	8.59	3,716.6	9.27

Notes

† Bus with us for two weeks only in April 1964. Returned for a further week in July when figures marked * were obtained.

Test compressed into two weeks instead of three.

The 'Atlantean' demonstrator was accompanied by a Leyland driver ostensibly to advise our drivers unfamiliar with this type of vehicle. On the others our men simply took the controls and drove.

The 'Loline' had a four-speed gear box.

Appendix Two

Albion 'Nimbus' Engine Life

Bus No.	Date	Mileage	Remarks	Recent delay
250	27. 3.64	29,000	Broken con rod. New engine fitted.	
	5.11.64	15,000	Reconditioned crankshaft. New bearings. New rings. Cylinder head reconditioned. *New gasket.*	
	9. 4.65	57,000	New Sump.	
	12. 8.65	65,000	Engine seized. Engine fitted ex-256 bus (2,000 miles from new).	
	11. 9.65	4,000	Big end gone. (To Albion's 20.9.65.)	Away 1 week to date
251	28. 6.64	21,000	Cylinder head reconditioned. *New gasket.*	
	3.7.64	30,000	New bearings and con rod bearings.	
	29.9.64	34,000	New pistons. Cylinder head reconditioned. *New gasket.*	
252	1.4.64	27,000	*New gasket.*	
	16.4.64	28,000	*Cylinder block warped.* New engine fitted.	
	15.12.64	23,000	*New gasket.*	
	17.8.65	49,000	*Gasket trouble.* (Waiting to go to Albion's.)	7 weeks
253	2.3.64	23,000	*New gasket.* Cylinder head reconditioned.	
	8.10.64	45,000	Reconditioned crankshaft and bearings. New rings.	
254	17.1.64	21,000	Broken valve. Cylinder head fitted. *New gasket.*	
	29.2.64	23,000	Cylinder head reconditioned. *New gasket.*	
	23. 9.64	39,000	New con rod shells. New pistons. Cylinder head reconditioned. *New gasket.*	
	11.1.65	49,000	*Cylinder block warped.* New engine fitted.	
	21.9.65	52,000	*New gasket fitted.*	
	28.9.65	66,500	Pistons seized. (On Dock.)	
255	13.11.63	12,000	New No. 4. con rod sleeve, piston, head, *gasket.*	
	16.12.63	14,000	*Engine seized.* New engine fitted.	
	11.11.64	36,000	*New gasket.*	
	17.11.64	37,000	New pistons, etc.	
	24.3.65	48,000	*Cylinder block warped.* (To Albion's.)	
	3.6.65		*Engine seized.* New liners, etc. (To Albion's.)	
	16.7.65	56,000	*New gasket fitted.*	
	6.8.65	57,000	*New gasket fitted.*	
	9.8.65	57,000	*New gasket fitted.*	
	16.8.65	58,000	*New gasket fitted.*	
	17.9.65	60,000	*Gasket trouble.* Engine changed.	4 weeks
256	14.9.64	43,000	*New gasket.*	
	1.10.64	45,000	New main bearings. Pistons.	
	22.1.65	58,000	*New gasket.*	
	25.5.65	67,000	Engine trouble. *Cylinder block warped.* New engine fitted. (To Albion's.)	
	29.7.65	72,000	Engine trouble. Engine changed.	2 weeks
	12.8.65		Engine removed and fitted to 250 bus.	
	23.8.65		New engine fitted.	2 weeks

Bus No.	Date	Mileage	Remarks	Recent delay
257	20. 5.64	35,000	New bearings, etc. (To Albion's at Glasgow.) *New gasket.*	
	2.11.64	40,000	New rings. Cylinder head reconditioned. *New gasket.*	
	5.65	58,000	Engine trouble. Boils, fumes. New liners, new pistons, etc. (To Albion's.)	
	12.7.65	63,000	Engine trouble. New engine fitted.	2 weeks
258	26.5.64	34,000	Cylinder head reconditioned. *New gasket.*	
	9.9.64	43,000	New engine fitted.	
	19.2.65	60,000	*New gasket.*	
	3.3.65	62,000	Cylinder head changed. *New gasket.*	
	24.3.65	82,000	*New gasket.*	
	31.5.65	85,000	Engine trouble. Throwing oil from exhaust. (To Albion's.)	
	10.6.65	86,000	Engine trouble. Throwing oil from exhaust. New rings. New engine fitted. (To Albion's.)	
259	24.2.64	20,000	*New gasket.*	
	13.5.64	28,000	*New gasket.*	
	20.5.64	29,000	Knocking. New engine fitted.	
	25.3.65	27,000	*New gasket fitted.* No heater.	
	30.4.65	30,000	Engine trouble. Engine seized. New pistons, etc. (To Albion's.)	
	21.7.65	35,000	Engine trouble. New engine fitted.	4 weeks

My arrival back in Halifax was not uplifted by the sight of 10 almost new Albion 'Nimbus' vehicles carrying Weymann 31-seat bodies. True they had Albion 6-speed gear boxes and exhausters but that Albion engine and BMC rear axle remained. As bus Nos. 250 to 259 they were a dubious asset as this Appendix clearly shows.

Appendix Three

The Halifax Fleet at 31st March, 1974

'A' Services

Bus No.	Chassis No.	Reg. No	Date in service	Bus No.	Chassis No.	Reg. No.	Date in service
Leyland PSU 4B/2R Leopard chassis/Plaxtons 45-seat single-decker body							
1	7202388	SCP 341L	10.10.1972	6	7302898	UJX 916M	9.11.73
2	7202389	SCP 342L	10.10.1972	7	7302899	UJX 917M	23.12.73
3	7202390	SCP 343L	10.10.1972	8	7302900	UJX 918M	17.12.73
4	7202391	SCP 344L	10.10.1972	9	7302901	UJX 919M	21.12.73
5	7202392	SCP 345L	10.10.1972	10	7303491	UJX 920M	27.12.73
Leyland RT3/1 chassis MCW 42-seat single-decker body							
6	582243	KCP 6	10.11.1958	9	582350	KCP 9	10.11.1958
7	582319	KCP 7	10.11.1958	*10	582223	KCP 5	10.11.1958
8	582322	KCP 8	10.11.1958				

* Previously No. 5 fitted with 43-seat body.
Nos. 6-10 went to JOC as Nos. 376-380 on 1.1.74.

Bus No.	Chassis No.	Reg. No	Date in service	Bus No.	Chassis No.	Reg. No.	Date in service
Leyland PD2/37 chassis/MCW 64-seat double-decker body							
21	601194	MJX 21	19.11.1960	25	601258	MJX 25	30.11.1960
22	601195	MJX 22	13.11.1960	26	601259	MJX 26	27.11.1960
23	601196	MJX 23	1.11.1960	27	601260	MJX 27	1.11.1960
24	601197	MJX 24	8.11.1960	28	601261	MJX 28	6.11.1960
Leyland Leopard chassis/Weymann 42-seat single-deck body							
*31	611922	PJX 31	1.8.1962	34	611952	PJX 34	27.7.1962
32	611923	PJX 32	30.7.1962	35	612074	PJX 35	15.8.1962
33	611936	PJX 33	13.9.1962	36	612075	PJX 36	28.7.1962

* 44 seater.

Bus No.	Chassis No.	Reg. No	Date in service	Bus No.	Chassis No.	Reg. No.	Date in service
Leyland PD2/37 chassis/Weymann 64-seat double-deck body							
43	622180	PJX 43	26.11.1962	46	622215	PJX 46	5.12.1962
44	622181	PJX 44	26.11.1962	47	622216	PJX 47	1.12.1962
45	622214	PJX 45	19.12.1962	48	622217	PJX 48	10.12.1962
Leyland PD3/4 chassis/Weymann 72-seat double-deck body							
51	L01366	TCP 51	17.12.1963	55	L01421	TCP 55	1.1.1964
52	L01367	TCP 52	1.1.1964	56	L01422	TCP 56	17.12.1963
53	L01368	TCP 53	1.1.1964	57	L01423	TCP 57	23.12.1963
54	L01369	TCP 54	1.1.1964	58	L01424	TCP 58	1.1.1964
Leyland PD2/37 chassis/Roe 65-seat double-deck body							
59	L20934	CCP 159C	7.9.1965	63	L20946	CCP 163C	11.9.1965
60	L20935	CCP 160C	8.9.1965	64	L21074	CCP 164C	1.10.1965
61	L20944	CCP 161C	9.9.1965	65	L21075	CCP 165C	1.10.1965
62	L20945	CCP 162C	10.9.1965	66	L21076	CCP 166C	1.10.1965

Thanks to the abrupt road level changes, 'Fleetlines' could not be universally employed. Note the problem here at Rishworth New Road in 1972. Consequently Leyland 'PD2s' continued to dominate Ryburn Valley services but the time must have come when this and similar problems at Sowerby, Steep Lane and Hubberton would need to be solved.

Bus No.	Chassis No.	Reg. No	Date in service	Bus No.	Chassis No.	Reg. No.	Date in service
Leyland PD2/37 chassis/Weymann 64-seat double-deck body							
67	L41707	DCP 67D	10.1.1966	71	L42119	DCP 71 D	10.1.1966
68	L41708	DCP 68D	10.1.1966	72	L42120	DCP 72D	10.1.1966
69	L41815	DCP 69D	10.1.1966	73	L42121	DCP 73D	31.1.1966
70	L42118	DCP 70D	10.1.1966	74	L42256	DCP 74D	31.1.1966
*Daimler Fleetline chassis/Northern Counties 74-seat double-deck body, or * 75 seats*							
82	66119	RCP 272K	12.6.1972	94	62935	LJX 404H	5.2.1970
83	66120	RCP 273K	23.6.1972	95	62801	JJX 595G	24.10.1968
84	66121	RCP 274K	15.5.1972	96	62802	JJX 596G	21.10.1968
85	66122	RCP 275K	15.5.1972	97	61444	GJX 317F	20.9.1967
86	66123	RCP 276K	12.6.1972	98	61445	GJX 318F	22.9.1967
87	63941	MJX 14J	3.12.1970	*99	61242	ECP 679D	21.11.1966
88	63942	MJX 8J	1.12.1970	*100	61243	ECP 680D	8.10.1966
89	63943	MJX 9J	8.12.1970	*101	61244	ECP 681D	26.11.1966
90	63944	MJX 10J	9.12.1970	*102	61245	ECP 682D	28.11.1966
91	63945	MJX 11J	1.12.1970	*103	61456	BHD 222C	9.8.1971
92	63946	MJX 12J	1.12.1970	*104	61247	ECP 684D	29.11.1966
93	63947	MJX 13J	1.12.1970	*105	61248	ECP 685D	1.9.1966

Bus No. 103 new to Yorkshire Woollen District as fleet No. 624 on 1st May, 1966 (Alexander 75-seat body).

Daimler Fleetline 18 ft 6 in. chassis/Willowbrook 45-seat single-deck body							
106	61441	FJX 506E	16.6.1967	111	62931	JJX 371G	1.11.1968
107	61442	FJX 507E	17.6.1967	112	62932	KCP 422G	1.4.1969
108	61443	FJX 508E	17.6.1967	113	62933	KCP 423G	1.4.1969
				114	62934	KCP 424G	1.4.1969
Daimler Fleetline 18 ft 6 in. chassis/Pennine 45-seat single-deck body							
109	62805	KCP 379G	6.2.1969	110	62806	KCP 380G	4.2.1969
AEC Reliance 2 MY3RA chassis/Alexander 43-seat single-deck body							
123	3923	PCP 803	8.4.1971				

New to Hebble Motor Services 1.6.1962.

'B' Services

Bus No.	Chassis No.	Reg. No	Date in service	Bus No.	Chassis No.	Reg. No.	Date in service
Leyland PD3/4 chassis/MCW 72-seat double-deck body							
201	582209	KCP 10	1.1.1959	205	582269	KCP 14	2.1.1959
202	582210	KCP 11	1.1.1959	206	582270	KCP 15	2.1.1959
203	582211	KCP 12	1.1.1959	207	582271	KCP 16	15.1.1959
204	582220	KCP 13	20.1.1959	208	582272	KCP 17	15.1.1959
Leyland PD2/37 chassis/MCW 64-seat double-deck body							
221	601299	MCP 221	27.11.1960	225	601312	MCP 225	1.11.1960
222	601300	MCP 222	6.11.1960	226	601313	MCP 226	6.11.1960
223	601301	MCP 223	27.11.1960	227	601314	MCP 227	20.11.1960
224	601302	MCP 224	13.11.1960	228	601315	MCP 228	13.11.1960
Leyland Leopard chassis/Weymann 42-seat single-deck body							
229	612087	PJX 37	1.2.1971	235	612254	PJX 235	27.7.1962
230	612088	PJX 38	1.2.1971	236	612269	PJX 236	28.7.1962
231	602941	OCP 231	24.8.1961	237	612298	PJX 237	1.9.1962
232	612229	PJX 232	2.9.1962	238	612299	PJX 238	27.7.1962
233	612230	PJX 233	19.9.1962	239	621362	PJX 39	1.2.1971
234	612253	PJX 234	11.9.1962				

Bus Nos. 229, 230 and 239 renumbered from 37 to 39. New to Corp. 3.9.1962.
Bus Nos. 231 to 234 fitted with 44-seat bodies.

Bus No.	Chassis No.	Reg. No	Date in service	Bus No.	Chassis No.	Reg. No.	Date in service
Leyland PD2/37 chassis/Weymann 64-seat double-deck body							
241	622230	PJX 241	10.12.1962	246	622318	PJX 246	21.11.1962
242	622231	PJX 242	12.12.1962	247	622319	PJX 247	12.12.1962
243	622232	PJX 243	4.12.1962	248	622320	PJX 248	1.12.1962
244	622233	PJX 244	26.11.1962	209	622178	PJX 41	1.1.1971
245	622317	PJX 245	10.11.1962	210	622179	PJX 42	1.1.1971

Bus Nos. 209 and 210 formerly 41 and 42 in 'A' fleet. New to Corp. 21.11.1962, 3.12.1962.

Bus No.	Chassis No.	Reg. No	Date in service	Bus No.	Chassis No.	Reg. No.	Date in service
AEC Reliance 6MY 3RA chassis/Pennine 39-seat single-deck body							
249	6576	ECP 949D	17.10.1966	253	6580	ECP 953D	1.2.1966
250	6577	ECP 950D	18.11.1966	254	6581	ECP 954D	16.12.1966
251	6578	ECP 951D	2.1.1967	255	6582	ECP 955D	24.1.1967
252	6579	ECP 952D	10.2.1967				
AEC Reliance MY 3RV chassis/Plaxton 'Panorama' coach bodies 43 seats							
256	202	MBY 347	6.10.1967	258	463	NRK 350	9.2.1968
257	462	PXO 974	21.11.1967	259	407	TGJ 484	11.7.1968
AEC Reliance 6MY 2R chassis/Plaxton 43-seat single-deck body							
†260	7733	OJX60K	1.8.1971	†261	7734	OJX 61K	1.8.1971
AEC Reliance 6MY 3R chassis/Willowbrook 41-seat single-deck body							
262	6989	JCP 322F	10.8.1968	265	6574	EJX 65D	12.11.1966
263	6990	JCP 323F	10.8.1968	266	6575	UX 66D	12.11.1966
264	6999	JCP 324F	10.8.1968				
Leyland Leopard chassis/Willowbrook 41-seat single-deck body							
267	L42412	CJX 275C	13.11.1965	268	L60476	DJX 143D	6.4.1966

† Buses marked were currently allocated to Todmorden (Millwood) Depot.

Bus No.	Chassis No.	Reg. No	Date in service	Bus No.	Chassis No.	Reg. No.	Date in service

Leyland Leopard chassis/Willowbrook 43-seat single-deck body

Bus No.	Chassis No.	Reg. No	Date in service	Bus No.	Chassis No.	Reg. No.	Date in service
269	L122240	AJX 269B	16.10.1964	270	L122241	AJX 270B	16.10.1964

AEC Reliance 6MY 2R chassis/Plaxton 'Panorama' Elite' 43-seat coach body

Bus No.	Chassis No.	Reg. No	Date in service	Bus No.	Chassis No.	Reg. No.	Date in service
271	7744	WX 854J	1.7.1971	274	7169	KCP 874G	1.4.1969
272	7745	MX 855J	1.7.1971	275	7170	KCP 875G	1.4.1969
273	7168	KCP 873G	1.4.1969				

AEC Reliance 6MY 2R chassis/Plaxton 43-seat single-deck body

Bus No.	Chassis No.	Reg. No	Date in service	Bus No.	Chassis No.	Reg. No.	Date in service
†276	7171	KCP 876G	14.6.1969	†277	7172	KCP 877G	21.6.1969

Leyland PD2/73 chassis/Roe 65-seat double-deck body

Bus No.	Chassis No.	Reg. No	Date in service	Bus No.	Chassis No.	Reg. No.	Date in service
278	L21002	CCP 523C	3.9.1965	279	L21003	CCP 524C	4.9.1965

Leyland PD2/37 chassis/Weymann 64-seat double-deck body

Bus No.	Chassis No.	Reg. No	Date in service	Bus No.	Chassis No.	Reg. No.	Date in service
280	L21004	CJX 320C	1.12.1965	285	L42380	CJX 325C	15.12.1965
281	L21005	CJX 321 C	13.12.1965	286	L42381	CJX 326C	13.12.1965
282	L21044	CJX 322C	15.12.1965	287	L42408	CJX 327C	20.12.1965
283	L42258	CJX 323C	13.12.1965	288	L42409	CJX 328C	20.12.1965
284	L42379	CJX 324C	13.12.1965	289	L42257	CJX 329C	10.1.1966

Daimler Fleetline chassis/Northern Counties 74-seat double-deck body

Bus No.	Chassis No.	Reg. No	Date in service	Bus No.	Chassis No.	Reg. No.	Date in service
290	62803	JJX 579G	1.11.1968	†301	66128	RCP 281K	15.5.1972
291	63873	UX 403H	5.2.1970	†302	67579	RCP 332K	8.7.1972
292	62936	UX 402H	13.2.1970	†303	67580	RCP 333K	6.7.1972
293	61246	ECP 683D	12.8.1971	†304	67581	RCP 334K	6.7.1972
294	61480	WX 351 D	19.8.1971	†305	67582	RCP 335K	6.7.1972
295	66129	RCP 282K	1.6.1972	†306	67583	RCP 336K	8.7.1972
296	66130	RCP 283K	1.6.1972	307			
297	66124	RCP 277K	23.6.1972	308			
†298	66125	RCP 278K	1.6.1972	309			
†299	66126	RCP 279K	1.6.1972	310			
†300	66127	RCP 280K	1.6.1972	311			

Bus Nos. 307 to 311 due for delivery in 1973/4.

AEC Regent Mk V chassis/MCW 72-seat double-deck body

Bus No.	Chassis No.	Reg. No	Date in service	Bus No.	Chassis No.	Reg. No.	Date in service
211	2D3RA 756	UX 211	1.3.1960	218	2D3RA 763	LJX 218	22.2.1960
213	2D3RA 758	UX 213	6.2.1960	310	2D3RA 1528	AJX 410B	4.3.1971
215	2D3RA 760	UX 215	12.2.1960	313	2D3RA 1527	AJX 409B	10.2.1971
217	2D3RA 762	UX 217	30.1.1960	376	2D3RA 1131	RCP 237	8.6.1972

Bus No. 376 renumbered from 76.
Bus Nos. 310, 313 and 376 transferred from Hebble Motors. New on 26.10.1964, 26.10.1964 and 1.10.1962 respectively.

Seddon Pennine RU chassis/Plaxton 45-seat single-deck body

Bus No.	Chassis No.	Reg. No	Date in service	Bus No.	Chassis No.	Reg. No.	Date in service
315	46516	MJX 15J	20.10.1972	317	46518	MJX 17J	9.11.1970
316	46517	MJX 16J	9.11.1970				

AEC Reliance 2MY 4RA chassis/Park Royal 43-seat single-deck body

Bus No.	Chassis No.	Reg. No	Date in service
320	5709	BJX 134C	11.3.1971

New to Hebble 1.8.1965.

† Buses marked were currently allocated to Todmorden (Millwood) Depot.

Bus No.	Chassis No.	Reg. No	Date in service	Bus No.	Chassis No.	Reg. No.	Date in service

Leyland Leopard L1 chassis/Eastern coachworks 41-seat single-deck body

| 321 | 603155 | 1880 WA | 31.7.1970 | 323 | 603169 | 1882 WA | 1.8.1970 |
| 322 | 603156 | 1881 WA | 1.8.1970 | | | | |

New to Sheffield on 5.4.1961.

Leyland Leopard L1 chassis/Willowbrook 45-seat single-deck body

| †324 | 62672 | NWW 88E | 1.2.1967 | †326 | 62674 | NWW 90E | 1.2.1967 |
| †325 | 62969 | NWW 89E | 1.2.1967 | †327 | 62673 | NWW 91E | 1.2.1967 |

Nos. 326 and 327 fitted with 43 semi-luxury seats.

Leyland Leopard L1 chassis/Pennine 45-seat single-deck body

328	903682	BWU 688H	1.12.1969	331	903541	BWU 691H	11.11.1969
329	903683	BWU 689H	1.12.1969	332	903446	BWU 692H	11.11.1969
330	903445	BWU 690H	1.12.1969	333	903542	BWU 693H	11.11.1969

Nos. 328 and 329 fitted with 43 semi-luxury seats.

Leyland Leopard L1 chassis/East Lancashire coach Builders 44-seat single-deck body

†334	610337	634 WY	1.4.1961	†337	L02112	572 EYG	1.1.1964
†335	621728	520 BWT	1.9.1962	338	L02113	573 EYG	1.1.1964
†336	621729	521 BWT	1.9.1962				

Leyland PD2/12 chassis/Leyland 53-seat double-deck body

| †355 | 512865 | KWX 17 | 1.10.1951 | †356 | 512866 | KWX 18 | 1.10.1951 |

Leyland Leopard PSU4/4R chassis/Marshall 45-seat single-deck body

| 358 | 702235 | NHE 8F | 24.12.1971 | 360 | 702737 | NHE 10F | 1.9.1971 |
| 359 | 702236 | NHE 9F | 1.9.1971 | | | | |

New to Yorkshire Traction 1.4.1968.

Leyland RT3/1 chassis/MCW 42-seat single-deck body

| 371 | 582192 | KCP 1 | 8.6.1972 | 373 | 582194 | KCP 3 | 8.6.1972 |
| 372 | 582193 | KCP 2 | 8.6.1972 | 374 | 582222 | KCP 4 | 8.6.1972 |

Renumbered from 1, 2, 3, 4 respectively. Entered service on 20.10.1958 No. 1, 10.11.1958 Nos. 2, 3, 4.

Daimler CVG6 chassis/H. Roe 65-seat double-deck body

| 383 | 19079 | GJX 330 | 1.1.1971 | 384 | 19080 | GJX 331 | 1.1.1971 |

New to 'A' fleet as Nos. 18 and 19 on 1.10.1956 and 1.11.1956 respectively, later renumbered 118 and 119, renumbered again to 303 and 304 then later still as shown.

---

† Buses marked were currently allocated to Todmorden (Millwood) Depot.

Acknowledgements

I had the very good fortune during my years in the transport industry to make the acquaintance of many Municipal or Company Fleet Managers, and also numerous executives in the supply sides of the business. These people were invariably more than ready to answer questions I put to them such as, 'When did you cease to operate that particular Service?', or, 'Could you please let me have a photograph or drawing of a certain bus or tram'. I must here also fully recognise that part played by the members of those Transport Committees who saw fit to favour my application for the post they were offering, for without their coming to a decision that was to my advantage this story could never have been written. The same applies to those Senior Officers of the former London & North Eastern Railway, who gave me my first ever job, and then facilitated my transfer from office routines to the very different world that then existed inside the walls of Gorton Shed and Tank.

I have always been grateful to them, and I only wish that some of those who were particularly kind to me were still with us today so that I could express my gratitude in a more suitable personal manner.

Photographs

Over the years I have managed to acquire a considerable number of photographs and many of these are included were they are germain to the story in this publication. In many instances I have no knowledge as to who actually took them, and so they must remain unnamed, but I do pay full tribute to their excellent and much appreciated efforts. Sadly some old friends who were active in the field such as Bob Parr, Bob Mack and W.A. Camwell are no longer with us, but I look back with pleasure on the conversations that we had, and the way in which they were prepared to open their files to me, whenever I made a request.

Despite the size of my collection I found that I was short of several pertinent pictures and here I am more than obliged to David Wayman, Roy Marshall and Brian Render (like me a former member of the staff of the Leeds drawing office), old friends who took trouble to search out those that I was wanting.

Finally I must express my thanks to Mr Riley, the Editor of the *Halifax Courier*, for permission to use some of the excellent photographs that came to appear in 'Our local paper'.

Great Yarmouth's Leyland 'PS2' No. 17 (*see page 88*),was originally in the Hebble fleet as No. 42. It is seen here in Horton Street, Halifax, where the Hebble termini for Rochdale and Burnley were then located.